The Economics
of Inequality

BY

A. B. ATKINSON

CLARENDON PRESS · OXFORD

Oxford University Press, Walton Street, Oxford OX2 6DP

OXFORD LONDON GLASGOW NEW YORK
TORONTO MELBOURNE WELLINGTON CAPE TOWN
IBADAN NAIROBI DAR ES SALAAM LUSAKA
KUALA LUMPUR SINGAPORE JAKARTA HONG KONG TOKYO
DELHI BOMBAY CALCUTTA MADRAS KARACHI

Casebound ISBN 0 19 8770243
Paperback ISBN 0 19 8770766

© Oxford University Press 1975

First published 1975
Reprinted 1976 and 1977

PRINTED IN GREAT BRITAIN BY OFFSET LITHOGRAPHY BY
BILLING AND SONS LTD., GUILDFORD AND LONDON

PREFACE

This book has grown out of a course of lectures given for third-year students of economics, but it has been written with a wider readership in mind. The book assumes very little in the way of prior knowledge of economic analysis and I hope that it can be used by first- or second-year students as a supplement to introductory textbooks, which typically do not cover this ground. Nor is it intended solely for economists. The lectures were attended by students of sociology and politics, and I have tried to make the book intelligible to them. To this end, the more technical passages have been clearly marked. The fact that the issues discussed are topical and controversial may mean that the general reader will also find it of interest.

My first debt is to the students at the University of Essex who attended the lectures. Their interest in the subject encouraged me and their criticism led to substantial improvements in the exposition. Secondly, I would like to thank the friends and colleagues with whom I have discussed different aspects of the book, particularly Judith Atkinson, Christopher Bliss, Alan Harrison, Klaus Heidensohn, James Meade, Joy Skegg, M. Taussig and Peter Townsend. I owe a great deal to Christopher Trinder, who not only made valuable comments on the draft manuscript, but also prepared and checked many of the statistical tables and references. I am grateful to Adrian Sinfield for arranging for the draft to be read by two members of his course on social policy, Janet Gillinder and Jef Collingwood, whose comments from the perspective of non-economist students were most helpful. The manuscript was typed and retyped by Jill Adlington and Sheila Ogden with great accuracy and patience. Finally, Michael Shaw of Shaw Maclean and the staff of the Clarendon Press have been most helpful in making the arrangements for publication.

Lastly, I should explain about the system of references. In the text sources are indicated by the author's name and the date of publication: for example, Smith (1776). Where there are two works by the same author in one year, the second is referred to as Smith (1776a). The full citation may then be found in the 'References' at the end of the book. I have also given in the section 'Notes on sources and further reading' suggestions in case readers wish to explore further the issues discussed in this book. I hope that they do.

A.B.A.

University of Essex
August 1974

CONTENTS

LIST OF TABLES

LIST OF FIGURES

1
INTRODUCTION

The two greatest ends of economic inquiry seem to me to be the
furnishing of general answers to the two questions, first, why whole
communities are rich or poor, and, secondly, why inside each
community some individuals and families are above, and others below
the average in wealth... Economists sometimes vaguely wonder why
economic theory is so unpopular... Is there anything in this to excite
surprise, if we reflect for a moment on the inadequacy of the answer
furnished by the theory of distribution, as at present taught, to the
questions in which the ordinary person is interested?

(Edwin Cannan, 1905)

1·1 Economists and distribution

The subject of this book is the distribution of income and wealth. It is
concerned with incomes and needs, wages and profits, wealth and
poverty. These are important topics, and the questions they raise are
both difficult and controversial. Why is it that a doctor can earn in a
week what the average worker takes home in a month? Is it true that
wealth is concentrated in a few hands? Why are governments still
concerned about poverty and would a negative income tax be the
answer? Does the average Indonesian really live on 25 American cents a
day, or are such comparisons between countries meaningless?

Despite the profound implications of questions such as these, the
subject of income and wealth has not occupied the central position in
economics that one would expect. A glance at the titles in the
economic section of any bookshop will show that there are relatively
few books devoted principally to this topic. An analysis of two leading
professional journals in Britain and the United States, the *American
Economic Review* and the *Economic Journal*, reveals that of the more
than 1500 articles published in the last ten years, only some 100 dealt
with distributional questions in any form. It is probably fair to say that
most textbooks on economics give more prominence to economic
efficiency, growth (and pollution), full employment, and the balance of
payments, than to the issues with which this book is concerned. The
situation is not so very different from that which Cannan described
seventy years ago.

This relative neglect of the distribution of income and wealth has not
of course passed completely unnoticed and in recent years it has been
one of the main criticisms of 'mainstream' economics made by radical

economists in the United States and elsewhere: 'inequality is what economics should be all about. But, in fact, economics as it is taught and practised by economists deals very little with inequality' (Weeks, 1971, p. 75). Moreover, it is not simply radical economists who hold this opinion. In his 'outsider's view' of the political economy of the new left, Lindbeck agreed 'that the development of the theory and analysis of distribution problems has been considerably weaker than the development in many other branches of economics during the period since World War II' (1971, p. 10).

It would be wrong to suggest that economists have always neglected the subject of distribution; indeed classical writers gave it a great deal of prominence:

The popularity of distribution theory has had cyclical upswings and downswings. Certainly it enjoyed a peak during the time of Ricardo, who wrote to Malthus that 'Political Economy you think is an inquiry into the nature and causes of wealth. I thin' it should rather be called an inquiry into the laws which determine the division of the produce of industry among the classes who concur in its formation.' Just as certainly, distribution theory reached peaks of popularity during the time of Wicksell–Clark–Wicksteed and, in the early 1930s, of Hicks and Douglas. The Great Depression, World War II and the Keynesian Revolution brought about a marked decline in professional concern about distribution theory which, until recent times, revived only sporadically. (Ferguson, 1972, p. 437)

Ferguson goes on to argue that we are now due for another revival of interest. If such a revival takes place, then the work of the earlier writers mentioned by Ferguson, to say nothing of Marx, will no doubt influence the development of the subject, but it is unlikely to provide immediate answers. The classical writers, including Marx, were primarily concerned with the distribution among *factors of production* (land, labour and capital) and the distribution among *persons* received relatively little attention. How national income is divided among land, labour and capital is important in understanding the distribution among persons, but it is not by itself sufficient to explain all the aspects in which we are interested. At one time it may have been adequate to identify social classes with the ownership of particular factors of production, and to focus on the distribution between capitalists, landlords and workers. Today this identification does not necessarily hold and the link between the shares of factors of production in national income and the personal distribution of income is more complex. An explanation as to why wages and salaries represent three-quarters of total income does not help us understand why a managing director may earn fifty times as much as a labourer. The implications of a rise in profits may be quite different if it accrues to widows and orphans rather than to industrial millionaires. It is therefore important to go beyond the question of factor shares with which classical writers were concerned and to consider the distribution among persons.[1]

The purpose of this book is to examine what economic analysis can contribute to understanding the nature and causes of the differences between people in their income and wealth.

1. *How are income and wealth distributed?* This may appear at first sight to be a relatively easy question, but in fact it is far from straightforward. The amount of information available about the distribution of income, wealth and other resources is very limited. We know much less about this than about other aspects of the economy, a state of affairs which reflects the low priority attached to distributional issues by governments and economists in the past. Our knowledge of the extent of inequality consists mainly of information pieced together from sources which were not explicitly designed for the purpose, such as tax returns, and it may need careful interpretation.

2. *How can the differences in income and wealth which we observe be explained?* Having assembled the available evidence about the distribution of income and wealth, we need to examine the causal factors involved. What, for example, explains top salaries? Is it differences in training or skill? Is it bargaining power? Is it having had fathers with high incomes? Is it simply luck? In discussing such questions the primary emphasis of this book is on the role of economic factors, but this should not be taken as reflecting the view that economists' explanations are the sole ones which should be considered. The aim is rather to allow the reader to assess the relevance of economic explanations of inequality, which can then be viewed in the light of broader considerations. In asking, for example, how far the earnings of doctors can be explained by their long training period, there is no presumption that this is the only factor of importance: to obtain a complete picture one would certainly have to examine the social and political role of the medical profession.

3. *What is the impact of government measures to redistribute income and wealth?* In any explanation of the patterns observed, an important consideration is the effect of government policy. For example, in explaining the persistence of inequality in wealth-holding, account has

---

[1] That the tradition of emphasizing the question of factor shares dies hard is illustrated by two recent texts on income distribution theory by Bronfenbrenner (1971) and Johnson (1973). In the former only one chapter out of seventeen is devoted to personal income distribution, and in the latter the proportion is only slightly higher (two out of eighteen).

to be taken of the laws regarding the ownership of property and of the taxes levied on the transfer of wealth. In the same way, we can examine the effect of changes in policy. Would, for example, an alternative system of inheritance taxation lead to a reduction in concentration? In the course of the book a selection of policy measures are discussed. This discussion cannot be exhaustive, for the book would otherwise reach an inordinate length, but it covers a range of measures which are of current policy interest, including progressive income taxation, minimum wage legislation, income maintenance, and overseas aid.

Why are these questions of interest? Firstly, the distribution of income and wealth is a major feature of any social system and is therefore a phenomenon which requires explanation. There is an intellectual challenge in answering the questions outlined above which is parallel to that provided by explaining the origins of the universe or of the Second World War. It is, however, unlikely that intellectual curiosity is the only reason people have for reading this book, and concern about measures for redistribution is probably an important stimulus. Some people feel that present policies are inadequate, others that they go too far. The subject is controversial, and for this reason it is essential that the issues should be fully debated.

1·2 The meaning of inequality

The first question on which opinions differ is what is meant by 'inequality'. This is in large part because it is a social judgement, and no attempt is made here to review the procedures by which such judgements could be made. It is important to clarify, however, the way in which the term is used in this book.

As Bauer and Prest (1973) have recently observed, the term 'inequality' may either be applied quite generally to cases where incomes or wealth are simply different, just as we might refer to two people being of unequal height, or be restricted to cases where there is a moral content (i.e. a presumption that equality would be desirable). This may be seen as parallel to the distinction drawn in the *Oxford English Dictionary* between inequality meaning disparity in magnitude or quantity and inequality meaning 'the fact of occupying a more or less advantageous position' (see Wilson, 1966). The two uses of the term are clearly different. One person may have a higher income than another, but this may be considered not to be unjust because he will have a correspondingly lower income next year. The mere existence of disparities in income and wealth is not a sufficient basis for statements about justice or injustice; we need to establish that the people involved are comparable in other relevant respects.

The use of the term in its general sense of income differences is widespread. To take one example, Kuznets in his pioneering study of incomes in the United States set out by stating that 'When we say "income inequality", we mean simply differences in income, without regard to their desirability as a system of reward or undesirability as a scheme running counter to some ideal of equality' (1953, p. *xxvii*).

However, to avoid any possible misunderstanding, an attempt has been made in the text to refer to differences, or dispersion, or concentration, of incomes when all that is meant is that they are not the same. The term 'inequality' is confined to cases where we are considering people whose circumstances are comparable in other (specified) respects.[1]

This use of the term 'inequality' depends in turn on what other respects are considered relevant. Again this is a matter for social judgement, and here we simply point to some of the important factors which are likely to have to be taken into account.

Resources and needs The flow of income received by an individual or the amount he consumes has to be viewed in relation to his needs, as represented by such considerations as his age, the size of his family, and his health. What is generous for a single man may be felt to be inadequate for a family of six. What is enough for a child may not be enough for a working man. The distribution of income and wealth has therefore to be assessed in the light of individual differences in needs.

Tastes and choice Individuals differ in their tastes with regard to work, to saving and to risk-taking. As a result people with the same opportunities may make different decisions, leading to disparities in observed incomes or wealth. One person may prefer a job with low earnings but short working hours and little responsibility. A person who prefers to save while working to provide for old age may have more wealth when he retires than those who preferred to consume when they were younger.

Age and the life-cycle The distribution may be influenced by the systematic variation of income and wealth over a typical person's life. One person may be richer than another because he is older and has had longer to save. Individuals may differ in the time when they receive their peak incomes. One person may choose to forgo earnings when young to train for a skilled job, whereas another does not.

Opportunity and outcome The impact of random chance factors on the distribution means that people who start out with the same opportunities ahead of them may still end up with very different

[1] There are a few occasions—as in the title—where it has been used more generally, on the grounds that 'existing usage is so firmly established that it would be pedantic to insist on avoiding it completely' (Bauer and Prest, 1973, p. 23).

incomes. If we are concerned only with equality of opportunity, then all that is relevant is how they start out—whether the expectation of success is the same for everyone. If we are concerned with equality of outcome, then the working of chance becomes a matter for concern.

These factors, and others not mentioned, mean that it is not easy to move from statements about differences in income and wealth to statements about justice and injustice. There are many difficulties in reaching social judgements about (say) the allowance for differing needs, or in deciding between opportunity and outcome. The fact that these problems are hard does not mean, however, that we should give in. Sen has drawn attention in this context to 'the danger of falling prey to a kind of nihilism [which] takes the form of noting, quite legitimately, a difficulty of some sort, and then constructing from it a picture of total disaster' (1973, p. 78). Just as we should not assume that any difference implies injustice, so too we should not conclude that the difficulties of comparison mean that distributional questions should be ignored.

1·3 Plan of the book

The principal part of the book is concerned with different aspects of the distribution of economic resources—earnings, wealth, the shares of wages and profits, and the incidence of poverty—but before embarking on these subjects two preliminary chapters provide some of the necessary background. The first of these (Chapter 2) is intended to provide an overall view of different features of the distribution of income and wealth, which will allow the reader to see the problem in its perspective and to understand the kind of issues with which the book is concerned. Following this broad survey, Chapter 3 deals with some of the conceptual problems which recur in the fields considered. These two introductory chapters also provide some of the tools needed to understand subsequent chapters. They explain what is meant, for instance, by a Lorenz curve, by the discounted value of lifetime income, and by different measures of concentration.

The first of the main topics considered (Chapter 4) is the evidence about incomes in Britain and the United States, and how the distribution has been changing over time. The sources of information about this important topic are very limited. Surveys of incomes carried out by the tax authorities, for example, exclude a substantial number of people at the lower end of the distribution, and provide very little information about the needs of different people. Data collected from enquiries in which participation is voluntary typically understate the income from investment and certain other sources. For such reasons, the official statistics must be treated with caution, and Chapter 4 examines their reliability as a guide to how the distribution of income has altered over the postwar period. It also considers the need to interpret this evidence in the light of changes in the underlying economic and social structure, taking account of factors such as the level of employment, the age composition of the population, and the rate of inflation.

Most people derive their major source of income from work. Chapters 5 and 6 discuss the evidence about the distribution of earnings and the theories which have been put forward to explain the observed differentials. In practice these differentials represent the outcome of a number of forces, working quite possibly in opposite directions. A model based on training costs might indicate that clergymen would be paid more than the average working man, whereas a model of bargaining power might suggest the reverse. A range of factors are considered in detail in Chapters 5 and 6: education and training costs, ability (IQ), parental background, trade union bargaining power, and the structure of the labour market. After this general review of different theories, the last part of Chapter 6 examines their application to the problem of low pay. It considers a number of possible explanations for low pay and their implications for government policy, particularly the effectiveness of minimum wage legislation.

The difference between income and wealth may be expressed most simply as being that the former represents a *flow* of resources over a period, whereas wealth is a *stock* at a point in time. A person may have £1000 invested on 1 January. This represents wealth, whereas the £80 received in interest during the next year represents income. The distribution of wealth is the subject of Chapters 7 and 8. In the first, the evidence about the present situation and about the long-run trends in Britain and the United States is examined in detail. The aim of this examination is to establish what conclusions can be drawn from the limited available data about the extent of concentration, and how far it can be attributed to factors such as differences in age. In order to throw light on the changes over time, Chapter 8 examines the underlying processes of wealth acquisition: thrift, differential returns to investment, patterns of inheritance, and marriage. How do people get to be rich? What is the effectiveness of government policies, particularly the use of taxation as an instrument for redistribution?

The distribution between factor shares is not the central concern of the book, as explained earlier, but it is clearly an important ingredient in determining the distribution among persons, and Chapter 9 provides a brief survey of the literature on this subject. This literature is in part theoretical and in part empirical. The first part of the chapter presents some of the evidence about the behaviour of factor shares over time and in particular whether, as Keynes believed, they remain broadly constant, or whether, as others assert, there has been a steady rise in the share of labour. The second part of the chapter describes the leading theories put forward to explain the distribution between labour, capital, and other factors. These include the 'orthodox' competitive theory, those based on bargaining power and the accumulation of capital, and the new views of the radical economists.

In Chapters 10 and 11, attention is focused on the problem of poverty in Britain and the United States. 'Poverty' is a term which is used in many different ways and the first part of the analysis is concerned with defining more precisely what is meant. Chapter 10 goes on to analyse the evidence about poverty in Britain and the United States. How many people live below the official poverty line, and who are they? Is poverty associated with exceptional circumstances, such as sickness or losing one parent, or is it the normal expectation for many people at certain stages of the life-cycle? What is the relationship between poverty in the United States and racial discrimination? The persistence of poverty according to the official standards demonstrates a basic inadequacy in present policies for income maintenance, and Chapter 11 leads on to examine the shortcomings of the present system and to consider proposals for reform. It discusses the growth of means-tested benefits and their failure to provide a satisfactory solution. It considers whether the answer lies in a negative income tax.

The last main chapter (Chapter 12) deals with a subject of great importance: the world distribution of income. It begins with the evidence concerning the differences between countries in *per capita* incomes and the argument that such international comparisons are meaningless. It discusses the differences within developing countries, and the implications for the distribution of income in the world as a whole. The principal instrument for world redistribution is foreign aid; the last section of the chapter examines the objections which have been raised to present aid programmes from the right and from the left of the political spectrum, and the possible scope for future developments.

The final chapter does not attempt to summarize the findings of the book, or to draw any grand conclusions. Indeed the main aim of the book is not to provide definite answers to the questions raised, but rather to show how they may be investigated using the tools of economic analysis. The function of Chapter 13 is to draw attention to features of the approach adopted which are distinctive and may therefore be controversial.

1·4 Some qualifications

A book covering such a wide range of subjects must inevitably leave many avenues unexplored. The expert reader will be aware that in places there are difficulties of a theoretical or statistical nature which warrant fuller discussion than space here permits. The aim has been to provide as balanced an account as possible of the existing state of the art, while not losing sight of the readership for which the book is intended. The references, and the notes on further reading, do however go some way towards guiding the reader in the more technical areas.

A further limitation is that of geographical coverage. As will have become clear from the outline, the main focus of the book is on Britain and the United States. Indeed, it attempts in a number of places to provide a comparative treatment of the experience in these two countries: for example, in the policies adopted to combat poverty. However, reference has also been made wherever possible to other countries, and it is hoped that the theoretical analysis is of wider generality.

Finally, it should be re-emphasized that this book is concerned with *economic* inequality. Questions of equality before the law or in politics, of inequalities in social status or power, are not considered; nor is any attempt made to discuss the relationship between these dimensions of social inequality and the distribution of income and wealth.

2

AN OVERALL VIEW

Obviously not everybody in the world has two very nice houses, a couple of boats, a tennis court, a swimming pool, and a Rolls Royce or two in the family.

(Rose Fitzgerald Kennedy)

The aim of this chapter is to provide an introduction to some of the main questions with which we are concerned in this book. The intention is to give the reader an overview of the field and to indicate the way in which the material will be developed in later chapters.

2·1 The distribution of income in Britain

One of our principal concerns in this book will be with the distribution of income, and this first section examines the evidence about incomes in Britain today.[1] Later in this chapter we consider how the situation compares with that in other countries. For this purpose, we have taken the estimates of the distribution of before tax income published in the *National income blue book*. These official statistics have been severely criticized by Titmuss and others, and it has been suggested that they present a rather misleading picture; these criticisms are discussed at length in Chapter 4, but for the present we simply take the official estimates at their face value.

The official estimates for the year 1967 are set out in Table 2·1. The reader may wonder why figures for 1967 are used rather than more recent estimates. The answer is that the relevant table in the *National income blue book* was not published after that year and no comparable estimates are available for later years. The table was dropped on the grounds of 'the increasing amount of estimation required', but in view of the importance of the subject it is very much to be regretted that the government did not provide anything in its place. (The evidence from alternative sources, such as the *Family expenditure survey* discussed in later chapters, does not suggest that the figures would have shown a dramatically different picture in the early 1970s.)

Before considering what the official estimates can tell us about the distribution, we should explain what is being measured. (The precise

---

[1] Throughout the book, the term 'Britain' is used as a shorthand; the sources make clear whether the data refer to Great Britain or the United Kingdom (i.e. including Northern Ireland).

TABLE 2·1

Incomes in the United Kingdom 1967

Range of income before tax (£ per year, lower end of range)	Number of income units (thousands)	Average incomes (£ per year rounded)		% of total income units	% of total income before tax
		Before tax	After income tax and surtax		
50–	2338	210	210	8·4	1·8
250–	4956	375	365	17·8	6·6
500–	2068	545	525	7·4	4·0
600–	1904	645	605	6·8	4·4
700–	1729	750	685	6·2	4·6
800–	3435	895	805	12·4	10·9
1000–	6741	1200	1100	24·2	29·4
1500–	2769	1700	1450	10·0	16·8
2000–	1298	2350	2000	4·7	10·8
3000–	370	3700	2700	1·3	4·7
5000–	150	6700	4250	0·5	3·6
10 000–	35	13 500	6350	0·13	1·66
20 000 and over	7	33 000	8150	0·03	0·83
TOTAL	27 800	1010	875	100	100

Source: National income and expenditure, 1969, Table 23.

definitions are discussed further in Chapter 4.) The estimates are derived from income tax returns, and therefore relate to family units as assessed for income tax purposes. In broad terms, an income unit in Table 2·1 comprises a man, wife and dependent children: i.e. the nuclear family. It would not normally include other adults resident in the same household, such as grandparents or grown-up children. The distinction between income units, households and individuals is an important one; some idea of the difference is provided by the fact that there were, according to Table 2·1, some 28 million income units in Britain in 1967, whereas at that date there were around 18 million households and over 35 million adults. The second point which requires clarification is the definition of income. The figures for income before tax in the table cover in general terms wages, salaries, interest income, rents, dividends, and professional fees. This does not necessarily constitute a comprehensive definition of income, a point which will be taken up in later chapters. It should also be noted that it includes items not always considered part of original income, most importantly transfer payments such as pensions, family allowances, and student grants. In other words, part of the activity of the government in redistributing income through cash transfers has already been taken into account in these figures.

What do these official estimates of the distribution tell us about the dispersion of incomes? The most striking point at even a casual glance is the distance between the top and the bottom of the distribution. At the bottom there were nearly 2½ million income units with incomes of less than £250 a year in 1967; at the top there were 7000 with before tax

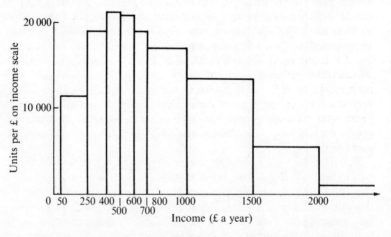

Fig. 2·1 Frequency of incomes, United Kingdom 1967 (*Source:* Table 2·1)

incomes of over £20 000. Those below £250 were likely to be mostly old age pensioners, since the pension was then around £4 a week, and they may well have had smaller needs, having no dependent children and not being at work. However, the difference in needs could not possibly correspond to a ratio of 150:1 between the average incomes of the top and the bottom ranges. Similarly, while income tax and surtax reduced the ratio of incomes after tax, it was still as high as 40:1.

A second feature of the distribution is that most income units are bunched around the middle, nearly two-thirds of the 28 million being found in the range £500–£1500, with a long tail spread out over the upper income ranges. One way in which this can be presented is in the form of a frequency distribution, as in Fig. 2·1, which shows the number of income recipients in each income range. For this purpose, the figures have to be standardized so that they correspond to income ranges of the same length. The range £1000 to £1500 includes more income units than the range £800 to £1000, but the former range is clearly wider than the latter and the frequency of incomes per £ of the income scale is in fact greater in the range £800 to £1000. There are 3·4 million divided by 200 (= 17 000) per £ in the range £800 to £1000, compared with 6·7 million divided by 500 (= 13 400) per £ in the range £1000 to £1500. The frequency distribution brings out clearly the bunching at the lower end of the income range. The most popular frequency (the mode) is around £500, which is considerably less than the average income (£1010). Moreover, it shows how the distribution spreads out above the average, with the tail stretching away to the right.

The frequency distribution is a useful presentational device, but it does not do full justice to the tails of the distribution. To the left, there should be people with negative incomes; that is people, typically in business on their own account, who have made losses during the year. These people are not covered adequately by the statistics. To the right, Fig. 2·1 is cut short above £2000, whereas the frequency distribution should really be continued until we have reached the richest man in the country. To do this, however, we would need a much larger page. The very size does indeed provide some indication of the extent of the gap. There were certainly people with incomes in excess of £100 000, and a graph incorporating them would stretch in fact for approximately 40 pages of this book.

The frequency diagram may, therefore, represent the middle, but it fails to bring out the full extent of differences in income, and in view of this Pen (1971) has recently suggested an alternative way of depicting the distribution of income. The device used is to imagine a parade in which every person (in our case each income unit) marches past in an hour and where his height in the parade corresponds to his before tax income. A person with the average income of £1010 in 1967 would therefore appear as being 5'10" tall and everyone else would be correspondingly taller or shorter. The attraction of this presentational device is that it not only brings out the relative positions of different people, but also allows one to identify who appears where in the distribution.

The highlights of Pen's parade may be summarized briefly. (The heights have been adjusted to fit the data shown in Table 2·1.) Right at the beginning come those who are walking upside down: businessmen and others who have made losses and therefore have negative incomes. Next, as we have seen, come old age pensioners dependent on the state pension. The height of the pensioners is not much over a foot. After them come low paid workers, with, as Pen says, the rule of women first for each occupation. Their height begins at about 2'6" and rises very slowly. The slowness with which height increases is one of the striking features of the parade, although it is exactly what we would have expected, given the bunching together of incomes indicated by the frequency distribution. It is only when we pass the average income (with 24 minutes to go) that events begin to speed up, but even when we enter the last 6 minutes (the top 10 per cent) we have only got to 6'6" headmasters. Heights then start to rise rapidly as we reach the top professional classes. At 18' there are MPs and army colonels; at 30' there are hospital consultants and senior civil servants; at 30 yards there are the chairmen of nationalized industries; and at over 120 yards there is the managing director of Shell. He is not, however, the last, since the final part of the parade is made up of people of whom Pen says 'their heads disappear into the clouds and probably they themselves do not even know how tall they are'. The last man in Pen's parade is J. Paul Getty, whose height he reckons to be at least 10 miles and perhaps twice as much. It is in fact important to watch the last few seconds of the parade carefully, since there is a great deal of difference between those who arrive at the beginning of the last minute (the top 1·7 per cent) and those who arrive at the very end. This difference is partly one of height, from a mere 6 yards at the beginning to 10 miles, but there is also a difference in the nature of their incomes. Those at the *beginning* of the last minute are the top salary earners, managers with possibly some £50 000 in savings, whereas those at the very end derive nearly all their income from wealth.

The differences in before tax incomes are clearly reduced by the taxation of income. Table 2·1 showed that in 1967 income tax and surtax reduced the ratio between the average incomes of the top and bottom ranges from 150:1 to some 40:1. The income tax, and the transfer payments already taken into account, are however the most

important in cash terms of the redistributive elements of the government budget. It has to be remembered that other taxes, notably social
security contributions, are if anything regressive in their incidence,
forming a declining proportion of income as we go up the scale. Even,
therefore, when allowance is made for government redistribution, the
dispersion of cash incomes remains very substantial. (Redistribution in
kind has not been discussed, but neither have important elements of
income in kind, such as fringe benefits; both are considered in Chapter
4.)

   Before leaving the overall distribution of income, reference should be
made to an alternative way of presenting data about the distribution of
income, through what is called a Lorenz curve. Although less dramatic
than Pen's parade, it is in many respects more useful and will be used at
a number of points in later chapters. The Lorenz curve corresponding
to the data given in Table 2·1 for before tax incomes is shown in
Fig. 2·2 and indicates the share of total income which is received by the
bottom x per cent of income units. From the dashed lines we can, for

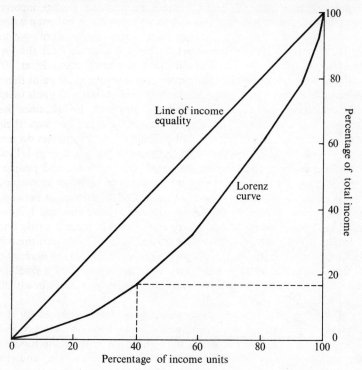

Fig. 2·2. Lorenz curve of income, United Kingdom 1967

example, read off that the bottom 40 per cent of income units received around 17 per cent of total before tax income. The construction of the Lorenz curve from Table 2·1 is straightforward. The last two columns in the table show the percentages of total tax units in the different income ranges and the percentage of total income they receive. The bottom group (those in the range £50 to £250) make up 8·4 per cent of tax units and receive 1·8 per cent of total income. This gives the first point on the Lorenz curve (because their share is so small, the point is very close to the horizontal axis). We now add the next group and find that the bottom 26·2 per cent (8·4 + 17·8) receive 8·4 per cent (1·8 + 6·6) of total income, which gives the next point on the Lorenz curve, and so on.

The Lorenz curve is useful because it shows very graphically the degree of dispersion of incomes. If all incomes are equal, so that every 10 per cent of the population receives 10 per cent of the total income, the Lorenz curve follows the diagonal 'Line of income equality' in Fig. 2·2. If the bottom 10 per cent receives less than 10 per cent of

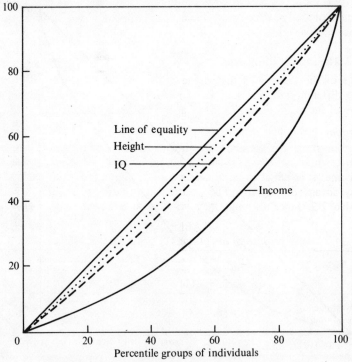

Fig. 2·3. Lorenz curves for height, intelligence, and income.
Source: Brown (1970), p. 114.

total income, then the Lorenz curve lies below the diagonal. In the extreme case where all the income is received by one person, the Lorenz curve follows the horizontal axis until we reach the last person and then rises steeply, so that it has an ⌟ shape. The closeness of the Lorenz curve to the diagonal, therefore, provides a means of assessing the extent of income differences. If, just to illustrate the working of the Lorenz curve, we look at the distribution of height, IQ and income, we can see (Fig. 2·3) that IQ scores are more unequally distributed than height and that income in turn is more concentrated than IQ.

As was emphasized in the previous chapter, differences in income do not necessarily imply the existence of injustice. It is possible that differences in income may reflect differences in needs. It is possible that they may be offset by non-pecuniary factors, such as longer hours of work. It is possible that they correspond to differences in age, as where people have saved for their retirement, or to longer periods of training. The hospital consultant who reached a height of 30 foot in Pen's parade was only 2'6" tall as a medical student. On the other hand, it is also quite possible that none of these factors can explain the full extent of income dispersion. One of the aims of this book is to examine how far this is the case.

2·2 The sources of income

One of the features of the parade of incomes was that it brought out the differences in the sources of income. In this section we examine two of the main sources: earnings and wealth.

Earnings

For most people, earnings are the single most important, if not the only, source of income, and a view of the distribution of earned incomes is essential to an understanding of the nature of inequality in any advanced economy. The position in Britain in 1973 is set out in Table 2·2. Since earnings may vary for a large number of reasons,

TABLE 2·2
Distribution of earnings in Great Britain 1973

| | Gross weekly earnings of full-time adult employees | | | |
| | Men (21 and over) | | Women (18 and over) | |
	£ per week	% of median	£ per week	% of median
Lowest decile	25·2	66	14·1	67
Lowest quartile	30·7	80	16·9	81
Median	38·4	100	20·9	100
Upper quartile	48·1	125	26·7	128
Highest decile	60·9	159	34·4	165
Mean	41·9	109	23·1	111

Source: 'New earnings survey',—*Department of Employment Gazette*, April 1973.

depending on the hours worked, age, sex and other factors, the figures in the table are based on adult workers employed full-time, both wage and salary earners, and show separately the distribution for men and women. The table presents the distribution in the form of the earnings at different *deciles* and *quartiles*. Their meaning may be understood as follows. Suppose that we were to line up workers in ascending order of earnings and to count off those making up the bottom 10 per cent, then the person just completing the bottom 10 per cent would be the lowest decile, and his earnings are those shown in the first line of the table. The lowest quartile is the person a quarter of the way along the line from the bottom; and the median is the man in the middle.

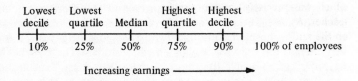

The table shows earnings both in cash terms in 1973 and as a percentage of the median person's earnings. To take one example, the earnings of the lowest quartile of men are only 80 per cent of those of the median.

These figures demonstrate once again the gap between the top and the bottom of the scale. The bottom 10 per cent of workers have earnings which are less than two-thirds of those of the median. On the other hand, the earnings of the top decile are some 60 per cent higher than those of the median, and as we have seen in Pen's parade there is considerable inequality within the top 10 per cent. A further feature of the distribution brought out by Table 2·2 is the difference between the median and the mean (or average). The median, or the man in the middle of the earnings line-up, earns only 91 per cent of the average. This reflects the bunching of the earnings distribution to the left, just as we observed in the case of income, with the average being pushed up by the long upper tail. Since the average earnings figure is one commonly quoted in popular discussion, it is important to remember that many more than half of all workers earn less than the average.

The right hand part of Table 2·2 shows the weekly earnings of women at the same date. The restriction to full-time workers is much more important in this case, since many women work part-time, and it has to be borne in mind that average hours are lower even for women working full-time. The figures demonstrate the large gap which exists between the sexes. The median earnings for women are only 55 per cent of those for men, and nearly 75 per cent of women earn less than the lowest decile of men. Even adjusted for the difference in hours worked, the median earnings of women are only 61 per cent of those of men. A less expected finding is that the shape of the distribution of earnings among women is very close to that for men. The ratios of the lowest decile and the lowest quartile to the median are almost exactly the same, and the other ratios are very similar.

It may be very helpful to put some flesh on to the statistics presented in Table 2·2, by examining just who appears at different points on the earnings scale. In the introduction to *The social foundations of wage policy*, Barbara Wootton says that one of the incidents which led to her writing the book was the discovery just before the Second World War that the elephant giving rides at Whipsnade Zoo earned £600 a year, which was precisely the same salary as she drew as a senior university teacher. As a result she started wondering what other occupations stood on the same rung of the ladder as the elephant and herself.

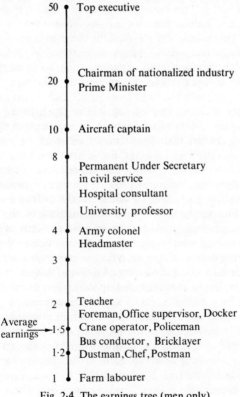

50	Top executive
20	Chairman of nationalized industry Prime Minister
10	Aircraft captain
8	Permanent Under Secretary in civil service Hospital consultant University professor
4	Army colonel Headmaster
3	
2	Teacher Foreman, Office supervisor, Docker
Average earnings → 1·5	Crane operator, Policeman Bus conductor, Bricklayer
1·2	Dustman, Chef, Postman
1	Farm labourer

Fig. 2·4. The earnings tree (men only)

In Fig. 2·4 we have set out an earnings 'tree' giving some idea of relative positions. Two points should be noted about this diagram. Firstly, the scale is measured not in £ but relative to the earnings of the person with the lowest earnings shown—the farm labourer. This presentation avoids the need to update the earnings with every general increase in money wages. Secondly, the vertical distances are measured on a logarithmic scale, which means that the gap between 1 and 2 is the same as that between 2 and 4, as that between 4 and 8, etc. This compresses the top part of the earnings scale so that we can get the very top earners on to the graph. Even so, we have had to squash most of the population into the bottom quarter of the diagram. The occupations shown in Fig. 2·4 are only a selection, but they give some indication of the relativities. The reasons why different people appear where they do are discussed in Chapters 5 and 6.

Wealth

We have seen earlier that the managing directors who appear at the top of the earnings ladder are not at the very top of the income distribution. This position is reserved for those with unearned incomes, that is incomes from wealth. This source of income is less important than earnings in absolute terms, since the share of property income in total income is only about a quarter or less, but it is highly concentrated and hence may add more to the differences in incomes.

The extent of concentration of wealth in Britain can only be determined within rather broad limits. As is explained in Chapter 7, the statistical sources are far from ideal and need to be interpreted carefully. It also depends on what one means by wealth and how it is valued. If, like the Inland Revenue, one values assets at what they could be sold for, then the estimates given in Chapter 7 suggest that in the late 1960s the top 1 per cent of adults owned around a third of total personal wealth and the top 5 per cent around a half. If, on the other hand, one includes assets, such as state pension rights, which have no market value but are worth something to the individual, these shares are reduced, but the degree of concentration remains substantial.

As in the case of the distribution of income, this concentration does not necessarily imply the existence of inequality. It has been pointed out that part may be explained by age differences and by people saving for retirement. The person who has paid off his mortgage on a London suburban house would not need a lot in the bank to qualify for a place in the top 5 per cent (although he might well be surprised to learn that he did!). This does not, however, account for the very rich, and in this context it is important to emphasize that there is an enormous gap between the moderately well off and the very rich. The top people are indeed millionaires and in some cases many times over. The property developer Harry Hyams was reputed to be worth £27 million in 1967; one member of the Sainsbury family held shares in the business estimated to be worth £30 million in 1973; and the late Sir John Ellerman was reported to be worth £150 million. These amounts are very hard to put in perspective; one way of looking at it is that £150 million would in 1973 have paid British Rail's whole wage bill for nearly four months. How these people get to be so rich is a question discussed in Chapter 8.

2·3 Changes over time

The evidence discussed so far relates to the late 1960s and the early 1970s. A much longer term view has been taken by Soltow (1968) in a study of the distribution of income before tax in Britain from 1688 to 1962–3. The evidence for the first of these years is based on the estimates prepared by Gregory King at that time, giving the number and average incomes of 26 classes of persons, ranging from temporal lords with £3200 per annum, through gentlemen with £280, to common soldiers with £14 and 'vagrants, beggars, gipsies, thieves and prostitutes' with £2 a year. (The reliability of these estimates is not discussed here!) From this information we can plot a Lorenz curve in the same way as if we had data on incomes by ranges and this is shown in Fig. 2·5, together with the curves corresponding to the income distributions available for 1801–3, 1867 and 1967 (this being the *Blue book* distribution described in Section 2·1).

From the evidence set out in Fig. 2·5, Soltow concluded that there was little change in the distribution of income between 1688 and the beginning of the nineteenth century; that the movement between 1801 and 1867 was rather unclear; and that there has been a clear reduction in inequality since 1867. These conclusions can be related to the position of the Lorenz curves. In the case of 1867, the Lorenz curve lies completely outside that for 1967 and, as with the diagram for height, IQ and income, we can conclude that the distribution was more dispersed in 1867. Comparing 1801–3 and 1867, however, the Lorenz curves intersect. While the bottom 30 per cent of the population had a larger share of total income in 1867 than at the beginning of the century, the share of the bottom 90 per cent fell, so that the top 10 per cent were better off in 1867.

On balance there appears from these estimates to have been a long-run trend towards less dispersion of incomes. This decline is attributed by Soltow to the reduced importance of income from land and he comments that 'the onslaught of the Industrial Revolution, with growth in profits from trade and professional income, could not have

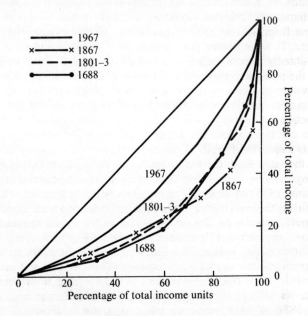

Fig. 2·5. Distribution of income in Britain 1688–1967
Source: Soltow (1968), p. 20 and data in Table 2·1.
Note: the data relate to England and Wales for 1688 and 1801–3, to Great Britain and Ireland for 1867, and to the United Kingdom for 1967.

introduced an element of greater inequality than that existing with property income' (1968, p. 28). Soltow goes on to suggest that the trend towards less dispersion has accelerated in the twentieth century. This view is certainly widely shared. At the beginning of the 1960s, Lord Boyle expressed the view in the House of Commons that 'we have a better and fairer distribution of incomes today than we had ten or eleven years ago'; and a member of the opposite front bench wrote that 'the distribution of personal income has become significantly more equal' (Crosland, 1964, p. 31). On the other hand, the examination by Titmuss of the official statistics on which these conclusions were based led him to conclude that 'there are other forces, deeply rooted in the social structure and fed by many complex institutional factors inherent in large-scale economies, operating in reverse directions' (1962, p. 198). In Chapter 4, we shall examine the relative merits of these different views.

Trends in the dispersion of incomes must reflect changes in the distribution of the two main components of income (earnings and income from wealth) or a change in the relative importance of these sources. If we consider first the distribution of earnings, there has undoubtedly been a decline in the position of upper earners as a group over the past sixty years. The estimates of Routh (1965) showed that the average earnings of higher professional workers fell from four times the average for all men in 1913/14 to three times the average in 1960. An extreme example was that of bishops of the Church of England, whose average income did not rise in money terms for over forty years, despite a more than fourfold rise in prices.

At the same time, there is remarkable stability in the distribution of earnings among manual workers. The study by Phelps Brown and Hopkins (1955) of building wages over seven centuries showed that in the fifteenth century the craftsman got half as much again as the labourer: 6d a day against 4d for the labourer. By the mid-nineteenth century, the rate for craftsmen had become 6d an *hour*, but the relativities were unchanged. Since then the differential between craftsmen and labourers has narrowed, but the same kind of stability is exhibited by the overall distribution among all manual workers. Table 2·3 shows data for the distribution of earnings among manual workers from 1886 to 1973, where the earnings of the lowest decile, etc., are expressed as a percentage of the median. (It should be noted that the data in this table relate to *manual* workers, whereas Table 2·2 covered both manual and non-manual workers.) From this table it appears that the dispersion of earnings among manual workers has changed very

TABLE 2·3

Changes in earnings distribution in Great Britain 1886–1973

Percentage of median	Gross weekly earnings of full-time male manual workers				
	1886	1906	1938	1960	1973
Lowest decile	69	67	68	71	67
Lower quartile	83	80	82	83	81
Upper quartile	122	127	119	122	122
Highest decile	143	157	140	145	145

Sources: 1886–1960 from Thatcher, (1968), p. 163.
1973 from 'New earnings survey', *Department of Employment Gazette*, April 1973

little in percentage terms over the best part of a century, a period in which median earnings increased from £1·20 a week to £37 a week. This does not mean that the earnings in all occupations have increased by the same percentage, but that the gains in one occupation have been offset by the relative losses in another (or by changes in dispersion within occupations) in such a way that the overall shape remains much the same.

The trend in unearned incomes depends on the underlying changes in the concentration of wealth and in the yield on wealth. The evidence about the distribution of wealth shows a clear decline in the share of the top groups over the past fifty years. This is likely to have led to a reduction in the dispersion of investment income, although it must be borne in mind that much of the increased wealth of the bottom 99 per cent consists of owner-occupied houses, consumer durables and other personal assets, which do not yield an income which appears in the official figures under consideration. The trend in the distribution of wealth raises wider issues. It has been argued that there is a spontaneous process of equalization which may be projected into the future, and the conclusion is drawn that there is no need for government intervention through measures such as a wealth tax. However, before we can project the trends of the past fifty years into the future, we must examine the forces underlying changes in the distribution of wealth. How far is it due to factors such as the use of gifts to spread property, the increased holding of wealth by women, the avoidance of estate duty, or temporary movements in asset prices? These questions are discussed in Chapters 7 and 8.

Finally, there is the division between earned and unearned incomes, or the distribution by *factor shares*. For a long time it was widely believed that the factor distribution was highly stable in the long run, the most celebrated statement of this view being that of Keynes, that 'the stability of the proportion of the national dividend accruing to labour, irrespective apparently of the level of output as a whole and of the phase of the trade cycle . . . was one of the most surprising, yet best-established, facts in the whole range of economic statistics' (1939, p. 48). This view was based on the estimates by Bowley and Stamp of the share of wages, which showed that it remained essentially constant between 1911 and 1924, despite the disruption of the First World War and the subsequent boom and depression. However, these figures were misleading in that they related only to wage earners, defined broadly as 'operatives', and excluded salaried workers (clerical, technical, professional, managerial, etc.). If salary earners are included in an estimate of the share of *total pay*, then the stability vanishes: the share, expressed as a percentage of gross national product, has risen from 48 per cent to 67 per cent over this century. 'Total pay' may not be the ideal definition, since it excludes the earned income component of self-employment income, but even if the whole of income from self-employment is included, there would still have been a substantial increase in the share.

In broad terms, it appears therefore that there has been a rise in the share of earned incomes and a fall in the shares of profits and rents. If it is assumed that unearned incomes accrue largely to upper income groups, then these movements would be consistent with a reduction in overall income dispersion. The relationship between factor shares in total national income and the distribution among persons is, however, less straightforward than this. Profits accrue not only to the wealthy with private means but also to the old age pensioner with a small holding in a unit trust. Rents go not only to Mr Hyams but also to the widow leasing out the shop her husband used to run. In Chapter 9 we examine the link between factors and persons in more detail, as well as describing some of the theories put forward to explain the observed change in factor shares.

2·4 International comparisons and the distribution of world incomes

International comparisons are often used to score debating points and it is frequently suggested that Britain has a greater or smaller dispersion of incomes than other advanced countries. Such international comparisons are difficult to make with any confidence, since, in addition to the deficiencies of each set of national figures, there are enormous problems of comparability. The data for one country are collected from tax returns and do not cover the whole population; those for another are based on special surveys which do not achieve a 100 per cent response; a third country relies on data from a census of population where certain types of income are likely to be under-reported. One must therefore treat such comparisons with great caution and this qualification should be borne in mind throughout this section.

The most obvious comparison to make is that between Britain and the United States. It might well be expected that the latter country, with its more capitalist *laissez-faire* ethic, less government intervention, and greater regional and ethnic disparities, would have much greater income differences than Britain. In this context, we can draw on the comparative study of Britain and the United States by Lydall and Lansing (1959). While rather dated (the results relate to 1953–4), it is a rare attempt to obtain figures on a comparable basis, and it suffers less than many other sources from the problems described in the previous paragraph. The results of this study showed, very interestingly, that although the dispersion of income appeared greater in the United

States, the difference was very slight: the share of the top 10 per cent
in total income was 31 per cent, against 30 per cent in Britain. The
authors concluded that 'pre-tax income per spending unit is, in general,
very similarly distributed in the two countries' (1959, p. 66). They
went on to look at the distribution of wealth, and here the situation
was quite different. In this case it was Britain that had a higher degree
of concentration, and the difference was very much greater. As Lydall
and Lansing comment, 'the two Lorenz curves deviate very substantially from one another, a pattern in marked contrast with the
relative similarity of the Lorenz curves of income' (p. 60). The fortunes
of the Rockefellers, the Mellons, the du Ponts and Howard Hughes
were, in the 1950s at least, no match for the steady accumulation of
wealth over centuries by the wealthy families of Britain. In Chapter 7,
we examine how far this is still the case.

TABLE 2·4
Income distribution in Europe, North America, and Japan

| | | Share in total personal income before tax | |
		Top 20%	Bottom 40%
Canada	1965	40·2	20·0
Norway	1963	40·5	16·6
USA	1966	44·0	15·0
Sweden	1963	44·0	14·0
United Kingdom	1964	44·2	15·3
Japan	1962	46·0	15·3
Netherlands	1962	48·4	14·0
West Germany	1964	52·9	15·4
France	1962	53·7	9·5

Source: Economic Commission for Europe (1967), Table 6·10.

If we turn from the United States to Europe, data have been
assembled for the distribution of income in seven different European
countries by the Economic Commission for Europe, and some of this
information is reproduced in Table 2·4, together with estimates for
Canada, Japan and the USA. While efforts have been made to ensure
comparability, there are still important differences which are likely to
introduce systematic biases into the comparison. For example, the unit
of analysis is in general the nuclear family—man, wife and dependent
children—but in France it is the household, which could include other
adults, and in Sweden the incomes of husband and wife are not
combined. In general terms, the broader the income unit the lower the
degree of concentration, a point which is developed in the next chapter.

Another difference is that the figures for West Germany include the undistributed profits of companies, which appear as separate units in the statistics and are likely to increase the number of high income units. Finally, the definition of income differs, with that for the Scandinavian countries being income assessed for tax purposes and that for the other countries being an estimate of total income.

Bearing in mind these deficiencies of the data, we may compare Britain with the other countries in terms of the shares of income received by different groups. From this it appears that Britain occupies an intermediate position, with Canada, Norway and Sweden apparently characterized by a rather lower degree of inequality, and France, the Netherlands and West Germany having a higher degree of concentration. In the case of France, the share of the bottom 40 per cent is considerably smaller than in all other countries and the share of the top 20 per cent is larger.

A rather similar picture emerges from the estimates of the distribution of earnings in different countries presented by Lydall (1968), who discusses the differences in definition in considerable detail. Within the group of industrialized countries, the degree of dispersion is broadly the same, with France having an exceptionally high degree and Australia and New Zealand noticeably less. The data also cover two other groups of countries: Eastern Europe and a selection of developing countries. The Eastern European countries appear for a given level of development to have rather less dispersion of earnings and this is particularly marked in the cases of Czechoslovakia and Hungary. Finally, in the developing countries earnings differentials appear to be considerably greater, although given the unreliability of the data it would be very dangerous to draw any definite conclusions about the relationship between the distribution of earnings and the level of development.

The reference to developing countries brings us to the last subject of this section—the world distribution of income. There can be little doubt that income differences on a world scale are of a quite different order of importance from those within a single country. This is brought out if we consider the distribution of average per capita incomes in different countries. The available evidence is subject to a number of qualifications (for example, exchange rates are often used to convert into a common currency), and thus may not accurately reflect differences in standards of living. However, it is shown in Chapter 12 that even when adjustments are made for such factors, the income differences *between* countries are even greater than those found *within* a country such as the United States. India, for example, accounted in 1962–3 for a quarter of the population covered by the estimates of Beckerman and

Bacon (1970), but for only 4 per cent of total world consumption. Moreover, the small share received by poor countries is itself unevenly distributed. If the average income in India is so much lower than the average in the United States, the gap between the poor in India and the rich in the United States must be many times larger.

3
CONCEPTUAL PROBLEMS

The setting up of reasonably clear, and yet difficult specifications is not merely an exercise in perfectionism. For if these specifications do approximate ... the real core of our interest when we talk about the shares of economic classes or long-term changes in these shares, then proper disclosure of our meaning and intentions is vitally useful. It forces us to examine and evaluate critically the data that are available; it prevents us jumping to conclusions based on these inadequate data ... and most important of all, it propels us toward a deliberate construction of testable bridges between the available data and the income structure that is the real focus of our interest.

(Simon Kuznets)

The features of the distribution of income and wealth described in the previous chapter raise a number of questions of a conceptual nature. The aim of this chapter is to clarify these before proceeding to the main part of the analysis. We discussed, for example, the distribution of income among tax units in a particular year, but this left a number of issues unresolved. Is it with income that we should really be concerned? Should we consider the distribution among individuals, families or households? Is it sufficient to look at annual incomes or should we take incomes over the life-cycle?

The conceptual framework set out in this chapter is intended to apply throughout the book, but it is important to remember that the approach adopted may depend on the subject under discussion. When considering the incidence of poverty, we may be more concerned with week-to-week variations in income than if we are trying to form an overall assessment of the distribution of life-chances. More generally, many issues depend on judgements which have to be made by society, and the focus here is on bringing out the implications of different social decisions.

3·1 Access to economic resources and the definition of income

Access to economic resources has several different dimensions and it may be helpful first to distinguish between income, expenditure and wealth. For this purpose, let us consider the hypothetical life history of a single man, Mr A, reserving for later discussion the problems which arise if he marries and has children. In any year he is in receipt of resources from a number of different sources: earnings, investment income from the assets he owns, transfers from the government (student grant when young, pension when old) and capital receipts (legacies and gifts). After allowing for tax, he can dispose of the resources in three ways: he can use them for personal expenditure, he can pass them on to others as a capital transfer, or he can add them to his stock of wealth (saving). In the last case, his investment income in the next year will be correspondingly greater. Schematically, we may set out the process as follows:

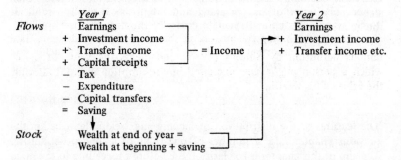

	Year 1		*Year 2*
Flows	Earnings		Earnings
+	Investment income		+ Investment income
+	Transfer income	= Income	+ Transfer income etc.
+	Capital receipts		
−	Tax		
−	Expenditure		
−	Capital transfers		
=	Saving		
Stock	Wealth at end of year =		
	Wealth at beginning + saving		

(The definition of income is discussed more fully in the next section.)

From the diagram we can see how annual decisions about flows of resources affect the stock of assets which the person possesses. The stock provides a link in money terms between different periods of his life. (There are obviously other links: for example, his earnings in year 2 may depend on decisions about training in year 1.) The process goes on year after year from his reaching the age of economic independence to the day he dies. At his death, his wealth is by definition zero, since his estate is transferred to his heirs (and the government in estate tax, if he is wealthy). Over his life as a whole, just as he proceeds from dust to dust, so his wealth goes from zero to zero, and all the resources received during his life are disposed of, through either expenditure or capital transfers (including the final transfer at his death).

In assessing the economic position of Mr A in year 1 (we take up later the question whether it is right to consider his position in a single period), there are, therefore, a number of indicators which we could take:

Income before tax
Income after tax
Expenditure
Wealth.

Of these income, before or after tax, is that most commonly employed, and it is the main aspect considered here. It is important, however, to consider its relationship to the other measures.

The most natural measure may in fact appear to be not income but expenditure, since this represents the purchasable benefits which a person enjoys. To echo the question posed by Hobbes in *The Leviathan*, should we regard a person who 'laboureth much, and sparing the fruits of his labour, consumeth little' as being of higher economic status than a person who 'living idlely getteth little, and spendeth all he gets'? Expenditure has, however, been used as a measure of economic status much less frequently than income. The reason for this may lie in the relative availability of evidence, but it also reflects the fact that income represents *potential* spending power. As expressed in the famous definition by Simons (1938), income is the value of rights which a person *might have* exercised in consumption without altering the value of his wealth.

What difference does it make if we take income as a measure of potential spending power, rather than actual expenditure? In any one period of Mr A's life, the difference between his income (after tax) and his expenditure consists of capital transfers and saving. In the latter case, it can be argued that if he decides to save and thereby postpone consumption, this will be taken into account at a later date, so that over his lifetime as a whole net saving is zero. The difference in this respect is therefore one of timing. The case of capital transfers is rather different, since these would not usually be counted when measuring expenditure, even if we consider the whole lifetime of Mr A. An important difference between the use of income for measurement or expenditure is, therefore, whether or not one considers that the control exercised through gifts or bequests should be taken into account. A miserly millionaire who lived on virtually nothing would from one point of view appear rich, and from the other poor.

This brings us to the question of control over economic resources, related not to flows but to the stock of wealth that a person owns. The possession of wealth may generate income but is that all wealth means? A person may save 'for the sake of increasing his control *per se* of the economic institutions of a capitalistic society, and for the sake of the various satisfactions ... which such control brings over and above [that] derived from the expenditure of the income from this capital' (Vickrey, 1947, p. 340).

This is most obvious in the case of owner-controlled firms, such as the Getty Oil Company or the Sainsbury food chain, and in trusts and charitable foundations, such as the Rockefeller or Nuffield Foundations. At the same time, the links between personal wealth and control are far from straightforward, and we need also to take account of the other aspects of control, vested in executives, civil servants and politicians. For this reason no systematic treatment of the relationship between resources and control is attempted in this book. Moreover, the links depend crucially on the form in which wealth is held: whether Mr A's wealth is in the bank, in physical assets such as his house and furniture, or in shares in the A Manufacturing Company Ltd. Money invested in a building society does not provide the owner with any control over industry, whereas the same amount invested in shares in a private company may be associated with considerable influence over its activity.

This last point draws attention to the fact that although we shall be primarily concerned with aggregate variables, there are cases in which certain components may be more significant than others. This may be illustrated by expenditure, where particular items may be regarded as being of especial importance. We may be more interested in the equality of access to medical care than of access to theatre tickets. We may want to single out food consumption, because we are concerned with the distribution of nutritional intake in relation to recommended standards. Such 'specific egalitarianism', or the view 'that certain specific scarce commodities should be distributed less unequally than the ability to pay for them' (Tobin, 1970, p. 264), is not examined here, but may be an important explanation as to why governments pursue certain redistributive policies.

Finally, the impact of the tax system on the distribution of resources, while not a primary concern of this book, is of major importance. In the schematic history of Mr A, he was shown as paying tax on his income, but he clearly comes into contact with the fiscal system at many different junctures. He may be taxed, under a value-added or sales tax, on his expenditure and he may be subsidized. He may pay taxes on his house to local authorities. The capital transfers he makes may render him liable for duty. In the discussion above, attention was focused on the resources available to the individual after tax and it appears from the point of view of spending power, either actual or potential, and of control over economic decisions, that this is the relevant indicator. Two qualifications should, however, be mentioned. Firstly, income before tax may be more relevant as a measure of status or of social respect. It is gross earnings 'which tell people how they stand compared to others, how they are valued by their employers compared to colleagues and how they are progressing compared to similar reference groups outside work' (Daniel, 1968, p. 236). Secondly, the benefit side of government activity has to be taken into account, and consumption clearly depends not only on personal expenditure but also on publicly provided goods such as hospitals, parks and schools.

The definition of income

In the schematic representation of a year in the life of Mr A, we defined his income as being equal to the sum of his earnings, investment income, transfers and capital receipts. This definition does, however, raise a number of issues (many of which also apply if we are concerned with expenditure).

At first sight, 'income' may appear to be a straightforward, everyday concept. There have, however, been years of controversy about its correct definition, and there is a wide divergence between income as defined for the purposes of income tax and the definition which would now be accepted by most economists. This latter definition is that described earlier: *income in a given period is the amount a person could have spent while maintaining the value of his wealth intact.* Or, as it was described in the classic treatment by Simons: 'Personal income may be defined as the sum of (1) the market value of rights exercised in consumption and (2) the change in the value of the store of property rights between the beginning and end of the period' (1938, p. 50).

The first significant feature of this definition is that it is comprehensive. As was pointed out by the Minority Report of the Royal Commission on the Taxation of Profits and Income, in a much quoted passage: 'No concept of income can be really equitable that stops short of the comprehensive definition which embraces all receipts which increase an individual's command over the use of society's scarce resources—in other words, his "net accretion of economic power between two points in time" ' (1955, p. 355).

It is in its comprehensive nature that the definition departs from the practice of the tax authorities, and hence from much of the statistical data on the distribution of income, and this will prove of great importance when we examine the evidence about incomes in the next chapter. For the present, attention is drawn to the kind of items which would be included under the comprehensive definition but are often excluded from the statistics on income distribution (the list is far from exhaustive):

Capital gains According to the Simons definition, capital gains and losses clearly form part of income. As is noted by the Minority Report, income 'includes the whole of the change in the value of a man's store of property rights ... irrespective of whether the change has been brought about by the current addition of property [or] by accretions to the value of property' (p. 356). If Mr A had invested £500 in shares which increased in value over the year by £50, he could have spent £50 more without reducing the value of his wealth, leaving on one side for the moment the effects of inflation. This capital gain, even if not realized by the sale of the shares, should be regarded as part of his income in just the same way as if he received £50 in dividends. Conversely, if his shares had fallen in value, the capital loss should be deducted from his income.

Fringe benefits In many jobs there is payment not only in cash but also in kind in the form of fringe benefits, ranging from free canteen meals and concessionary coal at the bottom end of the income scale to the company car and penthouse for the top executive. Moreover, the use of the term 'fringe' may give the misleading impression that they are of subsidiary importance. At the same time, there are serious problems of valuation. The benefits may not be marketable, in which case the value to the individual is hard to assess. One example is foreign travel by a businessman: 'is he giving himself a holiday under the bogus guise of a commercial purpose, or is he spending all day and half the night trying to sell a product in which he has no interest to people he dislikes in a place from which he is longing to get away?' (Runciman, 1974, p. 94). Yet it would clearly be wrong to assume that no fringe benefits provide any addition to economic resources and an attempt should be made to include estimates of the amount involved.

Production for home consumption Although the Simons definition refers to 'market value', this does not mean that the consumption must arise through a market transaction. The consumption of home-produced output, for example by farmers, clearly represents the exercise of command over resources and should be taken into account. This is likely to be important when making comparisons between countries, particularly those at very different stages of development (see Chapter 12).

Imputed rent Another example of income in kind which does not arise through a market transaction is the rent which should be imputed to physical capital which is owned by persons and yields them services. The most important instance is the benefit received by home owners. Owning a house does not provide a cash income, but it has much the same effect, in that it saves the owner from paying rent. If Mr A lived in his own house, we should therefore want to add to his income an amount equal to the market rent he could have obtained (similarly an addition would be made to his expenditure). The same consideration applies to other assets, such as cars, pictures, yachts, clothes, and consumer durables, but their quantitative significance is likely to be considerably less.

A second feature of the ideal definition is that it is concerned with *real* income, or its purchasing power, and that allowance should be made as far as possible for differing price levels. This is relevant, for example, where prices vary within a country, so that a given money income represents different spending power for people living in different places. In the United States, an index of the cost of living in 1967 (St Louis = 100) ranged from 91 in Houston, Texas, to 109 in New York (Taussig, 1973, p. 24). The most obvious source of such variation is housing costs, and when we come to consider poverty we shall see that the criterion employed in Britain takes into account differences in rents. The variation in prices is not only geographical. It has been argued in the United States that in certain cities the rents paid by blacks are higher than those paid by whites for comparable housing (Kain and Quigley, 1972). Similarly, the poor may pay less than the rich for the same goods because they have more time to shop around or they may pay more because they cannot purchase in bulk.

The definition of income in terms of purchasing power means that in any comparison of distributions at different dates the changes in the relative prices of goods must be taken into account. If all prices have risen by 15 per cent, then all money incomes have been reduced by the same amount, and relative purchasing power is unaffected. However, if prices have risen more for the goods which are bought by low income households than for those bought by the rich, then the movement in money incomes overstates any trend towards reduced concentration, and vice versa. In the next chapter, we examine how far this has been the case in the recent inflationary years.

The interpretation in real terms applies not just to the flow of income but also to the value of wealth: it means that the value of wealth has to be maintained in terms of purchasing power. As a result, allowance has to be made for inflation when calculating the return to wealth-holding. Earlier we referred to Mr A's making a capital gain of £50 on his shareholding of £500, but part or all of this gain may simply reflect a general rise in prices. If prices had increased generally by 8 per cent over this period, then £40 of his capital gain is simply keeping up with inflation. The real gain is only £10. However, it is not simply those who hold shares who are affected. Anyone holding assets is subject to a capital loss on account of inflation. A person with money in the bank is equally suffering a real capital loss of 8 per cent and this should be deducted from the interest received to give the *real* return. The adoption of a definition based on real income implies, therefore, that an allowance should be made in the case of all assets for the effect of inflation.

3·2 Definition of the time period

Earlier we referred to the income of Mr A accruing over a year. In this section, we consider whether the period of assessment should be a week, a year, a decade or a whole lifetime.

The shortest period of measurement which could realistically be taken is the week, but for many people weekly income is subject to considerable variation: in any particular week a person may have worked a short shift or received a special bonus. The weekly income may vary with the weather, as for a window-cleaner, or with the season, as for a shop-keeper. Income may be received monthly or annually (in the case of investment income). As a result of these short-run fluctuations, the distribution of weekly income appears more unequal than when income is measured over a longer period, such as a year. This is illustrated by the numerical example in Table 3·1, where Mr A is joined by Messrs B–J. The first two columns show their earnings in two pay-weeks, where in each case the distribution of weekly earnings is the same. In each week, there is a uniform frequency (of two men) at each

TABLE 3·1
*Hypothetical example of earnings distribution
and averaging over time*

Mr	Earnings week 1	Earnings week 2	Average for two weeks
A	32	32	32
B	32	36	34
C	34	38	36
D	34	38	36
E	36	32	34
F	36	40	38
G	38	34	36
H	38	34	36
I	40	36	38
J	40	40	40

of the earning levels. The third column shows the total earnings averaged over the two weeks and the distribution is clearly less dispersed. There is only one person whose average earnings for the two weeks are at the lowest value of 32 a week, and four people now have earnings equal to the average (36). The example is obviously based on rather large changes in earnings from week to week, but it illustrates the basic effect of averaging income over a longer period.

From this analysis it appears that taking a longer period of assessment tends to reduce the observed degree of dispersion. How far we want to proceed in this direction is likely to depend on the extent to which short-term fluctuations in income have an important effect on the individual: i.e. how far he can even out such fluctuations by spreading his income over good and bad periods. This in turn is influenced by the terms on which he can lend and borrow, or the effectiveness of the capital market. It may well be that there is considerable scope for averaging incomes over time at the upper end of the scale, but not at the lower end. The millionaire whose shares have fallen in value may not be too worried if he feels confident that they will rise again later, but the manual worker whose plant is put on short-time may be quite unable to borrow in anticipation of better times ahead. The family whose social security payment is delayed in the post may have no reserves on which they can draw: the only way in which they can borrow to finance living expenses may be by not paying the rent or the electricity bill. The important factor is clearly possession of assets which can be used to meet any temporary drop in income, or the ability to borrow on the capital market, and in both cases the low income groups are likely to fare least well. Moreover, on the lending side, they typically obtain a lower rate of interest on short-term savings, and in times of inflation the value of such savings is more likely to be eroded than for wealthier people holding real assets (such as houses).

The varying scope for averaging incomes over time means that we may want to apply different periods of assessment for different income groups, but this would be very difficult to put into effect. We can, however, use different periods for different purposes. If we are measuring the number of people in poverty, and if it is correct to assume that averaging is difficult for low income groups, then we may be concerned with weekly income. We would want to know how many people have incomes in a particular week which are below the prescribed minimum, independently of the fact that in two months' time they may be much better off. On the other hand, if we are concerned with the distribution of income among the population as a whole, we may feel that income averaged over a year is more appropriate. Such a judgement would be based on a view that for the majority of the population some averaging of income was possible, and that at the upper end of the scale it would be quite misleading to take any shorter period.

So far we have been concerned with measuring income in a *current* period, but we should consider the arguments for moving to a concept of *lifetime* income. This would clearly give quite different results. At any moment there are people who currently have low incomes, but will have higher incomes later (e.g. students or apprentices), or have had higher incomes in the past (e.g. pensioners). Lifetime incomes will, by the same argument as that used earlier, in general be less unequally distributed than current incomes.

The significance of this factor may be brought out by a very simple example of a society in which everyone has the same lifetime income, in that a person's income at forty is the same as that of everyone else of the same age and as that of his father when he was forty. This would be regarded as a completely egalitarian society from the standpoint of lifetime income, but there could still be considerable dispersion in the distribution of current incomes. Again, let us suppose that all those at work receive the same wage, but that pensioners receive only one-third of the wage. There are the same number of people (1 million) in each age group, and people work from 25 to 60 and are retired from 61 to when they die at the age of 75. The retired population therefore number 15 million and constitute 30 per cent of the population, ignoring those below the age of 25. The pensioners' share of total income may be calculated to be:

$$\frac{15 \text{ million} \times \frac{1}{3} \times \text{wage}}{35 \text{ million} \times \text{wage} + 15 \text{ million} \times \frac{1}{3} \times \text{wage}} = \frac{5}{40} \text{ or } 12\frac{1}{2} \text{ per cent}$$

In this society we should find therefore that the bottom 30 per cent received decidedly less than 30 per cent of total income, and in fact their share is virtually identical to that found to be the share of the bottom 30 per cent in Britain using the figures described in Chapter 2. This is purely a coincidence, but it serves to demonstrate that life-cycle differences can lead to a marked divergence between the distributions of lifetime and current income. (It should be emphasized that this does not imply that the actual distribution can be explained in this way.)

Whether we should adopt a lifetime assessment period depends again on the question being asked. If our concern is with measuring poverty, then the lifetime approach may not be regarded as very relevant, the fact that an old person had a high income thirty years ago not making up for his having a pension which is below his needs today. On the other hand, we may be concerned with the distribution of life-chances, as represented by a person's work career, by the capital he inherits, by his investment opportunities, by his pension and other access to state benefits. In that case, it can certainly be argued that these are better measured by his lifetime income than by his income in any single period. The use of lifetime income takes account of factors such as investment in education (human capital): the earnings foregone while training are offset by higher earnings later in life. It deals with the fact that 'the short working life of a baseball player means that the annual income during his active years must be much higher than in alternative pursuits open to him to make it equally attractive financially' (Friedman, 1962, p. 170). The lifetime approach allows for people with differing preferences about consumption at different ages.

Lifetime income is defined here to mean the total value of all receipts in the form of wages, capital transfers and state benefits, discounted to a common date. (We take the *discounted* value rather than a simple sum in order to allow for the fact that income accruing later is worth less to a person than if he received it today, since he loses the interest.) In other words, for Mr A, who had a bequest in the second period of his life, his lifetime income discounted to the beginning would be of the form:[1]

$$\text{Earnings in period 1} + \frac{\text{Earnings in period 2} + \text{bequest}}{(1 + \text{rate of interest})} + \dots$$

The difficulties in applying this definition arise from the choice of the rate of interest and of the base date to which the value is discounted (here period 1). The problems with the rate of interest have been brought out by our discussion of imperfections in the capital market. The rich may be able to lend or borrow on much better terms than the poor. Moreover, any one person may face different rates for borrowing and lending, paying rates of 20 per cent and higher on instalment credit but only being able to obtain 4 per cent from the savings bank. [2]

A more immediate problem with the lifetime approach is that of obtaining the required data. If we were to start collecting information now about individual cohorts, we should not have any complete cohorts for fifty years or more. Obtaining figures retrospectively involves serious problems. Information supplied from memory would be unreliable and piecing together figures from tax returns on a national scale would be an immense undertaking even if access were granted to them. There have, however, been some interesting steps in this direction. For example, Soltow (1965) has studied lifetime incomes in the Norwegian city of Sarpsborg. He collected information from the tax returns, which are available for inspection by the general public, on the annual income of a group of men over the period 1928—60 and showed

---

[1] Only the first two elements in the sum are shown. The value of £1 received in the second period is given by $1/(1+r)$ where r is the rate of interest; the value of £1 received in the ith period is similarly $1/(1+r)^{i-1}$.

[2] An example of the high interest rates at which people effectively borrow is embodied in the rates for car licences in Britain: a person choosing to license his car for four monthly periods rather than a year at a time is in effect borrowing at a rate of over 30 per cent per annum (in 1973).

that the concentration in total income over this period was significantly less than that in single years.

Given that this kind of information is unlikely to be generally available we may be able to make some deductions about the lifetime distribution from the degree of dispersion within age groups. In the simple example given earlier, of a society where incomes were the same for everyone in an age group but varied with age, the distribution over all age groups showed inequality; however, the absence of lifetime inequality would have been revealed by looking at individual age groups. This is not fully adequate, since the life-cycle pattern of incomes differs between social groups, the earnings of manual workers reaching a peak earlier than for professional workers. Nonetheless, an examination of the extent to which inequality is attributable to differences between age groups allows us to eliminate those life-cycle differences which are common to all individuals.

Up to this point we have concentrated on income, but it could be argued that in the case of expenditure the divergence between current and lifetime measures would be less, since current expenditure is determined more by lifetime income than by current income. Explanations of consumption such as the permanent income hypothesis advanced by Friedman (1957) suggest that individuals implicitly make calculations of the kind described above and that these are reflected in consumption decisions. There may therefore be an argument for using consumption as an indicator of lifetime income, although consumption would in this case have to be defined to include capital transfers.

Finally, we should consider the relationship between lifetime income and the concept of inter-generational mobility. Suppose that Mr A has a higher lifetime income than his school friend Mr B. If there is no inter-generational mobility, the children of Mr A will similarly be better off than the children of Mr B; on the other hand, if there is significant inter-generational mobility, the positions may be reversed in the next generation. Just looking at the lifetime distribution for one generation will not reveal the extent of mobility, and for this reason we may want to take a *dynastic* view, taking the incomes of different generations of the same family together. This question will be considered further in Chapter 8, which deals with the sources of concentration in the distribution of wealth.

3·3 Families, households and differing needs

We have so far discussed the case of a single individual, but Mr A is likely to marry and have children and we need to consider the treatment of the family or household. The income data presented in Chapter 2 were effectively based on the nuclear family (man, wife and dependent children), but this is not the only possible unit for analysis. We could use a household unit, which would include other non-dependants who lived with the nuclear family, such as a grandmother or a grown-up son, as was the case with the data for France discussed in Section 2·5. (The definition of a household used in the *Family expenditure survey* in Britain is 'a group of people living together at the same address with common housekeeping'.) Alternatively, we could use the smallest possible unit—the individual—although income distributions are not typically presented in this form.

The implications of these different units of analysis can be seen in terms of the degree to which a group of people share their resources. Suppose, for example, that we were to decide to take the individual as the basic unit of analysis. We would then find a large number of individuals with virtually no recorded income, notably children and wives who do not go out to work. These people may well, however, be enjoying a high standard of living as a result of sharing the income of their parents or their husbands. In our society most married women do share their husbands' income (perhaps not equally) and most children are supported by their parents, so that there is a very important degree of income-sharing. If the extent of these intra-family transfers was known with reasonable accuracy, it would be possible to add them to the income of the wife and children, and we could then retain the individual unit.

Such calculations of intra-family transfers are not likely to be possible, and we may therefore decide to take a wider unit of analysis than the single individual. A natural candidate, in view of the extent of income-sharing, is the nuclear family. Adopting this unit would be equivalent to assuming that all income received by members of the family was shared, and for any given distribution of individual incomes the amalgamation into family incomes would tend to reduce the overall degree of dispersion. It means in effect replacing the individual incomes of husband and wife by the average of their incomes, and unless all marriages are between people with the same income, the relative differences in income decrease. If we were to go beyond the nuclear family, and take the household as the basic unit, then the degree of dispersion would be still further reduced. We would be assuming in effect that not only the family but also other household members pooled their incomes equally. The investigation by Cole and Utting (1957) of incomes in Cambridgeshire showed, for example, that the switch from an individual to a household basis had the effect of reducing the share of the top 10 per cent from 37 per cent to 25 per cent. In the same way, the study by Morgan (1965) of poverty among the aged in the United States demonstrated that 48 per cent were below the poverty line on a nuclear family definition, compared with 39 per cent on a household basis.

The choice between the different units depends in part on the empirical question of how far incomes are in practice shared, and on this there is very little evidence. Earlier it was suggested that within the nuclear family there is an important degree of income-sharing, but we know very little about just how *equally* income is divided among different members. The same applies when we consider people who are not members of the nuclear family but who live in the same household. It seems likely in practice that income is pooled to a considerable extent, but it may still be true that working teenage children enjoy a higher, and grandparents a lower, standard of living than the basic family unit.

Equivalence scales

From the above discussion it appears that the choice of the unit of analysis lies between the family and the household. Both of these involve units which vary in size. In the United Kingdom *Family expenditure survey*, there is typically the following range of households (Department of Employment, 1973):

	Percentage of total
Single person	17
Married couples with no children	28
Couples and 1, 2 or 3 children	26
Other	29
	100

These households clearly have differing needs which must be taken into account. In this respect, the income distribution figures discussed in the last chapter are unsatisfactory, since they make no allowance for the composition of the unit.

Allowance for household or family composition can be made in a number of different ways. The simplest is to treat all members as having the same needs and to calculate the income per head. This does not however recognize the variation of need with age, and the possible economies of scale (the 'two can live as cheaply as one' hypothesis). In order to allow for these factors, attempts have been made to construct *adult equivalent scales* to allow comparison between different types of unit.

Two main approaches have been used to construct equivalence scales. The first is based on *a priori* consideration of the needs of children and adults, and effectively consists of listing what are considered the minimum requirements. The equivalence scales derived in this way are clearly subjective, being based in large part on the judgement of the investigator. An early example is the study by Rowntree of poverty in York in 1899, for which he obtained an equivalence scale based on dietary needs plus estimated 'minimum necessary expenditure' on rent, clothing and household sundries. The relativities are shown in column 1 of Table 3·2, and it can be seen that the amount allowed for children is between a third and a half of that for a single adult. A rather similar approach was adopted by Beveridge in 1942. On the basis of dietary standards laid down by the League of Nations Technical Commission on Nutrition and by the British Medical Association, he arrived at the estimates shown in column 2, again with an (essentially arbitrary) allowance for clothing, fuel, rent and sundries. The allowance for children is in this case rather smaller. In the United States, the official poverty line is derived in the same way, using the 'economy' food plan of the Department of Agriculture. The implied adult equivalence scale shown in column 3 appears to lie between those of Beveridge and Rowntree.

TABLE 3·2

Equivalence scales for different households (married couple = 100)

	Rowntree	Beveridge	US poverty scale	Nicholson
Single person	60	59	78	–
Couple	100	100	100	100
and 1 child	124	122	123	127
and 2 children	161	144	157	141
and 4 children	222	188	208	–

Sources: col. 1, Rowntree (1901), p. 143.
col. 2, Beveridge (1942), pp. 88–9.
col. 3, US Bureau of the Census (1972), Table M (figures for 1, 2, 3, 4 and 6 person families).
col. 4, Nicholson (1949), pp. 387–8.

The second approach is based on observed differences in consumption patterns for households of different sizes. The method may be most easily understood by reference to a simplified case. Suppose that we consider the demand for a commodity, such as beer or adult clothing, which is consumed only by adults and can be taken as an index of the adult standard of living. If we then compare households with and without children, we shall expect that at any given income level the consumption of beer will be higher for the household with no children, since the adult standard of living is higher—see Fig. 3·1. (It is assumed that beer is not an inferior good: i.e. the adults do not switch to whisky as their standard of living rises.) The horizontal distance between the two curves then measures the increase in income which would be necessary to raise the household with children to the same standard of living, and from this the equivalence scale can be calculated. Column 4 of Table 3·2 shows the results obtained by Nicholson (1949) for a family with an average standard of living. This method also suffers from a number of shortcomings, which even the later, more sophisticated, applications of the basic technique cannot overcome. The income required to compensate for the needs of children may vary with the adult standard of living (with the Y chosen in Fig. 3·1). Parenthood may be accompanied by a change in tastes: parents of a family may consume the same amount of beer not because they have the same standard of living, but because the children drive them to it.

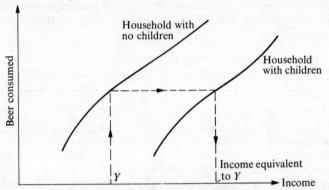

Fig. 3·1. Derivation of equivalent incomes

These two approaches suggest that the allowance for the needs of a child should be between a quarter and a third of that for a married couple. As we have seen, the methods are subject to a number of reservations. Moreover, they do not of course mean that this allowance *should* be made; that is a matter for social judgement. Indeed it might be argued that the benefits of having children are such that in a country where birth control is widespread no allowance should be made for the cost of children.

Finally, we should note that children are not the only group for whom special adjustments might be made. It could be argued, for example, that the needs of the retired are less than those of the working population. The fact that the food requirements of old people are usually estimated to be less may, however, be offset by greater needs for fuel, light and domestic help. There are a wide range of other needs which may also be taken into account: for example, those of the blind and the disabled.

3·4 The measurement of inequality

In discussions of the distribution of income and wealth, reference is frequently made to summary measures of concentration. These summary statistics, which include the Gini coefficient, the variance, and the relative mean deviation, are widely used for two purposes:

(i) to compare distributions: e.g. the distribution in 1950 and that in 1970, or that in Britain and that in the United States;
(ii) to attach some absolute measure to the degree of inequality, or to give some idea whether the inequality is 'large' or 'small'.

The most popular of these summary measures is the Gini coefficient, named after an Italian statistician. This coefficient may be interpreted in two ways. Firstly, it may be seen geometrically in terms of the Lorenz curve defined in Chapter 2 (see Fig. 2·2):

$$\text{Gini coefficient} = \frac{\text{Area between Lorenz curve and diagonal}}{\text{Total area under diagonal}}$$

The coefficient may be seen to range from 0 when incomes are equal (the Lorenz curve follows the diagonal) to 1 at the other extreme (the Lorenz curve has an ⌋ shape). For those who do not like geometry, its meaning may be presented in another way. Suppose we choose two people at random from the income distribution, and express the difference between their incomes as a proportion of the average income, then this difference turns out to be on average twice the Gini coefficient: a coefficient of 0·4 means that the expected difference between two people chosen at random is 80 per cent of the average income.

The Gini coefficient is used in official publications in Britain to summarize the distribution of income and wealth. The government statistics show, for example, that the Gini value for the distribution of wealth has fallen from 0·76 in 1960 to 0·65 in 1970 (Inland Revenue, 1972, p. 157). The likely effect of a value-added tax on the distribution of income was summarized in terms of increasing the Gini coefficient by 0·002. It is far from clear, however, what these statements mean. Is there any reason to doubt that the direction of movement is in fact as shown? Would all summary measures give the same answer? Does the use of such an apparently neutral statistic conceal judgements about the desirability of different forms of redistribution?

TABLE 3·3
Income distribution in the United Kingdom, the Netherlands, and West Germany

Cumulative share of bottom %	United Kingdom 1964	Netherlands 1962	West Germany 1964
10	2·0	1·3	2·1
20	5·1	4·0	5·3
30	9·3	8·2	10·0
40	15·3	14·0	15·4
50	22·8	21·4	21·9
60	31·9	30·0	29·1
70	42·9	40·0	37·5
80	55·8	51·6	47·1
90	70·7	66·2	58·6

Source: see Table 2·4.

To show how questions such as these may be answered, let us take for purposes of illustration the data for three different European countries referred to in Chapter 2: the United Kingdom, West Germany, and the Netherlands. A rather more detailed version of the income distribution for these three countries is given in Table 3·3, from which we can construct the Lorenz curves. If we consider first the United Kingdom and the Netherlands, the Lorenz curves have the form shown in Fig. 3·2 and in particular we can see that the curve for the United Kingdom lies everywhere inside that for the Netherlands. (In terms of Table 3·3 this is equivalent to the share of the bottom x per

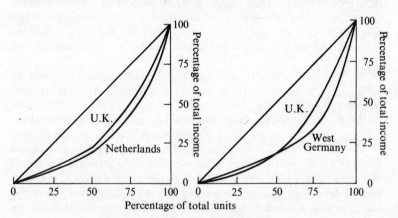

Fig. 3·2. Comparison of Lorenz curves

cent being larger in each case for the United Kingdom.) Now *if the Lorenz curves for two distributions do not intersect, then we can say unambiguously that the distribution closer to the diagonal is less unequal than the other,* subject only to the condition that we are ranking the distribution independently of the average levels of income (Atkinson, 1970). (In making this statement, it is assumed that people are otherwise identical.)

This means that any of the summary measures referred to on p. 45 would indicate that there was a higher degree of income inequality in the Netherlands. On the other hand, if the Lorenz curves intersect, it is quite possible to reach different conclusions using different summary measures. This is shown by the comparison of the United Kingdom and West Germany. The Lorenz curves intersect (see Fig. 3·2): the shares of the bottom 10 per cent, 20 per cent, 30 and 40 per cent are higher in West Germany, but above that point the distribution becomes less unequal in the United Kingdom. We can see by eye from Fig. 3·2 that the Gini coefficient, which ranks according to the area between the Lorenz curve and the diagonal, will give a lower value for the United Kingdom (it is in fact 0·40 as opposed to 0·47 for West Germany). However, a measure which attaches more weight to the bottom income groups may indicate less dispersion in West Germany: for example, in the extreme case we might only be concerned with the share of the bottom 10 per cent, and this group fares better in West Germany.

This example has brought out a number of important points about the use of summary measures. First, *the degree of inequality cannot, in general, be measured without introducing social judgements.* Measures such as the Gini coefficient are not purely 'statistical' and they embody implicit judgements about the weight to be attached to inequality at different points on the income scale. The fact that the Gini coefficient shows a decrease does not necessarily mean that everyone would agree that there has been a decline in inequality. Secondly, the Lorenz curves play a key role in determining in which cases summary measures will agree and which cases there is likely to be ambiguity. If we are concerned solely with comparing two distributions of income and wealth (and the ranking is being made independently of the average levels), then the first step should be to draw the Lorenz curves.

An alternative approach[1]

Given that the conventional summary measures inevitably introduce distributional values, it may well be preferable to consider such values explicitly. Only then can it be clear just what distributional objectives

---

[1] This section is more technical.

are being incorporated as a result of adopting a certain measure. One method by which this can be achieved has been suggested in Atkinson (1970). The measure proposed there introduces distributional objectives through an explicit parameter ϵ. This parameter represents the weight attached by society to inequality in the distribution. It ranges from zero, which means that society is indifferent about the distribution, to infinity, which means that society is concerned only with the position of the lowest income group. This latter position may be seen as corresponding to that developed by Rawls (1972) in his contractual theory of justice, where inequality is assessed in terms of the position of the least advantaged members of society. Where ϵ lies between these extremes depends on the importance attached to redistribution towards the bottom.

TABLE 3·4
An alternative measure of inequality

Value of ϵ	Value of index (I) United Kingdom	West Germany
0·5	0·12	0·17
1·0	0·24	0·29
1·5	0·34	0·38
2·0	0·43	0·45
3·0	0·55	0·54

Source: calculated from the data in Table 3·3.
Note: the formula for the index I is

$$I = 1 - \left[\sum_{i=1}^{n} \left(\frac{Y_i}{\bar{Y}} \right)^{1-\epsilon} f_i \right]^{\frac{1}{1-\epsilon}}$$

where Y_i denotes the income of those in the ith income range (n ranges altogether),
 f_i denotes the proportion of the population with incomes in the ith range,
 $\bar{Y}$ denotes the mean income

The precise formula for this alternative measure is given in the notes to Table 3·4. It may look intimidating, but the measure has a very natural interpretation as the proportion of the present total income that would be required to achieve the same level of social welfare as at present if incomes were equally distributed: a value of 0·12 means that we could reach the same level of social welfare with only

(1·00 − 0·12) = 88 per cent of the present total income. Alternatively, the gain from redistribution to bring about equality would be equivalent to raising total income by 12 per cent. In this way the measure is an index of the potential gains from redistribution, and provides a tool which can be used for the second of the two purposes outlined at the beginning of this section.

A key role is played in this alternative approach by the distributional parameter ϵ. How can people make up their minds about what value it should take (between zero and infinity)? One way of interpreting ϵ may be seen from the following 'mental experiment'

Suppose that there are two people, one with twice the income of the other (they are otherwise identical), and that we are considering taking 1 unit of income from the richer man and giving a proportion x to the poorer (the remainder being lost in the process, for example in administering the transfer). At what level of x do we cease to regard the redistribution as desirable?

If the person is at all concerned about inequality, then $x = 1$ is considered desirable. What is crucial is how far he is prepared to let x fall below 1 before calling for a stop.[1] The answer determines the implied value of ϵ from the formula $1/x = 2^\epsilon$. For example, if the person stops at $x = \frac{1}{2}$, this corresponds to $\epsilon = 1$, but if he is willing to go on until only a quarter is transferred, then the implied ϵ equals 2.

Returning to the comparison of the United Kingdom and West Germany, we can calculate the value of the alternative measure (I) for different values of ϵ (see Table 3·4), where a higher value denotes a greater degree of inequality. The value of the index is lower in the United Kingdom for all values of ϵ up to 2·0, but for $\epsilon = 3·0$ and above the index is lower in West Germany. This reflects the fact that as ϵ rises, more weight is attached to the lower income deciles, which have a higher share in West Germany. In terms of the interpretation of ϵ given in the previous paragraph, those who would be willing to accept a transfer of one-eighth or less would regard West Germany as having a less unequal distribution.

---

[1] To calibrate ϵ fully we should have to consider different gaps between the rich and poor man; the calculation described in the text is only illustrative.

4

INCOME DISTRIBUTION IN BRITAIN
AND THE UNITED STATES

> The wayfarer,
> Perceiving the pathway to truth,
> Was struck with astonishment.
> It was thickly grown with weeds.
> 'Ha,' he said,
> 'I see that no one has passed here
> In a long time.'
> Later he saw that each weed
> Was a singular knife.
> 'Well,' he mumbled at last,
> 'Doubtless there are other roads.'
>
> (Stephen Crane, quoted by Miller (1966)).

This chapter examines the evidence about the distribution of incomes, before and after tax, in Britain and the United States, paying particular attention to the changes which have taken place since the end of the Second World War. It draws heavily on the framework described in the previous chapter, and tries to show how the concepts developed there may be applied to actual income distribution data.

4·1 Popular beliefs and official statistics

The extent of inequality in the distribution of income, and how it is changing over time, is a subject about which people hold very definite views. In Britain, as we saw in Chapter 2, it is widely believed that the distribution of income has in recent years been moving clearly in the direction of equality:

Much has been written in recent years about the strongly egalitarian effects of the social and economic policies pursued by British Governments since the end of the Second World War ... Full employment ... was leading to a steady reduction in wage and salary differentials ... Above all, it was considered that the wealthy were a disappearing class in Britain (Titmuss, 1962, p. 15).

This led Titmuss to write a book-length critique of the evidence on which such views were based, and since then optimism has become rather more restrained. However, the Sunday newspaper reader is still told that the evidence about incomes shows that 'up to 1970, there was a fairly marked trend towards equality' (*Observer*, January 1974), and in 1972 the Inland Revenue concluded that 'the broad picture of the last twenty years is of a tendency for variations between incomes to diminish' (*Survey of Personal Incomes*, 1969–70, p. 4).

In the United States, Miller (1966) referred to the view 'shared by influential writers and editors' that incomes are becoming more evenly distributed, and quoted the announcement by *Fortune* that 'though not a head has been raised aloft on a pikestaff, nor a railway station seized, the US has been for some time now in revolution' (1953). The same magazine returned to the subject twenty years later and concluded that 'we seem to be making progress towards greater equality'. Other observers have been less sanguine. In 1969 an official report stated that 'since the mid-1940s, there has been little observable change in the overall distribution of income' (US Department of Health, Education, and Welfare, 1969, p. 42), a view which is shared by, among others, Miller (1966), Haley (1968), and Thurow and Lucas (1972).

The opinions just described are based largely on the evidence provided by official statistics for the distribution of income. Titmuss referred to the 'profound importance' of the report by the Inland Revenue in 1950 which suggested that there had been a very considerable redistribution of income between 1938–9 and 1948–9, and subsequent reports have been equally influential. The main source of these official statistics in the United Kingdom is the annual income

TABLE 4·1

Official estimates of distribution of income,
before and after tax, United Kingdom 1949–67

	Percentage share of total income					
	Before tax			After tax		
	Top 10 per cent	Next 60 per cent	Bottom 30 per cent	Top 10 per cent	Next 60 per cent	Bottom 30 per cent
1949	33·2	54·1	12·7	27·1	58·3	14·6
1954	29·8	59·3	10·9	24·8	63·1	12·1
1959	29·4	60·9	9·7	25·2	63·5	11·2
1964	29·0	61·4	9·6	25·1	64·1	10·8
1967	28·0	61·6	10·4	24·3	63·7	12·0

Source: Nicholson (1967), Table 3 and additional calculations (the data for 1967 are those given in Table 2·1). The years shown correspond (with the exception of 1967) to those of the Inland Revenue quinquennial surveys; the data for these years are more reliable than for the intervening years, particularly between 1950 and 1961.

survey carried out by the Inland Revenue, the basic material being the records of incomes for tax purposes. This survey in turn provides the source for the estimates of the distribution given in the *National income blue book*.

The *Blue book* estimates are set out in Table 4·1, which shows the percentage share of total income received by different groups over the period 1949—67. (As we saw in Chapter 2, the estimates have not been made for any later years.) If we consider first the share of the top 10 per cent, we find an apparent move towards less dispersion, this top group having suffered a fall of over 5 percentage points in terms of before tax income and a similarly marked reduction in the case of income after tax. This loss by the top group has not, however, been reflected in a corresponding gain by those at the bottom, the share of the bottom 30 per cent having fallen from 12·7 per cent to 10·4 per cent over the period. As Nicholson (1967), and earlier Paish (1957), pointed out, the redistribution has been from the extreme ends to the middle ranges, a feature brought out clearly by the middle column ('next 60 per cent'). Finally, much of the change seems to have taken place in the 1950s.

The official source most commonly employed in the United States is the annual sample survey carried out by the Bureau of the Census. The resulting estimates, summarized in Table 4·2, show a picture rather

TABLE 4·2

*Official estimates of distribution of income before tax,
United States 1947–72*

	Percentage share of total income				
	Top 20 per cent	Next 20 per cent	Middle 20 per cent	Fourth 20 per cent	Bottom 20 per cent
1947	45·5	23·8	16·8	10·5	3·4
1952	44·0	24·3	17·4	10·9	3·4
1957	43·4	25·2	18·1	10·3	3·0
1962	44·1	24·9	17·2	10·5	3·3
1967a	43·9	24·7	17·2	10·5	3·7
1967b	42·7	24·7	17·6	10·5	4·5
1972	43·9	24·6	16·8	10·5	4·2

Sources: 1947–67a from Budd (1970), Table 2.
       1967b–72 from US Bureau of the Census (1973a), Table D.
Note: The figures for 1947–67a relate to total families and unrelated individuals; those for 1967b and 1972 relate to total households. The main difference is that the former treats as separate units any unrelated individuals living with a family, and is likely therefore to give a higher degree of dispersion (as evidenced by the two estimates for 1967).

similar to that in Britain. The share of the top 20 per cent has declined, although by less, and the main gainers have been those in the next 40 per cent. Again redistribution appears to have been away from the top towards the middle, the share of the lowest group having shown much less improvement.

Popular belief in a trend towards equality is often accompanied by the assumption that this will continue into the future. Prediction of future developments can, however, only be made on the basis of an understanding of the underlying causes. If the changes in the distribution over the postwar period are attributable to factors of a once-for-all nature, then these changes clearly cannot be extrapolated into the future. In his criticism of comparisons of Britain before and after the Second World War, Titmuss drew attention to the large-scale changes in the social and economic framework which may have profoundly affected the distribution of income, and argued that 'we should be much more hesitant in suggesting that any equalizing forces at work in Britain since 1938 can be promoted to the status of a "natural law" and projected into the future' (1962, p. 198).

One important factor which is likely to have influenced the distribution of income is the level of unemployment. In the United States, Solow suggested that in the early part of the period 'the main cause of the equalization was the approach to full employment from the relatively depressed conditions before the war' (1960, p. 104). More recently, it has been argued that 'the improvement in the relative position of the poorest fifth [between 1964 and 1969] is probably due to the reduction in unemployment during the Vietnam escalation' (Ackerman et al., 1971, p. 209). These judgements are supported by a more thorough investigation of the link between the income distribution and macro-economic conditions undertaken by Metcalf (1969).

In Britain, Lydall concluded that the single most important cause of the egalitarian trend shown by his estimates was the achievement and maintenance of full employment, which entails 'the elimination of a large group of very low incomes, not only of the unemployed themselves but also of workers on the margin of unemployment whose wages are particularly depressed' (1959, p. 33).

A second example of social change which may have had major distributional implications is the increase in employment among married women, coupled with the trend towards earlier marriage. Lydall argued that this had clearly contributed to the equalization of income:

since a greater proportion of young married women—and especially of working- and middle-class women—go out to work [the effect] has been mainly to increase the incomes of the lower and middle income families ... At the same time the people who are already in the top 1 per cent of income units cannot usually benefit proportionately very much from their wives' earnings, since the earnings of wives are more equally distributed than incomes in general (1959, p. 23).

Similarly, Thurow and Lucas concluded that in the United States 'postwar increases in female participation rates have resulted in some relative equalization of the distribution of income' (1972, p. 8).

The reduction of unemployment and the expansion of employment opportunities for women may well have contributed to the reduction of income differences, but their effect is likely to have been of a once-for-all nature. If they were important factors leading to the observed redistribution, then it cannot be assumed that the trend will continue automatically in the future.

Deficiencies of the official estimates

The fact that the figures shown in Tables 4·1 and 4·2 are based on official estimates does not imply that they are adequate to measure changes in the income distribution, as indeed the government statisticians would be the first to admit. There are many obvious deficiencies. The estimates make no allowance for the needs of families of different sizes. The concept of income falls a long way short of the theoretical definition described in the preceding chapter. No account is taken of inflation. Annual incomes may bear no relation to lifetime incomes. The only taxes considered are those on income, and other aspects of government activity may have a significant effect on the distribution.

These deficiencies have led many people to reject the official statistics and any conclusions based on them. Titmuss' case against the popular belief in declining inequality was based on a lengthy catalogue of the shortcomings of the Inland Revenue statistics. In many cases these criticisms were, and remain, valid, but he did not go on to try and correct for them or to assess their quantitative importance. He did not demonstrate that the observed trend in Britain over the 1950s would be reversed in more accurate statistics. Similarly, Johnson (1973) refers to the 'extremely naïve' statistics used to validate the demonstration of inequality, but does not give any indication of the likely quantitative importance of the objections he raises; nor does he attempt to produce any alternative.

There are in fact two choices open. One can either point to the deficiencies and conclude that nothing can be said, or one can try to allow for them, possibly making use of alternative sources, and see what (qualified) statements can be made. It is the latter approach which we set out to explore here.

In examining the objections to the official estimates, it may be helpful to distinguish three types of criticism:

—that given the basic data on incomes, the method of analysis is inappropriate;

—that the data do not provide an accurate measure of income;

—that conclusions about inequality cannot be drawn from a simple comparison of the distribution of incomes at different dates.

In other words, a person who felt that the figures in Tables 4·1 and 4·2 exaggerated the dispersion of incomes might argue under the first heading that the distribution should be computed on a *per capita* basis rather than per income unit (and that units with higher incomes were simply larger) or under the second that substantial amounts of income accruing to the poor had been left out. Under the third heading, he might criticize the estimates as throwing no light on the distribution of lifetime incomes. In what follows, we consider examples of all three types, although clearly space does not permit an exhaustive treatment.

4·2 Methods of analysis

In this section we consider two objections to methods commonly employed in presenting official statistics: the fact that summary measures of inequality may conceal divergent movements in the distribution, and the neglect of differences in needs associated with family size.

Measurement of inequality

The evidence shown in the tables above was presented in terms of the shares of different groups in total income, but this information is often summarized by a measure such as the Gini coefficient. Such a procedure is, however, potentially misleading. In cases where there have been divergent movements at different points on the income scale (i.e. where the Lorenz curves intersect), then, as shown in the previous chapter, different summary measures may give different answers.

The dangers are well illustrated by comparison of the *Blue book* figures for before tax income in the United Kingdom for 1949 and 1967. According to the Gini coefficient, there has been a (slight) reduction in inequality: the coefficient fell from 0·39 in 1949 to 0·37 in 1967. We have seen, however, that there has been, according to these estimates, redistribution away from the extremes towards the middle ranges—the rich have lost, but so have the poor. If this is so, then any judgement about inequality must depend on the weight attached to gains and losses by different groups. A person who attached more weight to the fall in the share of the bottom 30 per cent than to the redistribution away from the top 10 per cent might well conclude that inequality had increased. Reliance on any one summary measure is to be avoided.[1]

A rather different summary statistic was used by the Inland Revenue in Britain in reaching the conclusion that the variation of income had declined in recent years. This finding was based on the fall in the 'Pareto' index of inequality over the period 1949–50 to 1969–70.[2] Closer inspection reveals not only that the Pareto index is open to the same objection as other summary measures—that it implicitly embodies judgements about the distribution—but also that the calculation of the index is based on only the upper range of incomes (above £1350 in 1969–70), so that the index cannot describe what is happening to the whole distribution. The lowest income ranges could be suffering a serious fall in their share of total income and this would not be detected. This brings home the dangers of presenting the evidence in such summary form; the choice of a single distributional index should clearly not be left entirely to the civil servants—or for that matter to economists.

Needs and family size

The estimates in Tables 4·1 and 4·2 made no allowance for the differences in needs between a one person household and a family of six. If those with low incomes tend to have fewer dependants than those with high incomes, then the degree of dispersion may be lower if income is defined per person or per equivalent adult. Trends over time may similarly be affected. If young people have tended to leave home sooner, and old people to continue living on their own longer, as they undoubtedly have, the differences in the size of income units may be widening, and hence the overstatement of dispersion increasing.

The possible quantitative importance of this factor may be illustrated by reference to the data for the United States in 1972. According to the table, the average income of the top 20 per cent was some ten times

[1] (This and the next footnote are more technical.) The alternative approach suggested at the end of the last chapter in effect allows a range of measures as the parameter ϵ varies between zero and infinity. It turns out that the distribution in 1967 would be regarded as more unequal than that in 1949 if ϵ is greater than 1·0. In terms of the interpretation suggested, if we think that taking £1 from a rich man and giving 50p to a man with half his income would be desirable, then we would not in fact consider that inequality had declined—contrary to the Gini coefficient.

[2] The ingredients for the Pareto index are as follows. Take a piece of graph paper. Plot on the horizontal axis the logarithm of income, and on the vertical axis the number of incomes in excess of this level, again in logarithms. The resulting line slopes downward to the right, and becomes approximately straight as higher incomes are reached. The Pareto index measures the slope of the straight part of the line.

that of the bottom 20 per cent. The average number of persons per
income unit was in broad terms 3¾ for the top 20 per cent, compared
with 2 for the bottom. In *per capita* terms, the gap between the average
incomes would be reduced to nearer 5:1; and even if the extra 1¾ were
children, and given a weight of one half (see Section 3·3), the gap would
still be reduced to 7:1. This crude calculation suggests that such
adjustments could be important, although in practice the effect of
adjusting for family size would be less marked, since the conversion to a
per capita basis would lead to changes in the ranking of income units.

A careful study of the precise effect of adjustments for family size
has been made in the case of Britain by Prest and Stark (1967), who
transformed the official *Blue book* figures to an equivalent adult basis,
using equivalence scales of the kind described in the preceding chapter.
Their estimates also include a number of other adjustments to eliminate
the double counting of income units in the original series. As expected,
their results show an inward movement of the Lorenz curve: in 1963,
the share of the top 10 per cent was reduced from 28·7 per cent to 26·9
per cent, while that of the bottom 30 per cent increased from 9·7 per
cent to 13·5 per cent. Moreover, the authors indicated that with the
adjusted figures there was a clearer trend towards equality over the
period 1949–63.

The effect on the degree of dispersion of the conversion to an
equivalent adult basis appears on the basis of these results to be smaller
than the crude calculation suggested. Prest and Stark chose to
summarize the distribution in terms of the Gini coefficient, and this is
reduced by the conversion from 0·38 to 0·33 in 1963. A study on
similar lines in the United States by Taussig (1973) showed a rather
smaller reduction in the Gini coefficient: from 0·36 to 0·34 (for
incomes after tax).

4·3 Towards a comprehensive measure of income

Objections may be raised to a measure of income on two different
grounds. Firstly, it may be argued that it does not record accurately
what it sets out to measure. Secondly, what it sets out to measure may
not coincide with the definition desired on theoretical grounds.

Accuracy

The United States figures shown in Table 4·2 were obtained from the
Current Population Survey, in which participation is voluntary. One's
immediate reaction is to ask why anyone should take part and why
people should tell the truth. The experience on the first point, however,
is that the response rate is surprisingly high: in 1972 only 12 per cent
of those who were asked the income questions failed to provide

complete information. On the second aspect—the accuracy of the answers given—there is evidence of understatement, particularly of investment income. Comparison with independent estimates of total income from different sources indicated that one half of property income was missing in 1972, compared with only 2 per cent of wage and salary income (US Bureau of Census, 1973, p. 15).

Differential reporting of income in this way may lead to a biased estimate of the degree of dispersion. Property income is likely to be more important at the top and the bottom (among pensioners). The attempt by Budd (1970) to adjust for the unreported income suggests in fact that the share of the bottom 40 per cent would be raised by approximately 0·7 per cent, while that of the top 5 per cent would increase from 11·5 per cent to 11·9 per cent.

The position with the British data, drawn as they are from tax returns, is rather different. Participation by the taxpayer is compulsory for those above the tax threshold, but there are definite incentives for income not to be recorded. Tax evasion is, unfortunately, a subject about which little is known. The Inland Revenue has continually expressed disquiet. In 1949 a government committee reported the serious and widespread nature of evasion, and counteracting steps were taken, but twenty years later the Inland Revenue was still referring to growing problems of non-compliance. It is hard to form any assessment of the quantitative importance of evasion, and harder still to predict its distributional implications. If the typical tax evader is the small shop-keeper failing to ring everything up on the till, or the labour-only subcontractor, then the true distribution may show less dispersion than the official figures suggest; if it is the rich who evade tax then the opposite is true. The same obviously applies to illegal income.

Even apart from tax evasion, it is possible that the underlying figures are inaccurate as a result of the methods employed in the British survey. For example, the Inland Revenue has made reference to the fact that the total investment income reported is less than expected on the basis of independent evidence, one explanation being that the previous year's investment income is reported when the current year's figure is not available. Although the Inland Revenue used to make an adjustment for this deficiency, this is no longer done, and it is noted that this may lead to an overstatement of the trend towards equality.

Definition of income

In the previous chapter we described the comprehensive definition of income which has been widely accepted by economists as the basis for assessing the equity of its distribution. This definition is very different from that employed in constructing the official estimates. In the case of

Britain, Titmuss (1962) lists at the end of his chapter on 'Statutory income and real income', nineteen kinds of income that were tax-free at the end of 1960 and did not appear in the Inland Revenue figures. In some cases these are of doubtful quantitative importance: for example, the expense allowances for members of the House of Lords. At £8·50 a day, even if every peer attended every day of the Parliamentary session, they would amount only to £2 million, a mere 0·006 per cent of total personal income recorded. In what follows, attention is focused only on some of the most important items of 'missing' income.

Capital gains

Capital gains and losses have effectively been omitted from the official estimates, and there can be little doubt that these are important. In the long run, assets such as real property (land and buildings) and company shares have generated substantial capital gains, at least in money terms (the adjustment for inflation is discussed in the next section); certain other assets, such as undated government bonds, have led to long-run capital losses. The impact of capital gains on the distribution of income depends, therefore, on the holdings of these assets by different income groups. With the exception of owner-occupied homes, it seems reasonable to assume that assets generating capital gains are held disproportionately by upper income groups. Personal holdings of ordinary shares, for example, are heavily concentrated in Britain in the hands of the top 10 per cent. Owner-occupied houses are an exception, because many pensioners own their own houses and among the working population home ownership extends some way down the income scale. Rising house prices may, therefore, lead to less of an increase in dispersion than capital gains on other assets, and may add to incomes at the bottom as well as the top.

Direct estimates of the effect of capital gains on the distribution of income are hard to obtain. In the United States, the tax returns provide information on realized gains (i.e. assets actually sold in that tax year), but not on the accrued gains which are relevant to the Simons income concept described in Chapter 3. In view of this, two indirect methods have been employed. The first, used in the United States by Goldsmith et al. (1954) and in Britain by Lydall (1959), is to take the value of retained company profits as a measure of capital gains accruing to share-holders. This assumes that the profits ploughed back into companies generate future profits, and that the expectation of these future profits leads to a rise in share prices. As Lydall himself stresses, this relationship may very well not hold, and retained profits may not in fact be reflected on a one-for-one basis in capital gains to the share-holders. A dramatic fall in share prices, such as occurred in 1974, means that share-holders have made capital losses, even though retained profits may be positive. The retained earnings method is probably best regarded as a measure of the 'permanent' income accrued. A further objection is that this method takes no account of capital gains on other assets.

The second approach, which does not suffer from the same drawbacks, is that employed by Prest and Stark (1967). They link the income data to the distribution of wealth and then calculate the increase in the value of different classes of asset during the period in question, using stock exchange price indices for shares, average house prices for land and buildings, etc. In this way all capital gains and losses are taken into account, and the estimates relate to actual gains accruing, rather than assumed gains, as in the case of undistributed profits. The method does, however, involve a number of approximations: for example, all share-holders are assumed to have enjoyed the same gains as indicated by the overall share price index, whereas some would have done considerably better and others considerably worse.

The results obtained by Prest and Stark, applying their method of estimating capital gains to the data for 1959, show that the share of the top 10 per cent is increased, as expected, and that the effect on the top 1 per cent's share is quite marked, rising from 8·3 per cent to 14·1 per cent. The bottom 30 per cent also benefited from capital gains, and it was the middle income groups whose share fell. The large gains accruing in 1959 were far from typical, reflecting in part the outcome of that year's general election, and for other years the estimated effect is less: in 1963 the Gini coefficient rose from 0·35 to 0·37 (Stark, 1972, p. 77). In the United States, a rather similar approach by Bhatia (1974) brought out the year to year variation: in 1962 capital losses reduced the Gini coefficient from 0·41 to 0·35, but the average gains over the period 1960–4 would have increased it by 0·02.

Imputed rent on owner-occupied houses

In Britain the position with regard to the imputed rent on owner-occupied houses is rather complicated. Until 1963 this imputed rent was taxable under Schedule A of the income tax and appeared in the income survey, but the valuation was based on prewar assessments and the imputed rent recorded in the survey had been falling steadily behind its true value. Since 1963–4, no imputed rent at all has appeared in the survey. In the United States estimates, it is missing altogether.

The inclusion of imputed rent could make a substantial difference to the distribution, as is illustrated by the figures for Britain: in 1954 the omitted rent was estimated at £139 million, by 1963 the figure had increased to over £500 million, and by 1971 it had reached £1200 million, or some 3 per cent of the total personal income. The impact depends, however, on the relationship between income and home ownership, and as explained above, this is not straightforward. The estimates of Kuznets for the period 1919–38 in the United States showed that inclusion of imputed rent led to a fall in the share of the top 5 per cent. In Britain estimates were made by Stark (1972), but were presented in combination with those for fringe benefits discussed below.

Fringe benefits

The *Blue book* figures in Britain include estimates of income in kind accruing to domestic and agricultural workers but make no other allowances for fringe benefits; the United States census concept of income excludes all employer-paid fringe benefits. There are, however, reasons to expect that these may be of substantial importance, and that their extent may have grown over time. In the United States, a study of 108 firms by Macaulay (1959) observed a rise in fringe benefits as a proportion of salary from 15 per cent in 1947 to 25 per cent in 1959. In Britain, Nicholson has pointed to the fact that 'high rates of income tax biting on gradually declining real incomes have encouraged a growth in expenses charged to business accounts' (1970, p. 278), although he notes that this growth may have been checked by recent changes in the tax law. If, as Nicholson indicates, the growth of fringe benefits over the postwar period has been greater in the upper income ranges, then this again causes the trend towards reduced dispersion to be overstated.

The estimates of Stark (1972) for the United Kingdom cover both fringe benefits and other forms of 'missing' income, such as the imputed rent on owner-occupied houses. The resulting figures show little change in the degree of dispersion for the earliest year (1954), but in 1963 the Gini coefficient rises by some 0·02 as a result of the adjustment.

Home production

It is often suggested that the value of home production is likely to be inversely related to income, not only because of the food grown for home consumption in rural areas, but also because 'people in the higher income groups spend less time doing work around the house' (Scitovsky, 1973, p. 115). Scitovsky goes on to quote an estimate that in 1964 allowance for such non-market services would have reduced the share of the top 25 per cent of families and raised that of the bottom 25 per cent. An earlier study (Morgan *et al.*, 1962) suggested, however, that the time spent on home improvements rose with income, there being more owner-occupiers at higher income levels, and that overall the money saved through home production was proportional to money income, although the range of items taken into account was more limited.

We have described above some of the main items missing from the official statistics and tried to assess their likely impact on the distribution, as revealed by the studies which have been made. It may be useful to bring together some of the main findings, although in doing so we have to bear in mind that the effect may go in opposite directions at different points on the income scale, and that it may not be possible to summarize the impact of an adjustment in any simple way.

Inaccurate reporting	Corrections for under-reporting of investment income raises share of top and bottom groups.
Tax evasion and illegal income	Effect unknown.
Capital gains	Allowance for accrued gains tends to increase share of top groups at expense of middle income ranges
Imputed rent	Allowance for imputed rent accruing to home owners probably benefits top and bottom income groups.
Fringe benefits	Allowance would probably raise share of top groups.
Home production	Allowance for non-market services may reduce dispersion(?)

4·4 Real incomes and inflation

In Chapter 3 it was emphasized that the definition of income related to *real* income, and this has important implications, especially at a time of rapid inflation and changing relative prices.

The first adjustment considered here is concerned not with changes in the price level over time, but with regional variation in prices. If prices are higher in New York than in Detroit, then account should be taken of this when comparing incomes. The effect of conversion to a common purchasing power standard depends on the relationship between money incomes and prices. If money incomes tend to be higher in high-price areas, then the variation in real incomes will be less; if there is no systematic relationship, then the variation will be higher. In an attempt to estimate the effect of such an adjustment Taussig used cost-of-living indices for twelve large urban areas. The results showed very little change in terms of the summary measures employed: the Gini coefficient was changed only by 0·001 (Taussig, 1973, Table 3). In Britain, where regional variation is unlikely to be greater, the effect may well be similarly small.

We come now to inflation as such, and the real capital loss which it imposes on those holding wealth. In principle, such an adjustment is straightforward, the decline in the purchasing power of assets being subtracted from money income, to give potential spending power *holding real wealth intact*. This reduces the net property income and is likely to lead to a fall in the share of top income groups. In practice, such an estimate would clearly have to be made in conjunction with adjustments for capital gains. For a person holding a real asset, the money value of which rose with the general price level, the net effect would be zero; and a person with liabilities fixed in money terms might be a net gainer. However, although there have been a number of recent studies dealing with the impact of inflation on the distribution of incomes (for example, Budd and Seiders (1971), Bach and Stephenson (1974) and Nordhaus (1972)), these have tended to focus on the adjustments of money incomes in response to inflation rather than the difference between money and real incomes.

A third factor of potential importance concerns changes in *relative* prices over time. If all goods went up in price at the same rate, the cost of living would rise by the same amount for everyone, and we could take money incomes in two different years as an indicator of purchasing power. It would be true that an income of £1000 meant less than it did ten years ago, but its purchasing power would be reduced by the same percentage as an income of twice that size. However, in fact not all prices go up at the same rate, as should be clear from everyday shopping. Taking a long view, from 1914 to 1968, shows that in Britain the price index for food rose by less than four times, whereas the index for clothing rose by over five times. Within the food group itself there was considerable diversity, with milk going up from 1¼d a pint to 10d a pint, but margarine only going up from 7d a lb to 1s 10d. In the more recent past, food prices have risen considerably faster than other prices: between October 1972 and October 1973, for example, food prices rose by 19 per cent compared with a rise of 7 per cent for durable goods and no change for tobacco. Differential price changes of this kind can, of course, occur even without there being any overall inflation; the question is one of *relative* price changes. The introduction of the value-added tax in Britain, for example, caused some goods to become cheaper and some more expensive.

The fact that prices go up at different rates would not be a matter for concern if the proportion of income spent on each class of goods were the same for all families. If food represented the same percentage of the budget of a millionaire as of a low wage family, then inflation would still reduce the purchasing power of all incomes by the same proportion. But household budgets do not in fact take the same form at different income levels. The proportion of income spent on food ranges from 20 per cent for a high income family to over a third for a pensioner household. It is therefore wrong to apply a single retail price index to all income groups. In estimating the changes which have taken place in the distribution of purchasing power, allowance has to be made or differences in the rates of price increase and for differences in family budgets.

The way in which such adjustments are likely to work may be illustrated from the data for Britain in Table 4·3. This shows the budgets of two low income groups in comparison with that of the 'average' household on which the retail price index is based. Pensioners spend a larger fraction of their income on housing, fuel and food, than

TABLE 4·3

Budgets and prices, United Kingdom

Commodity group	Proportion of budget (1966—7)			Rise in prices Jan. 1956— Jan. 1974
	Single pensioner	Low income family [a]	'Index' household[b]	
Housing	19	11	11	217
Fuel and light	14	8	6	146
Food	35	39	29	140
Alcoholic drink	2	3	4	80
Tobacco	4	7	6	76
Clothing and footwear	5	7	9	78
Durables	3	4	7	62
Transport and vehicles	3	8	12	122
Other goods	7	6	7	134
Services	8	5	9	177
All goods[c]	100	100	100	125

Sources: budgets from Department of Employment and Productivity, *A report of the Cost of Living Advisory Committee*, 1968; price data from *Department of Employment Gazette*.

Notes: [a]Married couple with three or more children and weekly income in range £10–£20 in 1966

[b]In constructing the retail price index, adjustments are made for the under-recording of certain items, such as drink and tobacco. No adjustments have been made in the figures given here.

[c]The budget data have been rounded and for this reason do not always add exactly to 100 per cent.

do the 'index' households, and spend less on clothing, durables and transport and vehicles. Low wage families with three or more children have a rather similar pattern, although housing is proportionately less important. The last column shows the rise in prices from January 1956 to January 1974. To illustrate the magnitudes involved, let us take the case of food. Food prices rose over this period by 15 per cent more than other prices, and food constituted 39 per cent of the budget of low income families compared with 29 per cent in the case of the average 'index' household. As a result of these two factors, the cost of living rose by (39 per cent − 29 per cent) x 15 per cent more for the low income family, or a difference of 1·5 per cent.

There is no necessary reason why prices should have risen faster for goods which form a larger part of the budget of low income groups, but this has in fact been the general picture in recent years in Britain. A few years ago the government began to publish special price indices for pensioner households, and these showed that in the ten years from January 1962 the pensioner index rose by 62 per cent compared with a 57 per cent rise for the corresponding general index of retail prices. The difference may appear small, but for a person living on an old age pension it is clearly very important. Tipping (1970) similarly estimated the retail price indices appropriate to different points in the income scale. He showed that the rise in prices over the period 1956—66 for a person 5 per cent from the top of the income distribution was 38 per cent, compared with a rise of 44 per cent for someone 5 per cent from the bottom. This kind of difference could well upset any calculation of the trend in the relative shares.

Experience in the United States has been rather different. Following the same approach, Hollister and Palmer (1972) calculated special price indices for those below the poverty line and for the aged poor. Although the differences in budget patterns follow the same kind of pattern as in Britain, relative price movements over the period 1947—67 were such as to cause the price indices to rise by a very similar extent: the overall consumer price index rose by 49·5 per cent, compared with a rise of 50·7 per cent for the 'poor' price index and 50·3 per cent if adjustment is made for the introduction of Medicare. They conclude that the 'effects of the type of inflation we have experienced since World War II, in general, have not been adverse for the poor' (1972, p. 249), although this may have changed in recent years.

4·5 Income, economic status and the life-cycle

We have described above a series of adjustments which would render the official figures a more accurate representation of the distribution of annual real income, defined comprehensively, among family units, allowing for differences in needs arising from size and composition. This measure of current potential spending power is an important indicator of economic status. It may, however, be argued that other measures are more appropriate to reaching judgements about distributional equity.

First it might be argued that income is too narrow a measure of current economic status. Even with allowance for missing income, it may be felt that there are other dimensions, such as leisure, work satisfaction, and security. Taussig (1973), for example, has examined the consequences of extending the measure of economic status to include two such elements. The first is the potential spending power associated with the ownership of wealth, over and above the income derived. A person with wealth can consume out of capital and Taussig, following earlier work by Weisbrod and Hansen (1968), takes an estimate of the annuity equivalent of the wealth held, in place of the actual income from investments. It is assumed that the family consumes all capital over its expected lifetime, so that the annuity is in general greater than the current income.

According to the results of Weisbrod and Hansen, such an adjustment shifts the Lorenz curve outwards at the top, the shares of top groups being increased. Towards the bottom, the presence of old people with a higher ratio of wealth to income means that the effect on the share of the bottom 25 per cent is relatively small. There are, however, a number of objections to this procedure. While it may be agreed that the value of wealth contributes more than current income, the assumption that a family seeks to consume all its wealth over its lifetime is essentially arbitrary. A more satisfactory procedure might well be to take the individual's own assessment, as represented by his actual consumption plus disposal of wealth through transfers: 'accruals from the various sources cannot be reduced to a common unit of spending power on any objective criteria. But each individual performs this operation for himself when, in the light of all his present circumstances and future prospects, he decides on the scale of his personal living expenses' (Kaldor, 1955, p. 47).

The study by Taussig also takes into account the value of voluntary leisure time. It is often argued that leisure hours are inversely related to income, and that high money incomes may represent compensation for a long working week. There are, however, two considerations: the number of hours, and the value placed on them. The estimates presented by Taussig show that where they are valued at a common wage rate (the then minimum wage of $1·60 an hour) there is a substantial fall in the Gini coefficient. However, a valuation based on the net market wage faced by the individual leads to virtually the same degree of dispersion as for money income. The combined effect of allowing for leisure defined on the latter basis, and for the annuity value of net worth, is summarized by Taussig in terms of the Gini coefficient rising from 0·34 to 0·38.

The second objection to the use of annual income considered here is that it does not provide an accurate guide to the distribution of *lifetime* incomes. Not only are there likely to be transitory variations in annual income (people in the top 10 per cent who will not remain there next year) but also, as we saw in the previous chapter, the systematic variation of income with different stages of the life-cycle means that the distribution of annual incomes is likely to overstate the degree of dispersion in the lifetime distribution. Many people have pointed to these factors, but there have been relatively few attempts to estimate their quantitative significance.

The impact of transitory components may be reduced by averaging over a longer period than one year, and this has been done in certain studies. An early treatment is that by Kuznets (1953), who drew on a variety of sources, including a sample of the Wisconsin tax returns for 1929—35. He found that the relative advantage of an upper group selected on the basis of its income in one year declined over time, but that such regression was definitely limited. He concluded that 'in passing from a distribution by size of income in a given year to a distribution of income status for five years to a decade, the share of the top 1 per cent of the former should be cut about a fifth; and that of the top 5 per cent, about a seventh' (1953, p. 140).[1] Prest and Stark (1967) calculated average incomes in the United Kingdom over two years and found that the Gini coefficient was 0·26, compared with an annual average of 0·28. This too suggests a significant, but limited, effect, although much fuller evidence is clearly needed, such as that due to become available from the University of Michigan panel study of the incomes over 5 years of 5000 families (Morgan 1974).

Direct information about lifetime incomes is in general hard to obtain. Some indirect evidence is, however, provided by the distribution within age groups: if life-cycle differences were important, we should expect there to be substantially less dispersion *within* age groups than in the population as a whole. It is not possible to obtain information about incomes by age from the Inland Revenue statistics in Britain, but the figures in Table 4·4, taken from the *Family expenditure survey*, provide some guide to the degree of inequality within age groups. This alternative source is preferred by some authors to the

[1] The evidence assembled by Friedman (1957) suggested that the transitory component explained about 20 per cent of the variation in annual incomes (for an explanation of what this means, see the note at the end of Chapter 5).

Inland Revenue survey, and it does have a number of merits (these are discussed more fully in Chapter 10 in relation to the measurement of poverty), but it is likely that incomes at the top are seriously understated. There are also differences in the definition: for example, the data relate to household rather than family income. As a result, the estimates are not comparable with those presented in Table 4·1; and it is the distribution in different age groups *relative* to that in the whole population that is the main concern.

TABLE 4·4

Distribution of income by age groups,
United Kingdom and United States

| | United Kingdom (1968) | | | United States (1967) | |
| | Share of top | | Gini coefficient | | Gini coefficient |
Age of head of household	10 per cent	50 per cent		Age of head of family	
Under 25	18·5	65·4	0·20	Under 25	0·33
25–9	19·3	64·6	0·20	25–34	0·27
30–9	20·0	65·3	0·21	35–44	0·29
40–9	21·6	68·2	0·24	45–54	0·33
50–9	23·1	70·9	0·27	55–64	0·40
60–4	23·9	73·1	0·30	–	–
65–9	29·3	75·6	0·35	65 and over	0·48
70–4	32·2	75·8	0·36	–	–
75 and over	31·5	76·3	0·36	–	–
All households	23·8	72·5	0·30	All families	0·38

Sources: United Kingdom, from Atkinson (1974), Table 2·9;
        United States, from Taussig (1973), Table 10 (income before tax).

There appears from Table 4·4 to be rather less concentration within age groups up to the age of 60, but above that age incomes are, if anything, more unequally shared than in the population as a whole. Moreover, even in the age groups 25–49, where inequality is least, standardizing for age does not make a very large difference, the share of the top 50 per cent typically being reduced from 72·5 per cent to around 65 per cent. The evidence of Taussig (1973) for the United States shows a similar picture—see the last column, where the Gini coefficients for approximately the same age groups are presented (for purposes of comparison, the Gini coefficients are also given for the United Kingdom). The results show less dispersion within age groups up to the age of 55 and greater dispersion among the elderly. Again, even for the prime age groups, the difference is not as large as might be expected. The coefficients indicate, following the interpretation given in the previous chapter, that if we take two people at random from the age group 25–34, the average difference in their family income would be $4300 compared with $5950 for any two persons drawn from the population as a whole. There remain considerable differences within age groups.[1]

Life-cycle lactors may be of significance when considering changes in the distribution over time. Trends in the age composition of the population may lead to a shift in the annual distribution when there has been no change in individual life histories of income. Over the period since 1949, one such factor of importance has been the growing proportion of the population over retirement age. In Britain in 1948 there was one pensioner for every 5·6 people at work; by 1980 this figure is expected to become one pensioner for every 3·2 people at work (Department of Health and Social Security, 1969, p. 10–11). A rise in the proportion of pensioners has the effect of increasing the number of low income units, and of increasing dispersion in the distribution.

While the age distribution cannot be expected to change without having other effects on the distribution (for instance, on the relative incomes of pensioners and workers), it is nonetheless interesting to examine the effect on the aggregate distribution of a change in the age composition, other factors being held equal. Prest and Stark (1967) calculated the change in the overall Gini coefficient by taking the distribution within age groups (and their mean income) in 1965 and the population structure in Britain in different years:

	Gini coefficient
1954	0·296
1965	0·302
1974 (projected)	0·307

In other words, the ageing of the population would by itself have led to an apparent trend towards increased dispersion. However, the effect, while discernable, is small. The conclusion reached by Morgan in the United States for a similar comparison of the age structure in 1957 with that projected for 1975 was that the effect of changes in that country was likely to be unimportant:

if nothing happened except the expected change in the age composition of the population we would 'observe' no appreciable increase in the

[1] Schultz (1969) shows that differences in average incomes by age and sex accounted for only 15 per cent of the variation in the logarithm of incomes in the United States in 1965.

inequality of the distribution of income. The increasing proportion of old people and of young people with low and unequal incomes would apparently be more than offset by an increase in the relatively equal 25–34 age group (1962, p. 274).

The trends over time may be affected not only by the changing age composition but also by changes in the profile of income by age. An example is provided by the growth of pension schemes. The contributions to private schemes are largely missing from the statistics, but the effect of the benefits in spreading income over retirement influences the distribution. Increased provision for retirement leads to income being more evenly spread over a person's lifetime, and hence tends to reduce the apparent degree of dispersion in the current distribution. The growth of pension schemes means that there is less dispersion due to age differences in the later period, so that any trend towards equalization of lifetime incomes is overstated.

4·6 Taxes, transfers, and the government budget

As indicated in the previous chapter, we may be concerned with income as potential spending power, in which case the relevant definition is income after taxation, allowing for the benefits from government expenditure; alternatively we may be concerned with income before government intervention, as a measure of status. The concept of income employed in the official statistics falls between these two stools. In neither Britain nor the United States are taxes and government expenditure fully taken into account, even in the 'after tax' figures in Table 4·1; but in both cases certain elements of government activity, notably transfer payments, have been included, so that the statistics cannot be taken as representing purely the outcome of the market process.

In this section, we examine some of the ways in which a fuller accounting may be made for government activity in order to reach a distribution of disposable income which allows for government expenditure. It should be stressed at the outset that no attempt is made to isolate the impact in itself of the government sector: i.e. to measure the extent of redistribution. The aim is to estimate the distribution after taxes and benefits, and not to say what it would have been in the absence of the government activity.[1]

---

[1] This involves a number of methodological problems. For example, pre-tax incomes are likely to be influenced by government activity, so that we would need to estimate what pre-tax incomes would have been in the absence of the public sector.

A useful starting point may be the estimates of the distribution after income taxation in the United Kingdom, shown in the right hand part of Table 4·1. A feature of these estimates is the closeness of the income shares before and after tax: the share of the top 10 per cent was 24 per cent after tax compared with 28 per cent on a before tax basis. The implication of this is not that income tax has no effect (as just noted, we are not trying to say what would have happened in the absence of taxation—before tax incomes might have been more dispersed), but that the use of before tax figures may not be too misleading. In the United States, Okner (1974) found that in 1966 income taxes and social security payroll taxes together reduced the Gini coefficient by only 4 per cent, reflecting the fact that the effective tax paid was proportional over a wide range. However, even if allowing for income and payroll taxes has no major effect on the estimated distribution, there are other aspects of the government budget, particularly the whole of the expenditure side. It could well be argued that the omission of the benefits from public services, which tend to be fairly equally shared and have been growing in importance, leads to an overstatement of the differences in real incomes and an understatement of the trend towards equalization.

Attempts have been made in both countries to estimate the distribution of income after allowing for all taxes and benefits. In the United States, the results of Gillespie (1965) and others indicate that the impact is progressive, in the sense that dispersion is lower when these are taken into account. Income after all taxes and benefits, compared with income after transfers (the concept employed earlier in this chapter), was estimated to be some 5 per cent higher in 1968 for those with incomes under $4000, and some 10 per cent lower for those with above $35 500 (Musgrave and Musgrave, 1973, Chapter 15). The effect does not appear very large, and Herriot and Miller concluded that 'while government fiscal operations promote a somewhat more equal distribution of income, the distribution remains highly skewed' (1972, p. 41).

In Britain, estimates by Nicholson (1974) give a similar impression. For 1970 it can be calculated that the weighted average Gini coefficients for six main types of family (which he uses as summary statistics) were as follows:

1. Income after transfers but before tax (approximate)   0·28
2. Income after direct taxes and benefits   0·23
3. Income after all taxes and allocable benefits   0·25
4. Income after all taxes and benefits   0·20
    (residual allocated equally)

The last two lines show two different methods of allocating the benefits from government expenditure. Line 3 takes account only of those forms of expenditure which can be directly allocated to households (e.g. education). It omits items which are not of individual benefit (e.g. defence), or which go to other sectors of the economy (e.g. support for industrial research), or which although directly benefitting individuals cannot readily be allocated (e.g. parks). Line 4 shows the effect of assuming that the benefits from this 'unallocable' expenditure accrue equally to all; an alternative assumption would be to allocate the benefits proportionately with income, which would give the same results as line 3.

These estimates have been the subject of considerable criticism. The underlying source (in Britain the *Family expenditure survey*) used as a basis for allocating benefits and taxes has a number of shortcomings, as noted earlier. The adjustments are made at an aggregate level and this may cause the reduction in dispersion to be overstated. It might be argued (see, for example, Hicks, 1971) that no account should be taken of indirect taxes, which are on balance slightly regressive. The method of allocating the benefits from education and health services is very crude. The treatment of 'unallocable' government expenditure can clearly be challenged, and it has been suggested that the benefits should be allocated in a way that rises more than proportionately with income (e.g. that the rich benefit more than proportionately from police protection).

4·7 Concluding comments

The reader may by now wish that, like Stephen Crane's wayfarer, he had taken a different road. In the face of the difficulties described in this chapter it is indeed tempting to conclude that nothing can be said. Such a nihilistic position is, however, a very limiting one. It means that we can say nothing about proposals to change the distribution of income—either for or against them. There can be no presumption that the distribution is equal unless proved otherwise. For those wishing to make statements about the justice or injustice of the present distribution, there is no road other than that taken in this chapter.

We have attempted to see how far the main difficulties posed by the official statistics can be overcome and what the likely effect would be of correcting for these shortcomings. The results of our survey of the existing state of knowledge suggest that adjustments can be made to arrive at a better measure of current economic status, to approach the goal set by Morgan of examining the 'relation between real, disposable, reasonably permanent income on the one hand and needs on the other' (1962, p. 279). There remain, however, problems of interpretation which have not been fully explored here. In particular, we have not obtained any direct evidence about the distribution of lifetime incomes. One of the aims of the following chapters is to throw more light on differences in lifetime opportunities—with regard both to earnings and to inherited wealth.

THE DISTRIBUTION OF EARNINGS
AND PERSONAL CHARACTERISTICS

It is not possible that a class which is compelled to leave off training at ten years of age can oust, by superior intelligence, a class which is able to spend four years more in acquiring skill.

(E. Thring, headmaster, 1864)

One of the principal sources of income inequality is the dispersion of earned incomes; indeed, earnings are for most people the major source of income. This chapter and the following one are concerned with some of the main factors which lead to such earnings differentials.

5·1 The evidence to be explained

The landmarks of the earnings distribution were described in Chapter 2, which demonstrated the existence of marked differences in earnings according to occupation. The earnings tree showed that a headmaster is likely to earn three times as much as a farm labourer, that a hospital consultant is likely to earn twice as much again, and top executives many times more. More complete information about the average earnings of men in different occupational groups in Britain is shown in Table 5·1. Unskilled manual workers receive some 80 per cent of

TABLE 5·1
Average earnings of men in different occupational groups
Great Britain 1913–60

| | Percentage of average for all groups (men and women) | | | | |
	1913/14	1922/4	1935/6	1955/6	1960
Higher professional	410	372	392	290	298
Lower professional	194	204	190	115	124
Managers and administrators	250	307	272	279	271
Clerks	124	116	119	98	100
Foremen	141	171	169	148	149
Skilled manual	124	115	121	117	117
Semi-skilled manual	86	80	83	88	85
Unskilled manual	79	82	80	82	79

Source: Routh (1965), Table 48.

average earnings; skilled manual workers some 40 per cent more than
unskilled; foremen 50 per cent more than average; and higher
professional workers, slightly ahead of managers, three times the
average.

The table also shows the changes in occupational differentials over
the course of this century, notably the relative fall in the earnings of
professional workers, especially between 1935 and 1955, and of clerical
workers. Within the manual occupations, as we saw in Chapter 2, there
has been much greater stability. In the United States there has been a
more marked tendency towards a long-term narrowing of occupational
differentials: the rate for skilled workers fell relative to that of
labourers from double in 1907 to only 40 per cent higher some fifty
years later. In the same way, the relative position of professional
workers has declined in the United States, as is illustrated by the fall
from 3·6 to 1·7 of the ratio of the earnings of university professors to
the average wage.

The occupational groups set out in Table 5·1 are broad, and the
figures conceal considerable variation. (The definition of an
'occupation' is clearly to some extent arbitrary, and some groups are
wider than others: in the United States census, for example, painters
are separated from paperhangers, whereas all accountants come in a
single category.) Within the group of higher professional workers,
actuaries earn on average nearly half as much again as accountants, and
architects earn only two-thirds the amount received by the average
doctor. Even within narrowly defined occupational groups, the degree
of dispersion remains very considerable. This may be illustrated by
figures for the distribution of earnings within selected occupations in
Britain in 1973 (from *Department of Employment Gazette*, 1974):

Weekly Earnings (per cent of median)	Lower quartile	Upper quartile
All full-time adult men (see Table 2·2)	80	125
Train drivers	84	117
School teachers	78	120
Doctors	84	175
Waiters	69	137

In each case the earnings of the quartile are expressed in relation to the
median *for that group*, so that the upper quartile of waiters earns 137
per cent of the median for waiters. This gives a rough indication of the
amount of dispersion within groups relative to that in the distribution
as a whole. For some groups, such as train drivers. the degree of
dispersion is less than for all men taken together. The lower quartile for

this group is only 16 per cent away from the median, compared with 20 per cent for all men, and the upper quartile is similarly nearer the median. However, in other groups the earnings of the lower quartile are a smaller percentage of the median (teachers), and again in others the upper quartile are a larger percentage (doctors), than for the overall distribution. Perhaps not surprisingly, both are true for waiters.

The variation of earnings within occupations is in fact such that knowing what a man's job is tells us relatively little about his likely earnings, which may rather surprising, since we are accustomed to thinking that it does. The proportion of the variation in earnings which can be explained by occupational differentials is fairly small: on the basis of the estimates for the United States, Lydall (1968, Ch. 4) concluded that not more than a quarter of the total variation in earnings could be attributed to the differences in median earnings between occupations.[1] In part this can be explained by factors such as age and location. For most occupations there is a clear pattern of variation of earnings with age, with the peak being reached relatively soon in the case of manual unskilled jobs and relatively late in the case of professional workers. For example, the position of the lower quartile of school teachers may be explained by the number of young teachers at the bottom of the scale. Earnings vary with geographical location. In the United States, Adams (1958) showed that, other things being equal, earnings tended to be on average 12 per cent lower in the south and were over 30 per cent higher in major conurbations than in rural areas.

A further feature of the earnings distribution described in Chapter 2 was the overall shape of the distribution. This was presented in terms of

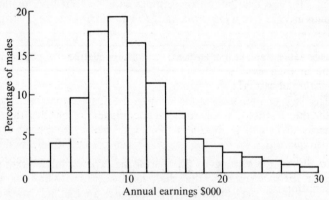

Fig. 5·1. Shape of the earnings distribution, United States 1971
Source: US Bureau of the Census, Current Population Report, No. 85, 1972.

[1] For an explanation of what this means, see the note at the end of this chapter.

the earnings of deciles and quartiles relative to the median, but it may be seen more clearly from examination of the frequency distribution (in Chapter 2 we presented a frequency distribution for *incomes* but not earnings). The distribution in Fig. 5·1 shows the pattern of earnings in the United States, where the data have been standardized to relate to white male employees working full-time in non-agricultural employment. As we saw to be the case with total incomes, the distribution is bunched around the middle, with over half the population being in the range $6000–$12 000. On either side of this range, the frequencies fall away, but the right hand tail is clearly much longer (even though in the figure it is truncated at $30 000). In other words, the distribution is not symmetric, but positively skewed. This skewness is also demonstrated by the decile figures for Britain. If the distribution was symmetric, then the distance between the lowest decile and the median would be the same as the distance between the median and the highest decile, but that is not the case:

	Percentage of median (all adult male employees)	
Lowest decile	66	
	Distance = 34	Ratio $\dfrac{\text{Median}}{\text{Lowest decile}}$ = 152%
Median	100	
	Distance = 59	Ratio $\dfrac{\text{Highest decile}}{\text{Median}}$ = 159%
Highest decile	159	

At the same time, it is interesting to note that the *ratio* is broadly the same in each case, so that if we were to plot not earnings but the *logarithm* of earnings, this would be much closer to symmetry.[1]

This lack of symmetry in the earnings distribution may be contrasted with the distribution of such characteristics as height: the lower quartile of heights in Britain is 1·76 inches below the median and the upper quartile is 1·74 inches above. The frequency of heights does, in fact, follow broadly the *normal* curve, which is bell-shaped and symmetric. Such a normal curve would clearly provide a poor description of the earnings distribution; however, the observation about the ratios suggests that the logarithm of earnings may follow the normal

[1] In this case the distance between the lowest decile and the median would be log (median) − log (lowest decile) = log (median/lowest decile).

distribution. In such a case, the distribution is said to be *lognormal* in form. In practice, frequency distributions do tend to follow this pattern in the middle range of earnings and from an examination of earnings data for a large number of countries, Lydall concluded that in general 'the central part of the distribution, from perhaps the tenth to the eightieth percentile from the top, is close to lognormal' (1968, p. 67).

As Lydall points out, the lognormal does not provide a good description of the upper tail of the distribution, because there are more people with high earnings than the lognormal would predict. He argues that the upper tail, in fact, follows more closely the *Pareto* distribution. On the basis of an examination of the distribution of income for an unlikely collection of places—Prussia, Saxony, eighteenth-century Peru and the cities of Florence, Perugia, Basle and Augsburg (in 1471)— Pareto concluded in 1897 that the distribution followed a particularly simple 'law':[1] 'These results are very remarkable. It is absolutely impossible to admit that they are due only to chance. There is most certainly a cause, which produces the tendency of incomes to arrange themselves according to a certain curve' (quoted in Lydall, 1968, p. 13–4).

Since then empirical work has cast doubt on the general validity of Pareto's law, and it is clear that it cannot provide an adequate description of the whole range of incomes or earnings, since it does not lead to the hump-shape characteristic of such distributions.[2] On the other hand, it often provides a reasonable fit to the upper tail, and Lydall concludes that 'tests of many ... distributions suggest that the Pareto function generally provides a good fit for approximately the top 20 per cent of earners' (1968, p. 66).

The range of explanations

A wide range of theories have been put forward to explain the evidence described above. These are in many cases based on very different assumptions about the labour market, and as a result they are difficult to present within a common framework. It may nonetheless be useful to classify the different explanations according to the assumptions

[1] (A technical footnote.) The law may be stated as follows: if Y denotes income, the number of people with incomes greater than or equal to Y is given by $A Y^{-\alpha}$ where A and α are constants. The α is in fact the Pareto index referred to in Chapter 4. One interesting feature of the distribution is that the average income of those in the range Y and above is always $\alpha/(\alpha-1) \times Y$. If, for example $\alpha = 1\cdot5$ (as Pareto supposed), then the average income of those above £1000 is £3000 and the average income of those above £10 000 is £30 000.

[2] The frequency falls with earnings throughout the range of the Pareto distribution, so that the highest frequency is at the left hand tail, which is clearly inconsistent with the pattern shown in Fig. 5·1.

made about three main factors: the working of the labour market, the extent of differences between people, and the differences between jobs.

Given a perfectly functioning, competitive labour market, and all people and jobs being alike, there would be no differences in earnings. If there were any differentials, then everyone would flock into the higher-paying positions and equality would be restored through the competitive process. If all people were alike, and if the labour market were perfectly competitive, but jobs differed, then there would be earnings differentials such that everyone was indifferent about which job he did: i.e. there would be an equalization of 'net advantages'. As it was described by Adam Smith:

the whole of the advantages and disadvantages of the different employments of labour [must] be either perfectly equal or continually tending towards equality. [If] there was any employment evidently either more or less advantageous than the rest, so many people would crowd into it in the one case, and so many desert it in the other, that its advantages would soon return to the level of other employment (1776, pp. 76–7).

Such equalization could apply to aspects such as the degree of responsibility, the pleasantness or otherwise of the work, the danger or health hazards, and the social prestige. The dimension which has probably received most attention, however, is the training required for a particular job, and it is this which provides the basis for the human capital theory discussed in Section 5·2.

This picture of the equalization of net advantages is clearly unrealistic. A person might prefer to be a policeman than a porter, but fail to pass the physical examination; he might prefer to be a surgeon rather than a butcher, but lack the money required to support him through medical school. Theories which emphasize differences between people—differences in abilities and differences in opportunities—are discussed in Section 5·3.

Finally, the assumption of perfect competition may well seem out of place in a world where wages appear to be largely determined by negotiations between trade unions and employers' federations, and by an increasing degree of government intervention, and where the working of the market is impeded by frictions of all kinds. In the next chapter we examine in greater detail the institutions of the labour market and the role played by factors such as status and custom.

5·2 Human capital theory

The human capital theory is of old vintage, Adam Smith having recognized that one major application of the principle of equal net advantages was that 'a man educated at the expense of much labour or time ... must be expected to earn over and above the usual wages ... the whole expenses of his education, with at least the ordinary profits of an equally valuable capital'. It is only recently, however, that the implications of this approach have been spelled out, as in the work of Mincer (1958) and Becker (1964). These authors have tried in particular to see how far human capital (education and training) on its own can explain earnings differentials. In order to focus on this aspect, the human capital theory in its simplest form makes strong assumptions about other aspects. The labour market is assumed to be competitive and perfectly functioning, so that a person can have a free choice of his occupation: if he wishes to train for a particular job, then there are no barriers to his doing so. Secondly, everyone has the same opportunities. There are no environmental inequalities, such as differences in intelligence, physical skills, or in home background. Everyone has access to the capital market on the same terms.

If these assumptions are satisfied, then, as Adam Smith put it, the occupations requiring a longer period of training have to provide a correspondingly higher level of earnings if they are to attract people. In order to bring this out more clearly, let us make a number of simplifying assumptions:

(1) Training involves postponement of entry into the labour force (i.e. there is no on-the-job training), where the number of years of training beyond the minimum school-leaving age is denoted by S;
(2) Everyone works for the same number (N) years after completing his training, so that those with longer training retire at an older age, and no one dies before reaching retirement;
(3) There are no costs of education apart from forgone earnings and there are no student grants;
(4) The earnings of a person who has S years of education, denoted by E_S, are assumed constant over his working life, and there is assumed to be no unemployment;
(5) All jobs are alike in every feature except the length of training required, and there is no intrinsic benefit from education.

These assumptions may be summarized in terms of the stylized lifetime for a person with S years of training:

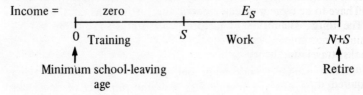

The decision to undergo training involves the person's borrowing to finance his living expenses for that period, and it is assumed that he can borrow (from parents, from the bank, etc.) as much as he requires at a constant interest rate, r per cent, per annum. Given this, and the fact that all jobs are otherwise alike, he chooses the length of his education according to the stream of earnings over his lifetime, discounted at this interest rate. (The stream has to be discounted since earnings at a later date are worth less than those at an earlier date.) This means that for a person to be indifferent between leaving school at the minimum legal age and training for a job requiring S years of education, the present discounted value of earnings must be equal. In the highly simplified case we are considering, this condition reduces to the formula (Mincer, 1970, p. 7):

Earnings with S years of training = Earnings with no training $\times (1 + r)^S$

Postponing entry into the labour force means that earnings are delayed and if the person has to borrow at an annual cost of r per cent, then E_S has to be higher to allow for this. The differential has to be larger, the longer the training period and the higher the interest rate.

Coupled with the assumption that everyone faces the same opportunities, this condition determines the distribution of earnings. If the condition did not hold, then everyone would flock into, or out of, jobs requiring training. On the basis of these strong assumptions, we have therefore a theory of the explanation of earnings differentials: earnings are directly related to the training required.

The simplifying assumptions made for purposes of exposition may readily be relaxed. Firstly, it would be quite straightforward to incorporate on-the-job training, either in the explicit form of apprenticeships or where it is implicit (e.g. where there are piece rates, so that an inexperienced worker earns less). In these cases, earnings are not zero during training but are simply lower than for jobs where no such qualifications are required. The second assumption about the expected working career can be modified to allow for different retirement dates and for the possibility of death in service (in which case the person is assumed to base his decision on the actuarial value of future earnings). Where people retire at broadly the same age, so that the working life for the highly trained is shorter, then the differential will have to be correspondingly greater.

The third assumption—that there are neither costs associated with training nor student grants—can be relaxed by taking account of fees, books, travel, and other costs specifically associated with the course of education. To the extent that there are such additional costs, the required differential is increased. (It should be noted that ordinary living costs should not be taken into acount, since these are incurred whether or not the person is in education.) Student grants work in the opposite direction, since they reduce the cost of education and provide some limited compensation for forgone earnings.

The assumption about the pattern of earnings over a person's lifetime is clearly unrealistic, but it can be modified. In the same way, an expected rate of unemployment can be introduced, where this rate is likely to vary with the level of training. A person with low education is more likely to suffer unemployment, and this factor narrows the differential required to make people indifferent between two occupations. It is also possible to incorporate uncertainty about the level of earnings. Adam Smith suggested that this uncertainty was greater for occupations requiring more training: 'Put your son apprentice to a shoemaker, there is little doubt of his learning to make a pair of shoes but send him to study the law, it is at least twenty to one if ever he makes such proficiency as will enable him to live by the business' (1776, p. 82). However, it is not clear that today earnings are more uncertain in jobs requiring more training. Finally, account can be taken of non-pecuniary features of different occupations. Casual observation would suggest that the more highly trained occupations are *on average* more attractive in terms of aspects such as safety, prestige, control over working environment, etc. This is further reinforced when one takes into consideration the fact that people may enjoy education to some extent as a consumption good.

To sum up, the human capital theory leads to the prediction that earnings differentials depend on the degree of training required, in terms both of formal education and of on-the-job training, and are just sufficient to compensate for the costs of this training, taking into account length of working life, uncertainty of earnings, unemployment and non-pecuniary benefits.

The evidence for the human capital explanation

At first sight, the human capital theory appears to promise an explanation for the occupational differentials described at the beginning of this chapter, the occupations with higher earnings being in general those which require more training. We need, however, to examine the *magnitude* of the differential required to compensate for the longer training. An early attempt to do this was the pioneering study by Friedman and Kuznets (1945) of earnings in the professions in the United States. They began by observing that in the 1930s there was a difference of some 85 to 180 per cent between the average incomes of professional and non-professional workers in the same community who had been in the labour force for the same number of years. They then proceeded to calculate the differential which would have been required to compensate the professional workers for the longer training required, which was on average seven years. After allowing for the specific costs of training (tuition fees, books, special equipment, etc.), for the longer life expectancy of professional workers, and for an annual cost of borrowing of 4 per cent, they estimated that the required differential would be in the range 55 to 70 per cent, or considerably less than that observed. They concluded that 'the actual difference between the incomes of professional and non-professional workers seems decidedly larger than the difference that would compensate for the extra capital investment required' (1945, p. 84), and went on to say that:

there is nothing surprising about this finding. It is clear that young men are, in fact, not equally free to choose a professional or non-professional career ... First, the professions require a different level of ability than other pursuits; second, the economic and social stratification of the population leaves only limited segments really free to enter the professions (p. 88).

The results of a more recent study, based on Canadian data for 1961, are shown in Table 5·2. This gives the present discounted value of

TABLE 5·2
Net present values of lifetime earnings after tax
for males, Canada 1961

	Present value (at age 14) $ 000		
Discount at interest rate of	5%	8%	10%
Labourers			
no high school	33·3	20·8	16·1
4 years' high school	36·4	21·7	16·2
Carpenters			
no high school	41·1	26·1	20·5
4 years' high school	44·3	25·1	19·9
Draftsmen			
no high school	59·3	36·5	28·2
4 years' high school	57·2	34·9	25·8
Engineers			
4 years' high school	72·5	41·6	30·6
university degree	76·5	40·8	28·3

Source: Wilkinson (1966), Table 3.

lifetime earnings in different jobs, allowing for differences within occupations in educational levels. In other words, a carpenter with four years of high school could have then expected to earn after tax $44 300 over his life, discounted at an interest rate of 5 per cent. The fact that these amounts vary considerably between occupations suggests that we are not observing the complete equalization of the present value of earnings: the lifetime earnings of engineers, for example, are around double those of labourers.

In the comparison of the present values of earnings in different occupations, the choice of the interest rate to apply could make a substantial difference, and the Friedman—Kuznets study has been criticized on the grounds that the rate of 4 per cent was unreasonably low.[1] As can be seen from Table 5·2, the use of a higher rate tends to narrow the difference; however, it would have to rise quite considerably before the gap between the net present values was eliminated. This can be illustrated by calculations of the *internal rate of return* to training, which is the (not necessarily unique) rate of discount at which the net present value of the job requiring qualifications is equal to that of the job where no training is needed. A recent study in the United States showed, for example, that the internal rate of return to training as a doctor was between 24 per cent and 29 per cent (Sloan, 1970). The fact that this is considerably in excess of the likely cost of borrowing again suggests that the human capital theory explains only part of the differential. In the same way, a study by Hansen (1967) showed rates of return to training as an engineer in the United States, which ranged from 10 per cent in government service to 19 per cent in research and development, with an average of 17 per cent.

So far we have considered the contribution of the human capital theory to the explanation of occupational differentials; we have seen, however, that there is considerable dispersion within occupations and we need to ask how far it can explain the distribution of earnings as a whole. (From Table 5·2 it appears, for example, that there is a broad equality of present values for different education levels within occupations.)

In testing the validity of the human capital theory as an explanation of the overall distribution, it is tempting to begin by applying the

---

[1] One important question is whether *r* is specified in money or real terms (i.e. allowing for inflation). If we assume that earnings are fixed in real terms, then it is the real cost of borrowing that is relevant, so that *r* = 4 per cent means a money rate of interest of 4 per cent plus the rate of price increase.

formula given on p. 81, from which it can be seen that by taking logarithms we obtain:

$$\log \left(\begin{array}{c} \text{earnings with } S \\ \text{years of training} \end{array} \right) = S \times \log (1+r) + \log \left(\begin{array}{c} \text{earnings with} \\ \text{no training} \end{array} \right)$$

This means that if it is plotted on graph paper the logarithm of earnings should go up linearly with the number of years of schooling: for every further year of schooling, it should increase by a factor of log (1+r). The evidence for the United States for the earnings of white men in non-farm employment in 1959 shows a clear positive relationship of this kind (Mincer, 1974, p. 46). The slope of the line is, however, rather lower than expected; moreover, only a small fraction of the variation of earnings can be explained in this way.

The test just described, while straightforward, is open to many objections. Even leaving on one side the effects of differential ability and other factors discussed in the next section, the data are in too gross a form for the question at hand. There is, for example, no reason to expect the age composition of the population to be the same at all educational levels. With the spread of education, the lower educational groups contain disproportionately large numbers of older people. To the extent that the pattern of earnings varies systematically with age, this will introduce a bias into the results. These issues have been discussed at length by Mincer (1974), using the data for the United States in 1959. He stressed the interaction between formal education and work experience, and argued that it was necessary to standardize at a comparable level of experience. On the basis of the earnings of men 8–10 years after they left school, Mincer estimated that differences in education explain about one-third of the variation in the logarithm of annual earnings for that group. Extrapolating to the distribution as a whole, he concluded that schooling accounts for a quarter of the variation for all age groups, and that this may be higher if allowance is made for the quality of education.

These findings are in contrast to earlier studies, which had concluded that less than 10 per cent of the variation was attributable to education. Mincer's own results show that schooling by itself accounted for only 7 per cent of the variation in the logarithm of total earnings. An important role is therefore being played by the 'experience' variable, which may in part simply reflect age. It should also be noted that the explanation of 25 per cent of the variation is still consistent with considerable dispersion of earnings among those with the same education and experience: the mean difference would in fact be 87 per cent of that for the population as a whole.[1] A striking, if rather exceptional, illustration of this is given by Rees (1973, p. 196): the distribution of earnings in 1967 of the Princeton class of 1942. These people had spent four years at the same college, and were about the same age, yet the spread was such that the upper quartile earned over one and a half times the median.

Overall, the evidence suggests that the human capital theory explains part, but far from all, of the earnings dispersion. The differentials required to compensate for the training necessary to enter skilled occupations are less than those actually observed, and considerable differences still exist in the present value of lifetime occupational earnings. In 1914, Cannan pointed out that if there were equality of net advantages, 'we should find well-to-do parents in doubt whether to make their sons civil engineers or naval stokers, doctors or road-sweepers' (1914, p. 207). Today, education explains only part of the dispersion of individual earnings, and people with the same schooling and experience may well be paid very different amounts. One reason for this, as Friedman and Kuznets pointed out, is that the simple human capital approach leaves out important elements: differences in individual abilities and background, and the fact that the labour market does not necessarily operate in the smooth, perfectly competitive way posited. These factors have important implications for the assessment of equity, since to the extent that lifetime net advantages are not equalized, we do have inequality of opportunity. The human capital theory has done a valuable service in pointing out that part of earnings differentials may be attributed to the return to training, but it does not explain away all earnings inequality.

5·3 Unequal opportunities and abilities

Imperfect capital markets

In the exposition of the human capital theory given above, it was assumed that everyone could borrow as much as he wished at a given interest rate, a situation which no student is likely to regard as realistic. It is, in fact, highly unlikely that the capital market will operate in this perfect manner; especially in the case of .education, the terms of borrowing depend on how much is involved and on who the borrower is. Difficulties in borrowing arise particularly because human capital cannot be held as a collateral, since that would be equivalent to a

[1] This is an example of the fact that the same statistical evidence may be summarized in different ways to give quite different impressions—see the Note on statistical methods at the end of the chapter.

person's selling himself into slavery, so that the lender has no security, as he would have if he held the title to a house or a claim against other physical assets.

The effects of such imperfections are likely to work in two ways. First, any one individual probably faces a rising cost of borrowing the larger the amount required. This means that to finance a further year of schooling he has to pay more than before and hence that the earnings differential must be enough to give a higher rate of return—see the cost of borrowing curve in Fig. 5·2. Initially, a person is likely to borrow from parents or relatives, and the cost is relatively low; he may then begin to borrow from the bank by running up an overdraft, which would involve a higher interest rate; and finally, he may be unable to borrow any more at all, as shown in the diagram by the line's becoming

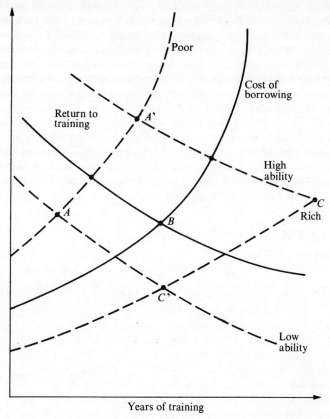

Fig. 5·2. Inequality of ability and opportunity

vertical. The second aspect of imperfect capital markets is that different people are likely to face different conditions of borrowing. A person coming from a wealthy family is probably able to borrow more from his parents and is regarded as more credit-worthy by banks and other lending institutions. Children from poor families may get little help from their parents (they may be under pressure to leave school as soon as possible) and are much less able to borrow on the market, although in the United States there are tuition programmes designed to help students from low income families. As a result, there is a range of cost of borrowing for different people, such as that illustrated in Fig. 5·2.

Inequality in access to borrowing, and hence to education, may lead to earnings differentials in excess of those predicted by the simple human capital theory. Suppose that the annual cost of borrowing to go on from university to three years at medical school is 15 per cent for a person from a poor family, compared with 5 per cent for a person with a wealthy father. The earnings differential required to make this attractive to the person from a wealthy background, leaving on one side any government grant received or other income, is (from the formula given on p. 81) $(1 + 0·05)^3 = 1·16$, or 16 per cent more than the earnings of an ordinary university graduate. The person from a poor background, however, would require a differential of $(1 + 0·15)^3 = 1·52$, so that the actual differential could lie anywhere between 16 per cent and 52 per cent without it being the case that poor people would flock into medical schools. The existence of high internal rates of return to training for many occupations is consistent with barriers to entry of this form, although it may also be explained by other factors, such as differences in ability.

Unequal abilities

It has long been believed that earnings are related to differential abilities, where these include physical characteristics (such as strength, energy, and dexterity), intellectual capacity, and personal qualities. Many authors were indeed puzzled by the fact that earnings did not follow the normal curve according to which abilities were thought to be distributed among the human population. Pigou, for example, argued that 'there is clear evidence that the physical characters of human beings–and considerable evidence that their mental characters' are distributed according to the normal curve (which he described as being shaped like a cocked hat), and that as a result 'we should expect that, if, as there is reason to think, people's capacities are distributed on a plan of this kind, their incomes will be distributed in the same way. Why is not this expectation realized?' (1952, p. 650).

The first explanation of Pigou's paradox is that abilities may not, in fact, be distributed according to the normal curve. While physical measurements such as height satisfy this relationship, there is no necessary reason why the abilities relevant to determining productive capacity should follow the same pattern: 'there is at present really no such thing as *the* distribution of ability: the distribution depends upon the measuring rod used and cannot be defined independently of it' (Mayer, 1960, p. 194). The arbitrary nature of the distribution of scores in the case of intelligence tests is brought out by a hypothetical example given by Mayer. Suppose that the test consists of ten questions, each involving the addition of two numbers. Most people are likely to score close to 100 per cent on such a test. On the other hand, if the ten questions involved solving differential equations, most of the population would score zero. By varying the ratio of easy and difficult questions, we can get almost any distribution that we like. The fact that most actual IQ tests lead to a distribution of scores which follows the normal distribution does not necessarily tell us anything, therefore, about the distribution of abilities; it may simply reflect the way in which the tests have been constructed.

A second explanation of the Pigou paradox is that the relationship between abilities and earnings is more complex than he supposed. The productivity of a worker may be related to a number of different dimensions of ability. If these operate multiplicatively, it may then be that output has an approximately lognormal distribution, even if the individual attributes are themselves distributed normally. Roy (1950) gives a number of examples, and although these are rather specialized (for example, 35 girls packing boxes of chocolates), they suggest that output has in fact an approximately lognormal distribution, so that if earnings are directly related to output, they will follow the pattern we observed to hold for the middle range of earnings.

An alternative way of linking abilities to earnings is in conjunction with the acquisition of training, and this brings us back to the human capital theory. Unequal mental abilities affect the operation of the human capital model in two respects. Firstly, the acquisition of education involves not simply a choice by the individual but also his or her acceptance by the educational institution. Entry into higher education is usually contingent on successful completion of secondary or high school, and graduation from college or university depends on the student's passing examinations and other hurdles. A person with higher intellectual abilities is more likely to be successful in this process, and hence we should expect the return to further training to be higher, other things being equal, for him than for someone with a lower level of intellectual ability who is less likely to pass examinations.

The second way in which differential ability affects the human capital theory is through a direct link between ability and earnings. Irrespective of its contribution to educational success, higher ability may raise the earnings of a person once he has qualified, more able lawyers earning more than less able, and so on. This does not, however, necessarily make education more attractive to the person with higher ability, since it may also mean that he would earn more if he did not train. The opportunity cost is also higher. If ability enters multiplicatively, so that one person would earn twice as much as another whether they were carpenters or accountants, then it would not affect the decision about the length of schooling (both sides of the formula on p. 81 would be double for the first person). It has, nonetheless, usually been assumed (e.g. by Becker, 1967) that ability and education are complementary: i.e. that the effect of ability on earnings increases with the level of education. This means that the marginal return to further education, taking account of both the factors mentioned, is higher for a person with higher ability. In Fig. 5·2 this is shown by the position of the dashed lines, the one for a person with high ability being above that for a person with low ability. (The downward slope of all the 'return to training' curves is based by Becker (1967) on the limited length of human life and the increasing cost of time.)

This discussion has tended to emphasize intellectual abilities, and the empirical work referred to in the next section is almost entirely concerned with ability as measured by intelligence and aptitude tests. It is important to remember, however, that these do not capture many different dimensions of ability. Jencks (1972), for example, points out that 'the ability to hit a ball thrown at high speed' or 'to persuade a customer that he wants a larger car' may be a more significant determinant of earnings. Moreover, qualities of personality or character, such as drive, determination or charm, may be very influential.

Unequal abilities and opportunities

The combined effect of unequal opportunity (cost of borrowing) and unequal abilities is shown in Fig. 5·2. The nature of the observed relationship depends on the relationship between ability and access to borrowing. If there is a positive correlation (ease of borrowing and high ability go together), then the observed pattern would be that marked *ABC* in the diagram, with the wealthy/high ability group being concentrated in occupations requiring considerably more education. In contrast to this, if there were a negative correlation, and the children of poor families were on average more able than children from rich families, then the pattern would be *A'B C'*, with much less marked differences in the years of education, but large differences in the rate of return.

It has been argued by Chiswick that the correlation is probably positive (i.e. the same person is likely to have high ability and to be able to borrow easily):

First, if ability is related to genetic factors it is reasonable to expect a positive correlation between the parents' and a child's 'genetic ability'. Since parental ability tends to be positively related to parental wealth, there would be a negative correlation between a child's ability and the marginal cost of funds. Second, wealthier parents presumably invest more in the non-schooling characteristics of their children [who may thus] appear to have a higher level of ability when they approach school-leaving age. Third, it is easier for youths of high ability to obtain . . . scholarships from schools (1969, p. 499).

There are a number of points here with which issue can be taken, particularly the statements about the hereditary component. It is not clear, for example, that parental ability tends to be positively related to parental wealth, especially where the latter has been inherited. However, on balance Chiswick's conclusion may well be correct, and the positive relationship observed between ability and years of education provides some indirect support for this position (Mincer. 1974).

The observed relationship depends also on the extent of variation in the distributions of ability and opportunity. If the differences in the cost of borrowing were relatively unimportant, we should observe a situation where the rate of return to extra years of schooling was greater at higher levels of schooling. The observed points would all lie close to the average cost of borrowing curve, most of the variation being due to differences in ability. (In terms of Fig. 5·2, the points A and A' would move down to the right, and the points C and C' up to the left.) On the other hand, were the differences in the cost of borrowing relatively much more important than the variation in ability, we should observe a downward-sloping relationship. The observed points would then all lie close to the average return to training curve. In fact the empirical study of Hanoch (1967) for white males in the northern United States shows a rate of return which declines from 21·8 per cent for staying on at school from 14 to 16 to a rate of 7·1 per cent on higher education from 18 to 23. In Britain the evidence is more mixed, with a first degree giving a higher return than taking 'A' level at school, and similarly in Canada the return does not decline consistently. However, a recent cross-country study by Psacharopoulos (1973) concluded that there is in general a tendency for the return to decline with the level of education. This suggests that differences in abilities may in fact be less important than inequality of opportunity, a finding which is reinforced by further evidence presented in the next section.

5·4 The explanation of earnings inequality and personal characteristics

The relationship between the different variables considered in this chapter is summarized schematically in Fig. 5·3. The human capital theory considered in Section 5·2 was concerned solely with the link between years of schooling and earnings, as indicated by the heavy line. The considerations introduced in the previous section are represented by the links from family background (cost of borrowing) and ability to years of schooling, indicated by dashed heavy lines in the diagram. The pure 'ability' theories discussed at the beginning of the previous section are represented by the direct link from measured IQ to earnings. These are not, however, the only links which may be important. The effect of family background may operate not just through schooling but also through measured abilities, and it may well make a direct contribution to the inequality of earnings. The determination of earnings may be influenced by chance events: a person in the top 1 per cent of the earnings distribution may have no superior abilities, may have left school at the earliest possible age, and may have no family advantages—

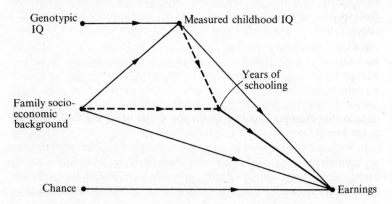

Fig. 5·3. The explanation of earnings

he just happened to be in the right place at the right time. Finally, random events may also influence the measured ability, and years of schooling, although these links are not shown in the diagram.

In recent years, a number of studies have attempted to measure the relative importance of the different elements outlined above. The findings are in many cases in conflict and all that is attempted here is a brief review of some of the main, if divergent, conclusions relating to the United States. Let us begin with the link between earnings and ability, or, more precisely, measured IQ, since it is this variable which has most often been considered. This subject has been surrounded by controversy, most recently since the publication in 1969 of Jensen's essay (1969) 'How much can we boost IQ and scholastic achievement?', which attacked the compensatory education programmes of the War on Poverty on the grounds that IQ was largely inherited and uninfluenced by environmental factors. As Bowles and Nelson (1974) point out, this attack is founded on two propositions:

(1) that IQ has a large heritable component;

(2) that IQ is a major determinant of earnings or economic success.

Jensen's position on the first of these propositions has been subjected to detailed, and often critical, scrutiny; however, the second proposition—the one central to the present discussion—has received much less attention. Jensen, himself, devoted little space to this issue, apparently considering that the intrinsic importance of intelligence as a determinant of earnings could be taken for granted.

The empirical evidence on the relationship between IQ and earnings suggests in fact that the direct influence of measured IQ is relatively unimportant. At first sight this is not the case, since there appears to be an association between intelligence and earnings. This is illustrated in the top part of Table 5·3, which is taken from a study by Bowles and Gintis (1973) of the earnings of non-Negro males aged 25 to 34 from a non-farm background in the United States in 1962, where 'economic success' is based on an individual's income and an index of occupational prestige. The association between IQ and economic success is portrayed in Table 5·3 in terms of the differing chances of people in different IQ classes entering different deciles of economic success: for example, a person in the top decile of IQ is 3 times as likely as the average person to appear in the top decile of success.

However, the immediate impression is misleading. If we were to draw up similar tables relating economic success to education or family background, they would show an even stronger association. The relationship between IQ and economic success may derive simply from the common association of both these variables with family background and the level of schooling. On the basis of a statistical analysis of the data, Bowles and Gintis argue that this is in fact so, and that the *independent* influence of IQ is very small. The magnitude of the effect, as estimated by them, is represented in the lower part of Table 5·3. Where education and social class background are held constant, a person in the top decile of IQ stands only a slightly higher chance than the average person of being in the top decile of economic success.

The results in Table 5·3 relate to the direct link between measured IQ and economic success. In order to measure the genetic contribution in full we need to allow for the indirect efect via years of schooling. The work of Bowles and Nelson suggests, however, that this too is small

TABLE 5·3
IQ and economic success, United States 1962

	Economic success by deciles									
	1	2	3	4	5	6	7	8	9	10
Probability of attainment of different levels of economic success by individuals of differing levels of adult IQ Adult IQ by deciles:										
Top decile	30·9	19·2	13·8	10·3	7·7	5·7	4·1	2·8	1·7	0·6
Third decile from top	14·4	14·5	13·7	12·6	11·4	10·1	8·7	7·1	5·4	3·0
Third decile from bottom	4·4	7·0	8·7	10·0	11·0	11·7	12·3	12·6	12·4	10·9
Bottom decile	0·6	1·7	2·8	4·1	5·7	7·7	10·3	13·8	19·2	30·9
Probability of attainment of different levels of economic success by individuals of equal levels of education and social class background but differing levels of adult IQ Adult IQ by deciles:										
Top decile	14·1	12·4	11·4	10·7	10·1	9·5	9·0	8·4	7·7	6·6
Third decile from top	11·4	10·9	10·6	10·4	10·2	9·9	9·7	9·4	9·1	8·5
Third decile from bottom	8·5	9·1	9·4	9·7	9·9	10·2	10·4	10·6	10·9	11·4
Bottom decile	6·6	7·7	8·4	9·0	9·5	10·1	10·7	11·4	12·4	14·1

Example of use: Suppose two individuals have the same levels of education and social class background, but one is in the third decile from top in adult IQ, while the other is in the third decile from bottom in adult IQ. Then the first individual is $11·4/8·5 = 1·3$ times as likely as the second to attain the top decile in economic success (lower part of table, row 2, column 1, divided by row 3, column 1).

Source: Bowles and Gintis (1973), Tables 1 and 4.

Note: It should be emphasized that this table has *not* been constructed by directly observing the decile position of different individuals. What the table brings out are the implications of the observed correlation between the variables in question. Rows do not necessarily add to 100 per cent because of rounding.

Moreover, to the extent that measured IQ *is* influenced by environment, the relationship between genotypic IQ and economic success is weakened (we have to subtract that part due to the link between family background and measured IQ). The conclusion reached by Bowles and Nelson is that 'the genetic inheritance of IQ is a relatively minor mechanism for the intergenerational transmission of economic and social status' (1974, p. 47).

The methods applied in arriving at the results described above are recognized by these authors to be subject to error and to a variety of interpretations. Nonetheless, the same conclusion about the relative unimportance of the link between IQ and earnings has been reached in other studies: Griliches and Mason (1972), for example, found a low independent contribution of ability measured according to the rather different Armed Forces Qualification Test. It seems that Cannan was right when he suggested in 1914 that:

even if road-sweeping were paid by the piece in strict proportion to the amount of service rendered, the most industrious and able man in the world would not earn £1000 per annum by it. There is clearly something more at the bottom of the differences of earnings as between one occupation and another (1914, p. 198).

A second important question concerns the relationship between earnings on the one hand and schooling and family background on the other. Here the evidence is more mixed. The apparent relationship between schooling and earnings described in Section 5·2 could again be explained by their joint association with other variables, such as family background. In his statistical analysis of earnings data, Bowles (1972) has attempted to isolate the two effects. His results indicate that the estimated increase in annual income (in 1962) associated with an additional year of schooling is $265, which is quite a substantial effect. This relationship is, however, less than 60 per cent of the gross return to schooling indicated if the effect of parental background is ignored. He concludes that socio-economic background has a significant effect on earnings. This works through the higher educational level achieved: 'a high status individual's origins—at the eighty-ninth percentile of the composite social class distribution—are translated into an advantage of 4·6 years of schooling over the respondent whose low status origins place him at the eleventh percentile'; as well as through a direct effect on earnings: 'even in the evidently unlikely event that both individuals attained the same years of schooling, the individual of high status origins could expect to earn $1630 more annually' (1972, p. S240).

Bowles goes on to suggest that length of schooling has a relatively minor influence on earnings independently of social background, but this conclusion is not based on a fully adequate treatment of the human capital variables and has not been universally accepted (see comment by Becker on Bowles, 1972). His results are in fact best interpreted, not as demonstrating the insignificance of education, but as bringing out the importance of socio-economic background, which has been neglected in the work of the human capital school (there is, for example, no treatment of it in the recent study by Mincer, 1974).

The final question concerns the importance of the three determinants of earnings discussed in this chapter—ability, education, family background—relative to other factors (represented by 'chance' in the diagram). It has indeed been argued recently by Jencks that these factors can explain only a small proportion of the variation in earnings. 'Neither family background, cognitive skill, educational attainment, nor occupational status explains much of the variation in men's incomes. Indeed, when we compare men who are identical in all these respects, we find only 12 to 15 per cent less inequality than among random individuals' (1972, p. 226). This leads him to conclude that an important role is played by sheer luck: 'chance acquaintances who steer you to one line of work rather than another, the range of jobs that happen to be available in a particular community when you are job hunting ... whether bad weather destroys your strawberry crop, whether the new super-highway has an exit near your restaurant' (p. 227).

The conclusions reached by Jencks have been widely reported, but his analysis is open to a number of objections. One immediate problem is brought out by the reference to 'incomes' in the first quotation. The data used by Jencks related to total money income and not just to earnings; and it is not surprising if ability and education can account for relatively little of the variation in income from investment. In the same way, the examples given in the second quotation (strawberry crops and restaurants) relate to income from self-employment, which again the theories do not seek to explain.

A second objection to the analysis by Jencks is that he does not take adequate account of short-term variation in earnings. Part of the unexplained variation may be due to purely temporary changes in earnings and not to any systematic factors. While such transitory inequality is clearly of concern, it is important to distinguish it from permanent differences between individuals. Jencks makes passing reference to this point but does not attempt to estimate how much of the variation can be explained in this way.

A third, related, problem is that the data employed by Jencks relate to all (white, non-farm) men aged 26—65, and he does not explore how far the variation is associated with age differences. Whether treated as a simple age profile, or related to work experience, as in Mincer (1974), the development of earnings over an individual life-history may lead to a systematic bias in the results, and it seems likely that the explanation of the variation in lifetime earnings is higher than suggested by the figures quoted by Jencks.

Jencks has probably, therefore, understated the contribution of ability, education, and family background to the explanation of earnings differences. At the same time, no one would suggest that they can explain all the observed dispersion. There will still remain substantial variation even when these factors are taken into account. This may be due to luck or it may be related to the features of the labour market described in the next chapter.

A (more technical) note on the presentation of statistics

At a number of points in the text, there are statements of the kind: 'variable S (e.g. years of schooling) explains 25 per cent of the variation in variable E (e.g. earnings or its logarithm)'. This is a short-hand way of saying that a linear least squares regression of E on S explained $R^2 = 25$ per cent of the variance. (The correlation coefficient is $R = 0.50$.) This means that the association between E and S is such that if we take people with the same S, the variance in their values of E is 75 per cent of that for the whole population. It should be noted that in most of the applications referred to in the text, particularly the work of Mincer, it is the *logarithm* of earnings which is regressed on S.

The effect of the choice of method of presenting the same statistical evidence may be illustrated by the following statements which can be derived from the analysis of Mincer (1974) and the assumption that earnings are lognormally distributed (i.e. the logarithm of earnings follows the normal distribution). They are broadly equivalent but may lead the reader to draw rather different conclusions:

(1) A person in the top fifth of the schooling distribution earns on average more than double a person in the bottom fifth of the schooling distribution of the same cohort;

(2) Differences in schooling explain one-third of the variation in annual earnings for people in the same cohort;

(3) If you take two people in the same cohort with the same schooling, the average difference between their earnings is only 18 per cent less than the average difference for the cohort as a whole.

The tables given by Bowles and Gintis (Table 5·3 here) are yet another way of presenting regression analysis.

6
THE DISTRIBUTION OF EARNINGS
AND THE LABOUR MARKET

The disputations of economists upon the validity in particular circumstances of the law of supply and demand, the principle of fair comparison or any other principle governing pay may lead to conclusions which in human terms and in their practical application leave something to be desired.

(Royal Commission on the Police, 1960)

The analysis in the previous chapter of the determination of earnings assumed a competitive and perfectly functioning labour market. In this chapter, we begin by describing two approaches which depart from these assumptions. The first emphasizes aspects of the labour market such as trade unions, employers' monopoly power and government intervention, which mean that there is no longer perfect competition; the second is concerned with the nature of the demand for labour, and the role of custom and status in wage determination. In the latter part of the chapter (Section 6·3), we consider the application of these theories, together with those discussed in Chapter 5, to the causes of low pay, and the effectiveness of policy measures, particularly minimum wage laws.

6·1 Institutions of the labour market—trade unions, employers, and government

The assumption of perfect competition in the labour market precludes consideration of aspects of wage determination which must appear to the average newspaper reader to be of considerable importance: the role of trade unions, collective bargaining, and intervention by the government. In this section we examine their impact on the structure of earnings differentials.

Unions and bargaining power

Trade unions have grown in importance over the past hundred or more years and now occupy a position of considerable influence in many industries. In Britain, membership has increased from 1½ million in the 1890s to over 10 million today (nearly half the labour force), with particularly rapid increases in 1910–13 and in the late 1930s. In the United States, union members comprised less than 2 per cent of the labour force in 1897, but this proportion has risen, notably between 1935 and 1945, to about one-third of the non-agricultural labour force today. There is considerable variation in union membership across industries. In the United States unionization has typically been high in mining, construction, manufacturing, and transportation, but much lower in agriculture, distributive trades, and the government sector. In Britain the proportion of union members varied in 1960 from 89 per cent in coal mining to 11 per cent in the food, drink, and tobacco industry.

The impact of trade unions on the structure of earnings depends on the objectives pursued, and these involve a complex variety of motives. Union leaders are concerned with many factors besides wages: employment, redundancy, control over working conditions and practices, fringe benefits, etc. It would be wrong, therefore, to regard unions as simply concerned with wage maximazation; at the same time it seems reasonable to suppose that raising wages is one of their main objectives:

we can probably assume with some conviction that *one* of the principal aims of a trade union will be to maintain and if possible improve the wage position of its members, though the degree to which it will pursue this aim will be governed by the union's need to take account of the consequences of that policy for employment, membership and other objectives (Hunter and Robertson, 1969, p. 275).

The power of the union to raise wages arises from the control which it can exercise over the supply of labour. In the older craft unions there is the natural restriction that all craftsmen have to serve a period of apprenticeship, typically five years, and the number of apprentices is often limited: for example, there may be no more than one apprentice per time-served craftsman. A second form of restriction is the closed shop, limiting recruitment to union members, or the union shop where the employer may recruit non-union workers on the understanding that they will join within a certain period after starting work. A third form of regulation is where the union does not simply restrict total employment but also insists on the right to nominate workers to fill vacancies. In addition to those over the supply of workers, there are controls related to the supply of effort (restrictions on output or on the allocation of labour) and the sanction of the withdrawal of labour through strikes, overtime bans, etc.

The employers' side of collective bargaining is often represented by employers' associations: for example, the Engineering Employers' Federation in Britain. Again such bodies have manifold objectives, and they are likely to be less cohesive in nature than the union side. However, it seems reasonable to suppose that employers, collectively and individually, are anxious to use their bargaining power to limit the wages paid. Where labour is unorganized, this may lead to labour receiving less than it would under perfect competition, as is shown in the textbook analysis of a firm with monopoly power in labour and product markets. The existence of such a gap was referred to by Pigou as 'exploitation' (for discussion of this concept in relation to Marxian analysis, see Chapter 9). Where labour is unionized, the level of wages depends on the relative bargaining strength of the two sides.

TABLE 6·1
Estimated effect of unions on relative wages, United States 1920–58

	Estimated effect (%)
1920–4	17
1925–9	26
1930–4	46
1935–9	22
1940–4	6
1945–9	2
1950–4	12
1955–8	16

Source: Lewis (1963). Table 64
Note: in fact Lewis used the equation set out below to explain the logarithm of relative wages, so the results here show the percentage difference.

The empirical importance of these factors may be examined by relating earnings in different occupations to the level of unionization, as a measure of employee strength, and to various indicators of the bargaining power of the employers. The best known study of this kind is that by Lewis (1963), who investigated the impact of unionization on relative earnings of different industries in the United States over the period 1920–58. These results, shown in Table 6·1, were based on an analysis of the average earnings of the group of heavily unionized industries, containing more than 80 per cent of union labour, relative to the average earnings of the rest of the economy. Lewis hypothesized that relative earnings would be determined by:

A x degree of unionization + other demand and supply factors

The coefficient A has the following interpretation: if 100 per cent of the labour force in the first sector were unionized and none of the second sector, then wages would be higher in the fully unionized sector by an amount A. It can be seen therefore as measuring the impact of unionization.

The results given in Table 6·1 suggest that the effect varied considerably over the period, showing a dramatic increase in the 1930s when union agreements prevented cuts in money wages, and a decline during the Second World War when the tight labour market improved the relative position of non-union labour. For the most recent period, Lewis concluded that 'the average union/non-union relative wage was approximately 10 to 15 per cent higher than it would have been in the absence of unionism' (1963, p. 5). This economy-wide analysis was supported by detailed studies of individual industries reviewed by Lewis, although these showed a wide range of results, from a relative wage effect of some 50 per cent in coal mining to no effect in suit manufacturing. Somewhat similar results have also been obtained in Britain by Pencavel, who concluded that 'in the early 1960s, trade unions raised the hourly earnings received by their members relative to the hourly earnings received by non-unionists by an average of some zero to ten per cent' (1974, p. 205), with the higher figure tending to apply in those industries where earnings are in excess of industry-wide agreed wage rates.

Studies such as that carried out by Lewis are open to the objection that they make inadequate allowance for differences in personal characteristics of the kind discussed in the previous chapter. Some of the differential might be explained by union labour being on average better educated, and this not being fully captured in the analysis. Weiss (1966) used data on individual earnings from the 1960 census in the United States to estimate the relationship between earnings, personal characteristics, and measures of union strength and the monopoly position of the employer (represented by the degree of concentration in the industry). He found that the effect of unionization was slightly smaller than that indicated by Lewis, although it was still significant, and this was confirmed by Boskin (1972), using data for wage rates in 1967. In the case of industrial concentration, Weiss found that wages do tend to be higher in highly concentrated industries, but he argued that this is explained by differences in personal characteristics; in other words it reflects the fact that monopolistic industries get a higher 'quality' of labour, rather than the ability of workers to extract part of the monopoly profits.

Trade unions are not, of course, the only bodies which use bargaining power to raise their relative earnings; many professional associations perform much the same function, although some members would no doubt be horrified by the thought. In certain cases professional bodies have a legal or effective monopoly over the supply of particular services. In Britain, solicitors have a legal monopoly of the drawing of documents under seal 'for gain' and of originating proceedings in court:

qualified accountants have a monopoly over auditing for public companies.[1]

The reference to professional bodies raises the question of how the gains from unionization are likely to affect the distribution of earnings. If the main gainers are doctors and airline pilots (Lewis estimated for the latter group a relative wage effect in the United States of 21 per cent to 34 per cent), then overall dispersion may be increased. Lewis did indeed conclude that unionization *increased* differences in average earnings between industries, although he pointed out that this may have been offset by reductions in dispersion within industries. This latter possibility has been the subject of a number of studies. Some authors argue that the lower paid are likely to gain in relative terms since unions tend to pursue fairly egalitarian policies: for example demanding equal cash increases for all members, which would narrow relativities. On the other hand, Friedman (1954) suggests that the better paid skilled workers would be more likely to gain, on the grounds that they represent a smaller part of the wage bill and hence face a less elastic demand. (This is Marshall's Third Rule of Derived Demand—'the importance of being unimportant'—and is only valid where there is limited scope for substitution. Airline pilots would be a clear example.)

In the United States, the study by Boskin referred to above suggested that labourers gained more from unionization than did craftsmen and operatives, and that by Rosen (1970), again for the United States, showed a gain in relative terms of 60 per cent for labourers, compared with less than 10 per cent for operatives. In Britain, it has been argued by Turner (1957) that the equal cash increases demanded by mass trade unions were responsible for the narrowing of differentials between the 1920s and the 1950s, and that where the unions were dominated by skilled workers and presented percentage wage demands, no such narrowing took place. The distributional consequences of unionization depend also on whether the relative gain of union members is achieved at the expense of non-union labour or at the expense of profits. This involves the general equilibrium of the economy as a whole, and this subject is taken up in Chapter 9, which considers the effect on the total share of wages in national income.

Government intervention

Government intervention in the process of wage determination takes a variety of forms. There is the statutory regulation of wages, which is primarily concerned with establishing minimum rates and the pro-

[1] It may be noted that in Britain doctors do not have a legal monopoly. Anyone can practise medicine for gain, but he must not call himself a doctor, imply that he is qualified, or sign prescriptions.

tection of low paid workers, and is discussed in Section 6·3. There are arbitration procedures which may be brought into effect in the event of the breakdown of collective bargaining: for example, the setting up of a formal board of arbitration or court of enquiry. More generally, the government may operate an incomes policy. Such policies range from the purely voluntary, based on exhortation, such as the Guideposts of the Kennedy years, through a statutory body making recommendations about wage increases, such as the Prices and Incomes Board in Britain from 1965–70 and a rather longer-lived body in the Netherlands, to legislated controls on wages, such as those operated by the Nixon administration and by the Conservative government in Britain in the years 1972–4.

In considering the impact of such government intervention on the distribution of earnings, it must be remembered that the aims of intervention have often been more concerned with maintaining industrial peace and with restraining the overall increase in wages than with distributional questions. Whether intended or not, however, the effect of such measures has been in large part to maintain existing differentials. In the case of arbitration procedures, this is reflected in the kind of arguments which are made to tribunals or courts of enquiry:

The claimants do not say: 'Concede this demand because we are a powerful union with a near-monopoly' ... nor do the employers respond by reference to the strength of their own economic position. The unions quote the failure of wages to keep pace with the cost of living, or the injustice of one [group] getting left behind in a general advance (Wootton, 1962, p. 99).

While it may be the bargaining power of the two sides which leads to the court of enquiry, the decisions appear to attach more weight to comparability than to other considerations. An illustration in the British case is the argument given by the Wilberforce Committee for recommending special treatment for the miners in 1972:

this is not to say that we take the view that the relative wage position of any industry should be immutable. Some changes are necessary from time to time as economic circumstances, technology and other factors alter. In our view, however, the fall in the ranking of coalmining pay has been quite unwarranted by any such changes (Hughes and Moore, 1972, p. 129).

At the level of statutory incomes policy, a somewhat similar picture appears to hold. The effect of successive policies in Britain and the

United States has been to provide in general for across-the-board percentage increases, or for an overall freeze. There have been certain exceptions. In Britain, the Labour government's incomes policy made provisions for higher increases where 'the existing wage and salary levels are too low to maintain a reasonable standard of living', but there was little evidence that the low paid made significant gains (Hughes in Bull, 1971). The Conservative £1 plus 4 per cent formula, and the subsequent threshold clauses, represented a partial return to equal absolute increases. This should have led to some narrowing of percentage differentials, although other factors, such as the limited coverage of low paid workers by threshold agreements, may well have reduced its impact. In the United States, the Guideposts of the mid-1960s allowed increases above the general guide rate where wage rates were exceptionally low on account of weak bargaining power. These exceptions were not, however, sufficient to lead to any major reduction in earnings differentials (Sheahan, 1967).

6·2 The demand for labour and the role of custom and status

In Chapter 5, relatively little attention was paid to the role played by the demand for labour. This reflected the underlying assumption that the labour market was in equilibrium, and that all workers identical in training, ability, and other respects relevant to their productivity received the same earnings. If they did not, then, as Adam Smith described, so many would crowd into the higher-paying job and so many desert the other, that wages would be brought into line. However, there are good reasons to believe that the labour market does not function in this smoothly equilibrating way, and that earnings may not necessarily be equal for people with identical qualifications. Indeed, this may be one explanation of the finding described in the last section of Chapter 5, that there is a large unexplained variation after taking account of personal characteristics. If this is the case, then the nature of the demand for labour may play an important role.

The view underlying the discussion of Chapter 5 that wages change in such a way as to bring about equilibrium in the labour market—to equate supply and demand—has long been the subject of criticism, particularly by economists of a more institutional orientation. Recently, there have been attempts to develop more explicit alternative theories of the labour market. These have taken a variety of forms, but the following passage from Thurow and Lucas is perhaps representative:

One set of factors determines an individual's relative position in the labor queue; another set of factors, not mutually exclusive of the first, determines the actual distribution of job opportunities in the economy.

Wages are paid based on the characteristics of the job in question and workers are distributed across job opportunities based on their relative position in the labor queue (1972, p. 2).

In this alternative view, the first central aspect concerns the hiring of workers by employers and the imperfect information available to them. The labour queue envisaged by Thurow and Lucas is the ranking of workers by employers according to the potential costs of training. The employer is not able to judge the suitability of any one worker with great accuracy, and obtaining further information involves substantial screening costs, so that he bases his decision on certain easily observed personal characteristics, such as age and education.[1] Where there is imperfect information about the true characteristics of workers in the labour queue, identical individuals may receive different earnings; on the other hand, it is possible that the rate of pay for a job will be in line with the *average* characteristics of the workers employed. We should then observe an equilibrium in a 'statistical' sense. Differentials are related to the personal characteristics of workers, but do not account for the whole variation in earnings, because of the limited information available to employers. Individuals with identical potential productivity as workers may end up with different earnings, depending on which characteristics employers use as a basis for hiring and on the luck of the draw.

Implicit in the view of Thurow and Lucas is the assumption that employers cannot simply learn by trial and error, and that there are costs of adjustment. This is based on the importance of on-the-job training and the associated concept of an *internal labour market* which has recently been emphasized by Doeringer and Piore (1971).

An internal labour market within a firm or plant is largely insulated from the outside labour market. It is characterized by a pattern of jobs, arranged in a line of progression, with entry into the labour force being limited to a number of points towards the bottom of the ladder and the remainder of the jobs within the internal labour market being filled by the promotion or transfer of workers who have already gained entry—see the hypothetical example in Fig. 6·1. As a result, these jobs are protected from direct competition by outside workers. An early illustration of this is provided by the 1907 enquiry into railway earnings in Britain: 'engine drivers are in the main recruited from the firemen, who in turn are recruited from the engine cleaners. Goods guards and brakesmen are largely taken from the ranks of shunters'

---

[1] The employer may also base decisions on the race or sex of applicants (subject to legal constraints on discrimination). Sex discrimination is discussed later in this section; racial discrimination is taken up in Chapter 10.

The labour force is in effect segmented; and indeed the concept of an internal labour market may be seen as a development of the idea of 'non-competing groups' associated with Cairnes and Taussig.

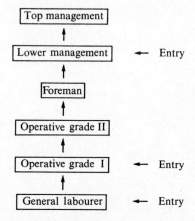

Fig. 6·1. An internal labour market

The key elements leading to the development of an internal labour market are seen by Doeringer and Piore to be the specific nature of skills and the role of on-the-job training. By a specific skill is meant one unique to a particular job in a particular firm, in contrast to a general skill, such as reading, which can be applied much more widely. As Doeringer and Piore point out:

Almost every job involves some specific skills. Even the simplest custodial tasks are facilitated by familiarity with the physical environment specific to the workplace ... Even mass-produced machines have individual operating characteristics which can markedly affect work performance ... performance in some production and in most managerial jobs involves a team element, and a critical skill is the ability to operate effectively with the given members of the team (1971, pp. 15−16).

When specific skills are important, then general training received through formal education is of little value to the employer and he selects workers on the basis not of skills already acquired but of potential training costs. Doeringer and Piore argue that 'by far the largest proportion of blue-collar job skills is acquired on the job' and that even in managerial positions on-the-job training may be a prerequisite for the successful application of formal education.

The specific nature of skills and the importance of on-the-job training provide a strong incentive for the employer to develop internal labour markets with a low degree of turnover and internal promotion. Similarly, the workers gain from a structured long-run career within the enterprise with job security and chances of advancement; and trade unions have a clear preference for the resulting stability, often reinforcing it through rules such as seniority governing promotion. It is for these reasons, Doeringer and Piore suggest, that the internal labour market characterizes a substantial fraction of the US economy. In industries such as steel, petroleum, and chemicals, for example, workers are hired almost exclusively into low-skill jobs and most blue-collar skills are developed internally. At the same time, they recognize that there is an important sector of the economy where the internal market is weak, where turnover is high, and jobs offer little prospect of a lifetime career. This 'secondary' sector is discussed in the next section, dealing with the causes of low pay.

The implications of the internal labour market for the determination of earnings are seen by Doeringer and Piore to be that, while textbook competitive forces place constraints upon wage differentials, they do not in general establish a unique wage rate. Rather, they provide upper and lower bounds on the range of possible variation. This reflects, first of all, the fact that both employers and employees take a longer view: 'When the [employment] relationship is permanent, neither employers nor workers necessarily concern themselves with the connection between wages and marginal productivity at any point in time' (1971, p. 76). There is therefore scope for flexibility in determining the wage for any particular job; however, we should still expect to find equality of *career* earnings for people with the same characteristics. (In this respect it would run parallel to the human capital theory of occupational choice.)

The second way in which the competitive constraints may be weakened is through the costs of adjustment. In the short run, wages may move out of line with those obtained elsewhere by workers with the same characteristics. In the worker's case, his scope for mobility is limited in an internal labour market by the restrictions on entry to other markets. Workers who have reached higher-level jobs may be earning well above the wages on entry jobs elsewhere. The employer, for his part, has invested in the hiring and training of the worker.

Such adjustment costs may lead to there being no short-run reallocation of labour; however, they do not explain a permanent disequilibrium. For there to be an enduring situation where workers with identical characteristics have different career earnings, we have to return to considerations of imperfect information and of restricted perceptions. For example, Thurow and Lucas argue that workers may compete, not on the basis of wages, but for the available jobs (what they refer to as 'job competition'). A worker may not be able to bargain his way into a high-paying sector; he may only be able to offer himself for the available jobs at a specified wage. The implications of such models of labour market behaviour have not, however, as yet been fully developed.

To the extent that wage differentials are not constrained by market forces, they are, according to Doeringer and Piore, influenced by considerations of custom and status. The former is particularly relevant in the case of short-run changes in the labour market. Any wage relationship, they argue, 'which prevails over a period of time tends to become customary; changes are then viewed as unjust or inequitable, and the work group will exert economic pressure in opposition to them' (1971, p. 85). This kind of customary wage differential applies not simply within a firm or an industry, but also across occupations. A well-known example is the tradition in both the United States and Britain that policemen and firemen get paid the same. Despite the shortage of policemen and the relative over-supply of firemen, this convention has been sustained over long periods. The role of custom over a long period is brought out by Phelps Brown:

Between 1412 and 1914 the rate for the mason . . . rose fourteenfold, but at one end of the five centuries as at the other . . . it was half as much again as the labourer's . . . the simple ratio of three to two appears far too widely and too long for us to suppose that it was reached each time by an equilibration of market forces: it must have been what it was primarily because men were following custom (1962, p. 132).

The force of custom does not prevent wage differentials from changing, the very differentials described by Phelps Brown having changed in Britain over this century, but within a given range of conditions, differentials are unresponsive to changes in the labour market situation.

The effect of custom is to reduce the sensitivity of differentials to economic conditions, but it does not in itself determine what these differentials will be (within the constraints imposed by competitive forces). Within the internal labour market, Doeringer and Piore stress the role played by the social status of the job in question and particularly its position in the hierarchy of production. They refer to the fact that workers whose jobs involve the direction of others must typically be paid more than their subordinates in order to perform this function effectively. Workers responsible for providing on-the-job training for new entrants may feel threatened by the trainee, and only give adequate training if their seniority is reflected in higher pay.[1] More generally, pay is seen as an indicator of status in society at large. A number of examples in the British context are given by Wootton: for example, the instruction to a government committee making recommendations for the pay of doctors to give 'due regard to ... the desirability of maintaining the proper social and economic status' of the profession, and the argument by *The Times* that 'it is of first-rate public importance that [judges] should continue to be men of substance and security. The vast moral authority of the law in this country is bound up in the public mind with the visible dignity of the men who dispense the Queen's justice' (1962, pp. 128–9).

The relationship between earnings and position in the hierarchy of production has been developed more explicitly in the theories of managerial salaries developed by Simon (1957) and Lydall (1968). They suppose that the hierarchical organization is broadly pyramid-shaped, so that each person has a certain number of subordinates below him, typically between three and ten. The salary of an executive is then assumed to be a constant multiple of that of his subordinates, or his salary span of control, which Simon describes as a widely accepted principle of executive remuneration. The resulting distribution of salaries turns out to be of the Pareto form described in the previous chapter.

Lydall goes further, and suggests that the hierarchical principle may explain why the overall earnings distribution follows the Pareto formula at the upper tail. This, however, involves a jump from the earnings distribution of an individual enterprise to that for the whole economy, which may not be warranted. Many highly paid employees do not work for hierarchical organizations, and even if they all did, the pattern of earnings would depend on the size of such organizations. Indeed, this brings out the dependence of the structure of jobs and earnings on the organization of production. The role of such status differentials is related to the extent of corporate and similar institutions and to the size distribution of firms. We should expect differentials to be smaller where production was typically in the hands of small enterprises and to be larger in a world of big business.

The analysis of the labour market described in this section is based on assumptions which have not been fully spelled out or examined in a rigorous way (it is, for example, much less thoroughly developed than the human capital theory), and it is clearly open to challenge. The extent to which it is valid can be determined only by extensive

[1] The example given by Doeringer and Piore is the threat to older, unmarried secretaries posed by pretty young girls.

empirical investigation, based on a more complete development of the underlying theory. It does however lead to a rather different view of earnings differentials and of the likely impact of government policy.

The differences between this view, the human capital theory of the previous chapter, and the bargaining power explanations discussed in Section 6·1, are clearly illustrated by the question of sex discrimination and equal pay. In Chapter 2 we saw that the median earnings of women are considerably below those of men. This differential is narrower when account is taken of age, education, hours worked, and other observed personal characteristics, but it remains the case that women's earnings are on average only some 70 per cent of those of men. Most authors (see, for example, the review by Oaxaca, 1973) have concluded that this largely reflects the concentration of women in lower-paying jobs rather than their being paid a different rate for the same job.[1]

This sex differential may be explained by discriminating attitudes on the part of employers, of male employees, or of customers (male and female). Such tastes for discrimination by employers and employees form the basis of the theory of discrimination advanced by Becker (1957), although there are reasons to expect such differentials to be eliminated in the long run through the operation of competitive forces (see Arrow, 1972). In addition to such direct discrimination, there may be other considerations, and the different views of the labour market described above do in fact suggest a range of factors.

Firstly, the human capital approach has been utilized by Mincer and Polachek (1974) to explain the earnings gap in terms of the differential work experience of married women and associated decisions about education. On this basis, the differentiation of roles within the family leads to women earning less than men who are otherwise identical, because they are able to acquire less human capital. Secondly, theories based on employers' monopoly power suggest that such role differentiation may be important in another way: that employers may be able to exploit the weaker supply position of women. Robinson (1933) discussed the case where men were unionized and women had a less than perfectly elastic supply, and showed that a differential emerged even where the two types of worker were equally efficient in production. Thirdly, a quite different explanation is suggested by the

[1] Although this clearly happens: cf. Ms Fawcett in the *Economic Journal* for 1918: John Jones earned good wages from a firm of outfitters . . . he fell ill and was allowed by the firm to continue his work in his own home. He taught his wife his trade, and . . . she did more and more of the work . . . as long as he lived it was taken to the firm as his work and paid for accordingly. When, however, it became quite clear, John Jones being dead and buried, that it could not be his work . . . the price paid for it by the firm was immediately reduced to two-thirds.

considerations of imperfect knowledge described in this section. If employers have no information about potential employees other than their sex, and if they believe that on average women are less productive than men, profit-maximizing behaviour may lead them to discriminate against women in employment. This may well mean that women are paid less than men with exactly the same productive skills: women 'may suffer from "statistical discrimination" by being treated as though their own behavior resembled the average' (Council of Economic Advisers, 1973, p. 106).[1] Women may not be recruited into occupations with well developed internal labour markets, and their prospects of promotion to the top jobs may therefore be restricted.

These three explanations could all account for women being paid less than men who have the same (potential) productive skills. They do, however, lead to people's making quite different policy recommendations. The human capital view indicates that attention should be focused on the intra-family allocation of time and the sex-linking of roles. The explanation based on employer exploitation has led to support for equal pay legislation; and the 'statistical discrimination' view has given rise to proposals for employment quotas: 'if women constitute 35 per cent of those who by objective criteria qualify for a given rung of an occupation, they should have approximately 35 per cent of those jobs' (Bergmann and Adelman, 1973, p. 513). The examination of the relative importance of the different factors, including direct discrimination, and of the impact of measures such as employment quotas, is a task of considerable urgency.

6·3 Low pay

We have considered a variety of explanations for the distribution of earnings, and in this section we show them 'in action', as applied to the problem of low pay. How far can low pay be explained by the different factors discussed, and what are the implications for policy measures, particularly the effectiveness of minimum wage legislation?

The first question is what one means by 'low pay', since a variety of definitions could be adopted. In the United States, two natural standards suggest themselves. The first is the level of the minimum wage set by the federal government for certain industries, or $1·60 an hour in 1972. The study by Perrella (1967) of earnings data for 1965, for example, took this standard as its basis. The second possible definition is the official poverty standard (see Chapter 10), set at around $4200 per annum for a family of four in 1972, which gives a rather higher

---

[1] The discrimination is of course no less real for being 'statistical'.

figure on an hourly basis ($2·10 an hour, assuming that a person works 50 weeks at 40 hours per week).

The use of the poverty standard raises the question why a family of four should be taken as the reference standard. In Britain, Wootton has pointed to the vacuous nature of the injunction in the 1924 Act to regulate agricultural wages so that they should be adequate 'to enable a man in an ordinary case to maintain himself and his family' (1962, p. 84). The impossibility of defining an 'ordinary case' means that an approach based on family needs is unworkable. In view of this, low pay has typically been defined in Britain directly in relation to average earnings: for example, where earnings fall below two-thirds of the national median. This has no inherent rationale, although it seems to correspond in broad terms to what surveys suggest people generally consider to represent low pay. A rather different approach, followed for example by the Prices and Incomes Board in Britain, is to define the low paid as those in the lowest 10 per cent of earners. While this definition has its uses, it clearly means that no statements can be made about the *extent* of the problem of low pay—there will on this definition always be 10 per cent of the population who are low paid.

The extent of low pay obviously depends on the definition adopted, but by all the standards described above the numbers involved are substantial. Taking the harsher definition in the United States, the federal minimum wage level, we find that in 1965 there were 3 million men who had worked a full year but earned less than this level, representing 9 per cent of the male labour force (Perrella, 1967). In other words nearly 1 in 10 male workers earned less than the amount laid down by the federal government as the minimum for industries covered by the Fair Labor Standards Act, a level which was then only half of average earnings in the economy as a whole. Moreover, figures for 1970 suggest that the number may not have declined. The minimum wage level in 1965 represented less than the amount required to support a family with one child at the official poverty standard, and in fact of the families below the poverty standard more than one in four had a breadwinner working full-time. In Britain the evidence from the 'New earnings survey' in 1973 shows that a substantial minority of adult male workers are employed full-time, yet earn less than two-thirds of the median:

Earning less than	Percentage of adult male workers
$\frac{2}{3}$ median	10·9
60 per cent median	6·4
½ median	1·8

The figure of 60 per cent of the median could well have been less than enough to support a family with two children (and average rent) at the Supplementary Benefit level, and, as in the United States, low wages are an important factor leading to poverty (see Chapters 10 and 11).

What are the causes of low pay? The human capital theory would clearly point to the role of training, predicting that the low paid would be those with poor educational qualifications and with limited on-the-job experience. The low paid would be those who lack productive skills. If the human capital theory is extended to allow for differential abilities, these too would be a determinant of low pay. The evidence discussed in Chapter 5 suggested that intelligence was a relatively unimportant factor, but at the extreme lower end of the ability spectrum it may become more significant. Finally, there is socio-economic background, as well as race and sex, which are clearly very important.

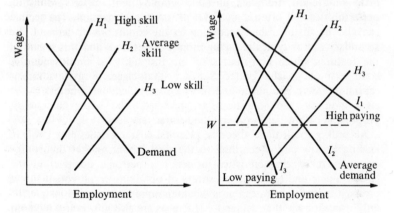

Fig. 6·2. Causes of low pay

The role of personal characteristics may be represented by the supply curves shown in the left hand part of Fig. 6·2. The curves correspond to people with high (H_1) or low (H_2) productive skills (the H stands for human capital); the more able or better educated person obtains a higher wage at any given level of employment on account of his greater productivity.

In contrast to the explanation of earnings in terms of supply factors, the theories discussed in this chapter have emphasized the institutions of the labour market. If earnings are influenced by bargaining power, we should expect to find the relatively low paid in industries where unions were weak and employers strong. This is represented in the right hand part of Fig. 6·2 by the different demand curves, one corresponding to a highly unionized, high-paying industry (I_1), and the other to a less organized, low-paying industry (I_2). (It should be noted that the term 'demand curve' is being used in a slightly unconventional way, in that it incorporates the effects of unionization.) A relatively unskilled worker in industry I_2 may earn as much as a worker with average skill in I_3 because of union pressures and barriers to mobility.

These different demand curves may also be seen as corresponding to the concept of a 'dual labour market' developed by Doeringer and Piore. They suggested that there are two broad sectors. The *primary* sector is characterized by a structured internal labour market, by employment stability and promotion from within, with the stability of the market often being reinforced by strong trade unions. Workers in this sector are typically well paid, in contrast to the *secondary* sector, where most low paid workers are concentrated. This sector involves little on-the-job training, unstable employment, poor promotion opportunities and often a low level of union organization. The sectors can also be distinguished according to the conditions of demand, the secondary sector typically facing more competition, and this is one of the features which contributes to the instability of employment. A good example in the United States is that cigarette manufacture is capital-intensive, unionized and faces a steady demand; whereas in the cigar industry, the conditions are reversed. The latter has a high proportion of low paid workers, the former very few.

According to all these theories, personal characteristics play a role in leading to low pay. According to the dual labour market theory, for example, these characteristics influence a person's position in the labour queue and hence his prospects of obtaining employment in the primary sector. The question is whether supply considerations are the only cause, or whether demand-side factors are also important. In terms of Fig. 6·2, if the labour market were competitive and perfectly functioning, then market forces would eliminate the difference between I_1, I_2 and I_3, so that only the difference between the H would remain—we should observe the left hand picture. The demand theory, on the other hand, assumes that there is disequilibrium in the labour market, so that people with the same supply characteristics may get paid different wages, as in the right hand diagram. This may come about because of the imperfect information available to employers or because of historical accident in a market which adjusts very slowly. Alternatively, it may reflect systematic barriers to mobility caused by trade unions or by the existence of internal labour markets.

If we look at the evidence about low pay among adult men, it appears that personal characteristics are important. In the United States, non-whites are more than proportionately represented among the low paid: 'whereas [Negro men] compose but one-twelfth of the non-agricultural male workforce, they hold one out of four low-wage jobs' (Bluestone, 1968, p. 3). (In Britain, the evidence on race and low pay is very sparse; see Stephen (1973).) In Britain, a substantial number of the low paid are over fifty, although age appears to be less important in the United States: 'by and large, the working poor are healthy and of prime age' (Bluestone, 1968, p. 3). Educational attainment appears to be related to low pay, although within occupations the association is rather weaker: 'we cannot easily write off the working poor as illiterate, unschooled, or for that matter, educationally inferior to workers in comparable occupations in high-wage industries' (p. 4). There is in fact considerable variation in the extent of low pay by industries—see Table 6·2. In the United States, the proportion earning less than $2500 a year in 1965 was as low as 4 per cent in transportation and as high as 17 per cent in personal services. Moreover, the broad industrial groupings in Table 6·2 conceal considerable variation. Within manufacturing, for example, there is a great deal of difference between industries such as chemicals, vehicles, and iron and steel, with few low paid workers, and industries such as textiles, clothing, and footwear, with a high proportion.

What we need to know is how far there is systematic variation in low pay across industries which is *independent* of personal characteristics. One attempt to disentangle the effects was made by Wachtel and Betsy (1972) using data on individual earnings in the United States for full-time workers in 1967. They first examined the influence of personal characteristics (education, years in present job, race, sex, age, and marital status), and then investigated how far the remaining variation was related to demand characteristics (occupation/industry, region, city size, and union status). They found that all these demand factors had independent significance, and indicated that a person with the same supply characteristics would have earnings which differed systematically across industries. Individuals employed as labourers, with the same personal characteristics, earned from $4708 to $6136 depending upon the industry in which they are employed. The statistical procedures used, and the interpretation of the results, may be questioned in a number of respects, but we must clearly consider seriously the hypothesis that low pay may be due to factors other than the personal characteristics of the worker. Tawney's view, that 'the problem of poverty is not a problem of individual character ... but a problem of economic and industrial organization' (quoted by Titmuss, 1958, p. 18) may be at least partly right, even though it runs counter to much of recent thought.

TABLE 6·2

Industrial distribution of low paid workers, Great Britain and United States

	United States 1965 (Year-round, full-time male workers aged 14 and over)		Great Britain April 1973 (Adult male workers)	
	% of low paid workers	Low paid as % of workers in that sector	% of low paid workers	Low paid as % of workers in that sector
Agriculture	34·0	43·4	4·9	35·2
Non-agriculture	66·0	6·2	95·1	9·1
Non-agriculture (selection)				
Mining	0·4	3·5	0·3	1·2
Construction	6·8	7·8	5·2	5·4
Manufacturing	16·5	4·3	24·7	5·6
Transport and utilities / Transport	4·3	4·1	1·0	6·6
Retail trade	13·5	9·6	9·6	25·2
Personal services / Miscellaneous services	10·6	17·3	11·6	24·4
Public administration	1·3	1·7	11·5	14·3
All workers / All employees	100	9·0	100	10·9

Sources: United States from Perrella (1967), Table 1. Low pay defined as below $2500 year (based on federal minimum wage). Great Britain from 'New earnings survey', 1973, Tables 41–2. Low pay defined as two-thirds of median earnings.

Low pay and minimum wage legislation

The view taken of the causes of low pay has major implications for the design of policy. In the 1960s the influence of the human capital theory led to a great deal of the discussion of public policy being directed towards the supply side of the labour market. Much of the War on Poverty in the USA was concerned with increasing the human capital of the low paid, through training programmes and the expansion of education. As described by an Assistant Director of the Office of Economic Opportunity, 'many of the poor have essentially zero productivity now. They lack skills, education, motivation, and sometimes even literacy. This is why there is so much emphasis on training and education in OEO programmes' (Kershaw, 1965, p. 57). At the same time, the setting of minimum wages was condemned by many economists: a survey of academic economists in the United States in 1966 showed that 88 per cent supported the War on Poverty but that 61 per cent opposed extension of the minimum wage law.

More recently, these policies have come into question. The alternative view of the labour market taken by Thurow and Lucas was seen by them as raising 'substantial doubts about the feasibility of altering the structure of American incomes with government programs that are exclusively focused on the supply side of the labor market' (1972, p. 39). Similarly, the Secretary of Labor recognized that the human capital formation approach is constrained by the structure of available jobs: 'our economy has a lot of jobs that pay low wages . . . we can only put people in the jobs that exist' (quoted in Wachtel and Betsy, 1972, pp. 127–8). One consequence has been a renewed interest in government intervention to influence the demand for labour and in minimum wage legislation. If human capital formation cannot be relied on to completely eliminate low pay, then other measures of this kind may be necessary.

In both Britain and the United States there has been minimum wage legislation for a long time. In the United States the federal minimum was established by the Fair Labor Standards Act of 1938, and in Britain there have been Wages Councils since 1909, dating back to the investigations of sweated labour by Charles Booth and Beatrice Webb. The coverage of this legislation is, however, far from complete. In the United States, the scope of the Act was extended in 1966, but even so in 1970 it covered only 46 million out of a total of 75 million employees. The gaps in coverage include sectors where low paid workers are particularly likely to be found: agriculture, retail trade and services. Incomplete coverage, coupled with violations of the law (the 1971 report referred to over 400 000 workers involved in detected violations), is responsible for the large number of workers earning less than the federal minimum. In Britain, the activity of the Wages Councils is directed more towards low wage industries, but their impact has been very limited, in that the minimum rates established have typically been well below the definition of low pay used earlier. For example, the weekly minimum for adult men in unlicensed places of refreshment was set in 1973 at less than one-third of national median earnings. The Wages Council sector includes, therefore, many workers who are low paid according to the definition adopted earlier.

There is, therefore, considerable scope for extending the coverage of legislation to bring about a national minimum wage, and for this minimum to be increased. What would be the consequences of such a move?

The standard textbook view is that minimum wage laws 'often hurt those they are designed to help. What good does it do a Negro youth to know that an employer must pay him $1·60 per hour, if the fact that he must be paid that amount is what keeps him from getting a job?' (Samuelson, 1967, p. 377). If the labour market is competitive and perfectly functioning, and differences in earnings reflect productivity, then minimum wages—without any accompanying measures—clearly reduce employment opportunities. The higher wage which has to be paid causes employers either to replace low paid workers (with more skilled workers or capital) or else to raise prices, in which case there will be substitution away from the product in question. The extent of the fall in employment depends on the ease with which the low paid workers can be replaced and on the elasticity of demand for the product.

What happens if these assumptions of competition and a perfectly equilibrating labour market are not satisfied? Even in the standard textbook treatments it is recognized that where the employer possesses greater bargaining power, the introduction of minimum wage legislation may have no adverse effect on employment. To this extent, the impact depends on the degree of competition:

If one thinks of labor markets as fairly competitive, then minimum wage legislation results in unemployment of low-skilled workers ... If one thinks of all capitalists conspiring together to exploit workers of low skills (many of whom may belong to particular groups in the population), then minimum wage legislation is an important element in the reduction of that exploitation (Stiglitz, 1973, pp. 294—5).

Although Stigler (1946) pointed out that industries with a high proportion of low paid workers are typically more competitive, so that this argument may not be relevant, the lower monopoly power of the employer may be more than offset by the lower level of union organization on the workers' side. To the extent that there is disequilibrium in the labour market, the link between wages and employment may be looser than assumed in the conventional theory. The pattern of jobs may not respond, at least not at all quickly, to the introduction of a minimum wage. Lester (1964), for example, draws attention to the possibility that minimum wages may stimulate a search for improvements in the productivity of a given labour force.

If the labour market is viewed as segmented, as in the dual hypothesis, into primary and secondary sectors, then the implications of minimum wages have to be assessed in terms not only of the employment within industries but also of the relative importance of the two sectors. Here there are conflicting opinions. Feldstein (1973) sees the minimum wage as reducing the incentive for employers to provide on-the-job training for young workers, and hence as forcing them to enter the secondary, low paid sector. Piore and Doeringer, on the other hand, see the impact as being confined to employment in the secondary sector and here they feel that 'the employment effects of such legislation may be exaggerated' (1971, p. 182). They do, however, draw attention to the possible effect on wages in the primary sector. Given the role of convention in determining wages, there is the possibility than an increase in minimum rates may have repercussions higher up the scale as customary differentials are restored.

If we turn to the empirical evidence, this too may be interpreted in different ways. At first sight it appears straightforward. As described by Friedman in *Newsweek* in 1966, the unemployment rate among black teenagers in the United States was about the same as that for white teenagers before the minimum wage went up from 75c to $1 in 1956, but within two years it rose to nearly double. He attributed the rise in unemployment among black teenagers, who were more likely to be affected by the legislation, to the increase in minimum wages, which had previously been unchanged for six years. However, the matter is less simple. We have to take into account the fact that the period 1956—8 was one of recession, when disadvantaged workers may have been particularly susceptible to unemployment. The movements in minimum wages have to be related to the secular rise in unemployment among black teenagers. This rise in teenage unemployment must also be seen against the background of a rapid increase in the teenage labour force, of changes in school enrolment, and of the draft. (For these reasons, it may be better to focus on the effect on employment rather than unemployment.) Finally, it is not just the level of the minimum wage that is important, but also its coverage.

There have been a number of more detailed investigations, considering the effect of minimum wages on employment and taking account of other factors operating at the same time. A recent example is that by Kosters and Welch (1972), who attempt to eliminate short-term or cyclical influences by distinguishing between permanent and transitional employment, the latter being employment in excess of that 'normal' for the economy given the long-run trends. During a short-term expansion, the transitional element is positive; during a recession, it is negative. On the basis of the changes in the level and coverage of minimum wages in the United States over the period 1954–68, they estimate that the employment vulnerability of teenagers, particularly blacks, is increased by minimum wages. Their share of permanent employment is decreased and that of transitional employment increased, so that their overall employment is less stable. In contrast, for adults, the overall effect is to stabilize their employment, particularly among whites. Their data are not disaggregated, but these findings could be interpreted as implying that minimum wages reduce teenage employment in the primary sector of the economy, forcing them into the secondary sector, where coverage and enforcement may be less complete.

Whatever interpretations are placed on the evidence, it is clearly not possible to reject decisively the hypothesis that minimum wages may reduce employment. Most of the recent advocates of a higher minimum, with extended coverage, have therefore proposed complementary measures to influence the demand for labour. One common suggestion is for the government to guarantee employment: 'the preferred method would be minimum wage legislation coupled with public employer-of-last-resort programs to guarantee that everyone who wanted full-time work at the minimum wage could have it' (Thurow, 1973, p. 80). On the other hand, those who feel that public employment would be 'unproductive', have argued for a wage subsidy to private employers (Feldstein, 1973); this would clearly need to be integrated with the system of income maintenance discussed in Chapter 11.

Finally, the analysis has brought out yet again the way in which policy recommendations depend critically on the way in which the labour market is believed to operate. The multitude of solutions proposed by economists stem not simply from differing objectives but also from differing views about the way in which wages and employment are determined.

7

THE CONCENTRATION OF WEALTH IN BRITAIN AND THE UNITED STATES

> I detest a man who conceals the extent of his wealth—it is as bad as leaving out the date of one's birth in *Who's Who*.
>
> (Lord Beaverbrook)

In this chapter we examine the distribution of the ownership of capital in Britain and the United States. How much of total wealth is really in the hands of the top 1 per cent or the top 0·1 per cent? What are the likely future trends in the distribution? How does Britain compare with the United States? What are the implications of the concentration of wealth-holding?

7·1 Sources and methods

There are three main methods by which information can be derived about the distribution of personal wealth:

A sample census of wealth

The ideal source of information about the distribution would be a regular census, possibly on a sample basis, giving the details of the wealth of all families or individuals. Everyone would be required to complete a form giving details of all assets and liabilities. The assets would include personal possessions, such as cars, houses, or consumer durables, and financial assets, such as money in the bank, cash, government bonds, shares, and so on. Liabilities would include items such as a mortgage on a house, overdrafts at the bank, and money owed. The value of assets minus the value of liabilities would then constitute one's net worth, or wealth, and from such a census we could derive the distribution of wealth among all families.

Such a census would run into a number of difficulties. The first would be that of securing an adequate response. In theory it would be possible to make compliance compulsory: for example, by including questions covering wealth in the population census. If this information were provided accurately, which would be hard to guarantee, then we would have a clear picture of wealth-holding at ten-year intervals. It seems unlikely that the census would in fact be extended in this way, since the introduction of questions about wealth would no doubt arouse considerable hostility and censuses are unpopular enough as it is. The alternative is to have a voluntary survey. The experience in Britain with the national savings surveys carried out by the Oxford Institute of Statistics in the early 1950s suggests, however, that it is difficult to secure anything approaching 100 per cent response, and there were good grounds for believing that the wealthy were under-represented. Moreover, there appears to have been significant understatement of wealth by those taking part. As it is described by Lydall and Tipping, 'The 1954 savings survey achieved a response rate of only 67 per cent amongst the "income units" approached for interviews; and there was almost certainly a substantial amount of understatement of assets even by those who were "successfully" interviewed' (1961, p. 85).

A second major difficulty concerns the definition of wealth and the method of valuation. In parallel with the earlier discussion of income we may want to adopt a comprehensive definition of wealth, including all assets and liabilities, but the significance of this turns on the method of valuation. A range of methods is possible, and two are considered here. The first corresponds to that adopted by the Inland Revenue in Britain and may be seen as a 'realization' value, that is the amount obtained if assets were sold on the open market. The person completing the census would therefore value his furniture at what he would get from a second-hand dealer. In contrast to this, we can consider a 'going concern' value, or what the assets are worth if they remain in his hands. On this basis, the furniture would be valued at what it would cost to replace. The difference between the two approaches is that the value as a going concern is likely in many cases to be higher than the realization value: for example, shares in a family business may be worth much more than the price obtainable on the market. In certain cases, for example, pension rights and interests in discretionary trusts, an asset may have no realization value but be worth something on a going concern basis.

There would be problems in obtaining accurate responses whichever method of valuation were adopted. With the going concern basis, these would be particularly acute, since for certain assets this would involve complex calculations concerning life expectancies etc. Even with the market valuation, there are assets with no ready market price: e.g. houses, jewellery, unquoted shares. To give a reliable answer might therefore involve the respondent in work which is time-consuming, and expensive if he employs a professional valuer. This is all likely to lead to inaccurate valuations.

The experience with sample censuses is not very encouraging. In Britain the Oxford savings surveys suggest that they are unlikely to provide by themselves an adequate source of estimates of the distribution of wealth (no survey comparable with the Oxford data has been undertaken since the mid-1950s). In the United States, an important contribution has been made by the surveys carried out by the University of Michigan and by the Federal Reserve Board, but these did not attempt, because of the valuation problem, to cover all types of asset. The 1953 Michigan survey, for example, excluded insurance policies, cash, annuities, state and local bonds, and consumer durables. In view of these difficulties with the sample survey approach, most studies have had to fall back on less direct sources of information.

Estate data

Under the present systems of taxation in Britain and the United States, the only occasion when a person's total assets and liabilities have to be revealed is at death, when a return is required for the purposes of estate taxation. The estate returns are therefore an important source of information about wealth-holding and they have provided the basis for nearly all estimates of the distribution of wealth in Britain and the United States.

In effect this method uses the estates of those dying in a particular year as a sample of the wealth of the living population. If we assume that those dying are a random sample of the living population of the same age and sex—clearly a strong assumption—then we can estimate the wealth of the living. To do this, we multiply up their wealth by what is known as the 'mortality multiplier'. The mortality multiplier is the reciprocal of the mortality rate, so that if the death rate is 1 in 100, the estates are multiplied by 100 to reach an estimate of the wealth of the living. In other words, if, in a given year, 15 men aged 45–54 died leaving over £200 000, and the mortality rate is 1 in 100, then we assume that there are 1500 such people in the population as a whole. Since there are systematic factors influencing the rates of mortality, the multipliers are in practice adjusted in certain respects, most importantly to allow for the fact that the wealthy tend to live longer. The mortality rate applied is that for the upper social classes rather than for the general population.

Despite such refinements, the estate method is liable to error on a number of accounts. The social class mortality rates may not in fact be appropriate for the wealthy. Mortality may be influenced by factors not taken into consideration, such as marital status. In the classification of estates by age and size, some of the cells contain very few estates, and there may be chance factors which cause the estimates to vary from year to year.

The very nature of the estate source brings with it certain problems. The tax authorities are only concerned with estates that are likely to be liable for duty, and the coverage below the tax exemption level is far from complete. The tax law does not necessarily embody the definition of wealth we should like to employ, and certain classes of assets may be excluded or given special treatment. The taxpayer has an incentive to reduce the value of his estate, and tax avoidance or evasion may lead to bias in the estimates. The problems are discussed further in the next section.

The investment income method

Although the estate method has been that most commonly employed in the past fifty years, a rather different approach was much used by early writers. This takes as its starting point the statistics for investment income collected by the tax authorities, and works back from these to the capital from which the income must have been derived. The estimates are obtained not from the recorded wealth of the dead but from the recorded investment income of the living.

The main feature of this approach is the use of a 'yield multiplier' to convert the distribution of investment income to an underlying distribution of capital. The yield multiplier is the reciprocal of the yield on the wealth: if, for example, the yield is 5 per cent, then the multiplier would be $1/0·05 = 20$. In other words, with such a multiplier, an investment income of £25 000 would be converted into wealth of £500 000. The yield multiplier clearly depends on the form in which wealth is held and the normal procedure has been to calculate a weighted average yield, based on the composition of wealth indicated by the estate statistics. In this calculation, allowance has to be made for the fact that the composition of wealth varies with the size of the holding—that cash and bank deposits (with no yield) tend to be held more by those at the lower end of the distribution and company shares (with a relatively high yield) more by the rich.

In Chapter 4, we saw that the income statistics were not necessarily accurate, and that there was in particular a deficiency of investment income. To some extent, these shortcomings can be taken into account in the construction of the yield multipliers. For example, the fact that capital gains and imputed rent on owner-occupied houses are missing from the statistics does not lead to any necessary bias in the use of the investment income method, since the yield multiplier is adjusted for these omissions, only the taxable yield being taken into account. There are, however, a number of problems which cannot readily be resolved, such as the limited coverage of the investment income returns, which relate only to the top 1 per cent or so. In view of this, the investment income method is unlikely to replace the estate data as the principal source of evidence about wealth-holding; it does, nonetheless, provide a valuable cross-check on their accuracy.

7·2 Wealth in Britain—evidence

Since 1960 the Inland Revenue has published annual estimates of the distribution of wealth in Great Britain. These estimates are derived from the estate duty returns, using mortality multipliers adjusted for social class. The main results are set out in Table 7·1, and show the number of people (not families or households) with net wealth in different ranges, together with the total amount of wealth owned. The Inland Revenue also presents this information in the form of the Gini coefficient of concentration, and this is given in the last line of Table 7·1.

TABLE 7·1
Inland Revenue estimates of distribution of wealth,
Great Britain
Numbers in thousands, amounts in £ thousand million

Range of net wealth (lower limit £)	1960 Number	1960 Amount	1965 Number	1965 Amount	1970 Number	1970 Amount
Nil–	9003	3·9	7626	3·6	3924	2·0
1000–	5817	10·1	5266	9·7	5423	9·8
3000–	1342	5·2	2598	10·0	2766	10·9
5000–	958	7·0	1795	12·6	3217	23·4
10 000–	314	3·9	491	6·0	710	8·5
15 000–	232	4·5	381	7·3	545	10·4
25 000–	170	5·9	263	9·1	318	10·9
50 000–	64	4·4	95	6·8	132	8·4
100 000–	20	3·0	34	4·5	40	5·0
200 000–	7	3·7	11	4·7	19	7·7
TOTAL	17 927	51·6	18 560	74·3	17 094	96·8
Gini coefficient of concentration	0·76		0·70		0·65	

Source: Inland Revenue statistics, 1971. Table 130 and 1972, Table 86.

While the tables do not, unfortunately, give the number of millionaires, it can be seen that in 1970 there were estimated to be 19 000 people worth more than £200 000. Their average wealth was over £400 000 and their share in the total wealth recorded by the Inland Revenue amounted to some 8 per cent. If we go down to holdings of £25 000, we see that in 1970 there were in all about half a million people with more than this amount, and they accounted for £32 000 million out of a total of £96 800 million. The Gini coefficient suggests a high degree of concentration; the value of 0·65 for 1970 is nearly twice that recorded for pre-tax income in the United Kingdom.[1]

[1] It should be noted that the wealth data relate to individuals, whereas the income data relate to tax units—see below.

The second main conclusion which seems to emerge from the Inland
Revenue statistics is that the degree of concentration is declining. This
is most obvious from the Gini coefficients, which fall from 0·76 in
1960 to 0·65 in 1970. The significance of such a change and whether it
can be projected into the future is taken up in Section 7·3.

Before such conclusions can be accepted, it is clearly necessary to
examine the reliability of the basic data. We have seen above that the
estate method is subject to a number of problems, and the Inland
Revenue itself refers to a number of major qualifications and recognizes
that its estimates are 'subject to fairly wide margins of error and are in
some respects incomplete'. Closer examination reveals a number of
reasons why the official estimates may give an inaccurate picture of
wealth-holding in Britain.

'Missing' people

The estate duty statistics cover those estates on which the duty was
paid in a given year or which require probate (official proof of the will),
and many estates not coming to the notice of the estate duty office are
missing from the statistics. In 1970, for example, there were 290 000
estates included in the Inland Revenue statistics, compared with a total
of 639 000 deaths. The omission of these estates from the estate duty
returns means that when the mortality multipliers are applied, the
number of wealth-holders falls considerably short of the total adult
population. The estimated number of wealth-holders in 1970 was 17
million, compared with a population of 39 million aged 18 and over, so
that well over half the adult population were missing.

The estates omitted from the Inland Revenue statistics are those
where no property has been left, or where the assets are of a kind which
may be transferred without probate: e.g. small sums held in the
National Savings Bank. It is clear, therefore, that none of the people
excluded from the Inland Revenue estimates is likely to own large
amounts of wealth. It follows that if the existence of these wealth-
holders is simply ignored, as it is in the Gini coefficients given by the
Inland Revenue in its main results (those presented in Table 7·1), then
the degree of concentration is understated. This point is recognized by
the Inland Revenue, which regards the Gini coefficient primarily as an
indicator of the *trend* in the degree of concentration; however, the
proportion of estates missing from the returns has varied over time, so
that it does not necessarily accurately reflect the trend.

'Missing' wealth

The estate duty returns may provide an incomplete picture of
wealth-holding not only on account of missing people but also because

the wealth of those covered is understated. This may result from the provisions in the estate duty law which allow wealth to be transferred without duty being paid or at a reduced rate of duty. In Chapter 4 we described the criticisms made by Titmuss of the official statistics on incomes, and many of his strictures apply also to the figures for wealth. While it is not true that all tax avoidance leads to wealth not appearing in the returns,[1] it is widely held that substantial amounts are 'missing' from the estate duty statistics: e.g. 'although the rich are not very well documented we do know that the Inland Revenue's estimates ... significantly underestimate the wealth of the very rich' (Runciman, 1974, p. 94). Among the items excluded are:

(i) property settled on a surviving spouse (who has no power to dispose of the capital) which is exempt on the death of this spouse;

(ii) property held under discretionary trusts (exempt before the 1969 Finance Act);

(iii) items treated as estates by themselves which do not appear if they do not exceed the exemption limit;

(iv) growing timber, which is not aggregated with the rest of the estate and on which duty is not paid unless and until the timber is sold;

(v) assets such as annuities and pensions which disappear on death.

Valuation

The list of items just given raises the question of the appropriate method of valuation. We distinguished earlier between the value of an asset obtainable on realization and the value to the person or household as a 'going concern'. The estate duty method of valuation, not surprisingly, is closer to the former. In the case of household goods, for example, the valuation is based on second-hand market prices, and, as has been pointed out by Revell (1967), these values 'are usually derisory' and would not be applicable if the household was viewed as a going concern. Similarly, the assets of unincorporated businesses may be valued for estate duty purposes on a second-hand basis, which may be quite different from the value to the owner on the assumption that he continues in business. On a 'sell-up' basis no value would in general be attached to pension rights, since the holder cannot realize the asset or borrow on the strength of it (even in the case of insured pension schemes it is not usually possible to pledge them against a loan). On the other hand, these rights are worth something to the holder as a going

[1] A person may, for example, purchase agricultural property; because of the lower rates of duty, this reduces his estate duty liability, but the full value of the assets is still shown in the return.

concern, and on this alternative basis some estimate should be made of their value.

Individuals and families

The estate duty statistics relate to *individuals* and the wealth of *families* is not aggregated. Just as in the case of incomes, there are good reasons why we may wish to take the family as the basic unit of analysis. The wife and dependent children of a wealth-holder share many of the benefits of his wealth and, as Daniels and Campion (1936) have argued, 'it would obviously be misleading to place the wives and children of persons with £50 000 in the same category as paupers'. Estimates of individual wealth-holding based on the estate data will tend to overstate the degree of concentration among families. The extent of the overstatement depends on the relationship between the wealth of husbands and wives (and dependent children). If rich men have poor wives, and vice versa, then there could be significant overstatement; on the other hand, if husbands and wives were equally rich, the estate duty data could give an accurate picture.

Adjusted estimates

These difficulties with the estate duty statistics have led some people to conclude that nothing can be said about the concentration of wealth-holding. The approach followed here, as in the case of the distribution of income, is to try and estimate the likely effect of adjusting for the problems described above. The results of such an attempt are presented in Table 7·2, which shows the shares of different percentages of the adult population (defined as those aged 18 and over, on the basis that it is the age of majority and probably corresponds to the average age at which children become financially independent of their parents). The first line gives the official estimates with no allowance for 'missing' people: i.e. on the same basis as the Gini coefficients shown in Table 7·1. The second and subsequent lines of the table allow for the whole adult population, so that all adults are covered, and give estimates based on a range of assumptions about 'missing' wealth, about the method of valuation, and about family versus individual wealth. The estimates relate to the most recent year for which data are available to make the necessary adjustments (1968); the changes in the distribution over time are discussed in the next section.

Line 2 of the table shows the first step in the adjustments—the inclusion of those missing from the estate returns, together with an estimate of their average wealth. This estimate, which is based on a 'sell-up' valuation, includes such items as household possessions,

TABLE 7·2
Adjusted estimates of distribution of wealth,
Great Britain 1968

	Share in total personal wealth Top % of adult population (aged 18 and over)			
	0·1%	½%	1%	5%
1. Official estimates (with no allowance for 'missing' people)	–	–	24·2	45·2
2. Adjusted for 'missing' people	13·5	25·6	33·5	58·3
3. Adjusted for 'missing' wealth				
(a) at sell-up value	14·5	27·2	35·5	59·9
(b) at going concern value	14·1	25·8	33·5	58·9
(c) plus state pension rights[a]	–	–	20·0*	37·0*
(d) plus state pension rights[a] and net worth of company sector	–	–	–	42·0*
4. Adjusted to a 'family' basis, on the assumption that[b]				
(a) All persons with wealth are married to spouses with no recorded wealth	11·3	21·7	28·4	50·8
(b) wealthiest males are married to wealthiest females	13·4	25·6	33·4	57·9

Source: line 1 from *Social Trends,* 1971, p. 81.
lines 2–4 from Atkinson and Harrison (forthcoming). The methods employed are described in Atkinson (1974*a*).
Notes: – denotes not available, *denotes approximate.
[a]Actuarial value of the flow of benefits minus contributions. The method is similar to that in Atkinson (1971), but differs in certain respects, including the valuation of the rights to pensions for dependants. The assumptions are such that the value of state pension rights is likely to be over-stated.
[b]The distribution is shown on a *per capita* basis: i.e. a married couple appears as two units, with each having half their joint wealth.

consumer durables, cars and small savings, together with an allowance for debt (for example, instalment credit commitments).

The estimates in lines 3(*a*)–(*d*) of the table introduce wealth 'missing' from the recorded estates and a range of different assumptions about the method of valuation. Line 3(*a*) is based on the 'sell-up' valuation closest to the Inland Revenue practice, whereas line 3(*b*) adopts the alternative 'going concern' valuation. This second estimate includes property held in trusts and occupational pensions, as well as adjustments to the appropriate valuation basis. An example of the latter is the higher value placed on unincorporated businesses on a going concern basis.

The figures in lines 3(c) and 3(d) raise more controversial issues. It is sometimes argued that if the value of occupational pensions is included, then there is no reason why this should not be extended to state pensions. Since the rights to state pensions are much more equally spread, at least within a given age group, than the rest of property, their inclusion leads to a reduction in the estimated degree of concentration. The second issue concerns the positive net worth of the company sector. Estimates of the net value of the company sector's assets suggest that this value is considerably in excess of the aggregate value of shares on the stock exchange, so that there is, as noted earlier, a positive net worth in this sector not attributed to individuals. It may be held that part of this net worth in fact belongs to the share-holders, representing considerations such as the value of a controlling interest, and should be allocated to them.[1] Revell (1967) has argued against this on the grounds that the net worth is not an item 'which individual economic units would regard as part of their wealth'. However, the same objection can be made to the inclusion of state pension rights.

The last part of Table 7·2 shows the effect of 'marrying up' estate duty returns to give estimates of the degree of concentration among families. Since dependent children are excluded from the estimates, the relevant unit is that of husband and wife. In these estimates no allowance is made for missing wealth, so that they should be compared with those on an individual basis given in line 2. Line 4(a) corresponds to the assumption made by Polanyi and Wood (1974), that the wealthy are married to people with no recorded wealth. This is clearly an extreme assumption, which gives a lower bound on the degree of concentration. Line 4(b) is based on the opposite extreme assumption, that rich men have wives rich in their own right. Where between these the true figure lies depends on the intra-family pattern of wealth-holding, but it is interesting to note that even on assumption 4(a) the shares of the top 0·1 per cent—5 per cent are reduced much less than is suggested by the statements of Polanyi and Wood.

The results described above are based on the estate duty data, and, as we have seen earlier, the mortality multiplier technique is not ideal. It is interesting, therefore, to see whether the estimates are broadly consistent with those obtained by the investment income method. This alternative approach does not permit estimates to be made covering the

---

1 It should not necessarily be allocated to *all* share-holders. The estimate in the table allocates to the top 5 per cent a share of the net worth proportional to their holdings, on the basis that this group accounts for the bulk of personal holdings of shares. If the value of control etc. is greater for institutional holders than for persons, this will be an over-estimate, and vice versa.

whole distribution, but at the very top it provides support for the estate method. In comparing the results, it has to be remembered that the basic estate estimates relate to individuals, whereas the investment income data relate to income tax units in which the wealth of husband and wife is aggregated. As a result, we should expect the investment income method to give higher estimates of the numbers above a given wealth level: a man worth £75 000 married to a woman worth £25 000 would appear as a single unit worth £100 000 in the investment estimates. Bearing this qualification in mind, the two methods appear to give broadly similar results. The numbers estimated to own £100 000 or more in 1968 are 60 000 (estate duty) compared with 100 000 (investment income); above £½ million they are 5000 (estate duty) compared with 5500 (investment income). (These estimates are not adjusted for 'missing' wealth—see Atkinson and Harrison, (1974).)

To sum up, it appears that the evidence for Britain in 1968 bears out the statements made in Chapter 2 about the degree of concentration. If we take a 'sell-up' basis for valuation (that is what people were worth in realizable cash), then the share of the top 1 per cent of adults was then around one-third of total personal wealth, and the share of the top 5 per cent was of the order of a half. If we move to a 'going concern' value, and include state pensions, the share of the top 5 per cent at that time was nearer one-third; finally, if we include the net worth of the company sector, the figure becomes 42 per cent. There is, therefore, a range of estimates, corresponding to different concepts of wealth, but it is clear that to reduce the share of the top 1 per cent at that time much below 20 per cent it would be necessary to bring in other items not commonly regarded as part of personal wealth.

While the conventional picture takes the share of these top percentage groups as relating to the really rich, it is important to remember that there are great differences within the top 5 per cent, and even within the top 1 per cent. The gap between Mr X who just qualifies for the top 1 per cent and the millionaire with a household name is much larger than that between Mr X and the average wealth-holder. It may therefore be more useful for the purposes of analysis to take a higher dividing line, closer to the level where people can begin to think about living a life of leisure (although not many, of course, choose so to do). One crude, but readily understood, criterion would be an amount equal to the total earnings that the average worker can look forward to over a working lifetime: that is, the undiscounted sum of what the average person could expect to earn, allowing for the fact that real earnings are likely to rise. This would have given a figure of some £125 000 in 1968, which corresponds in broad terms to the beginning of the top 0·1 per cent of the adult population, and this group will be the main focus of the analysis which follows.[1] While errors arising from year-to-year variations in mortality may be more important when considering such a small group, it appears from Table 7·2 that their share of total wealth was around 10 per cent in 1968.

7·3 Trends over time in the distribution of wealth in Britain

Over the course of this century, there has undoubtedly been a decline in the share of personal wealth owned by the top people. In this section we examine in more detail the significance of this and some of the factors underlying the reduced concentration. The need for such an examination is clear from the importance attached in some quarters to the continuation of this trend. Polanyi and Wood, for example, have referred to 'The spontaneous process of "levelling-up" as the incomes and savings of the majority rise. As this process is still in its early stages by comparison with the USA, further spreading of wealth may reasonably be expected to take place without deliberate government action' (1974, p. 76). If it is true, this statement has important implications for the way in which we think about the distribution of wealth; it means that the present concentration may only be a passing phase. In what follows, we investigate whether the trends of the past may in fact be projected into the future.

In making comparisons of the distribution of wealth at different dates, or between different countries, it is clearly important to ensure that the estimates are made as far as possible on a consistent basis and that any inconsistencies are taken into account when interpreting the findings. In the present case, this poses a number of problems. The figures usually referred to go back as far as 1911—13, and while estate data do exist in a form which can be used for this purpose, they need to be treated with caution. Estimates for that year, and for the interwar period, were given in the pioneering studies of Daniels and Campion (1936) and Langley (1950); estimates for the 1950s are given in the study of Lydall and Tipping (1961). Although the basic data used by these authors were of the same form, their estimates differed with respect to coverage and to the assumptions made:

Geographical coverage The early estate data were published only for England and Wales, and the earliest estimates for Great Britain are for 1938.

Mortality multipliers The multipliers applied by different investigators were in general adjusted for differences in mortality between social

---

[1] For future reference, the wealth required to enter the top 0·1 per cent is some 100 times the current average annual earnings.

classes, but the early estimates were based on less accurate multipliers than those employed today by the Inland Revenue.

Missing people The coverage of the estate returns has varied with the estate duty exemption level, which remained at £100 until 1946, and a variety of assumptions have been made to cover the wealth of those missing from the return.

Missing wealth The extent of missing wealth has varied with the evolution of estate duty law and with changes in social customs. In nearly all cases some allowance has been made for settled property, although other items were not in general taken into account (an exception is Lydall and Tipping, who included the value of rights to private pension funds).

Table 7·3 shows the results of an attempt to prepare estimates on a consistent basis in the light of the problems just described. There are two series, one for England and Wales covering the period since the 1920s, and the other for Great Britain going back to 1938. These estimates clearly demonstrate a downward trend in the degree of concentration in both cases (there is in fact little difference between estimates for Great Britain and for England and Wales).[1]

The trend over this century is often extrapolated into the future, with the suggestion that before long the present high degree of concentration will disappear. Whether it is legitimate to make such predictions on the basis of past experience depends crucially, however, on the causes of the decline. That the interpretation of the evidence is of central importance is illustrated below, with reference to four possible forces underlying the changes in the distribution.

Estate duty avoidance Over the course of this century, the nominal rates of estate duty have risen very considerably. In 1911 an estate of £1 million paid duty of 14 per cent; in the early 1970s the rate was 75 per cent. There can be little doubt, therefore, that the incentive to avoid estate duty has increased. This need not affect the interpretation of the evidence in Table 7·3. As we have seen, avoidance does not necessarily lead to property's being missing, and even where it does (as

---

[1] The recent official assessment suggests that in the early 1970s the shares of the top groups first rose and then fell. According to the Green Paper on the Wealth Tax, the share of the top 1 per cent rose from 29 per cent in 1971 to 31 per cent in 1972 but fell to 25 per cent by 1974; the share of the top 5 per cent rose from 53 per cent in 1971 to 58 per cent in 1972 and returned to 53 per cent in 1974. These estimates relate to the population aged 15 and over and are not adjusted for the wealth of those missing from the estate returns or other missing wealth.

TABLE 7·3
Trends in the distribution of wealth in Britain

| | Percentage of total personal wealth | | | | | |
| | England and Wales | | | Great Britain | | |
	Top 0·1%	Top 1%	Top 5%	Top 0·1%	Top 1%	Top 5%
1924	32	60	81	–	–	–
1929	28	56	79	–	–	–
1938	27	54	77	27	55	78
1951	18	42	68	18	42	68
1955	17	41	67	16	41	66
1960	15	37	63	15	38	63
1968	11	30	55	11	31	56

Source: Atkinson and Harrison (forthcoming).
Notes: apart from 1938 the estimates are three-year averages centred on the year given. They refer to the population aged 25 and over, and include allowances for the wealth of those not covered by the estate duty returns. The valuation is on a realisation basis.

in the case of certain settled property), an attempt has been made in these estimates to adjust for its omission. One important avenue of avoidance, however, is that of gifts, since these are exempt from duty if the donor survives for seven years (up to 1974). The wealth given away still appears in the statistics, but it belongs to someone else, and an increase of gifts may well affect the *distribution* of wealth. Revell (1965) has argued that wealthy persons have increasingly relinquished part of their capital to their heirs before death. This may be expected to reduce the share of wealth held by the top 1 per cent and to raise that of the heirs, who are probably in the top 5 per cent. For example, if a person worth £100 000 gives half of it to his two sons, divided equally, then the share of the top 1 per cent falls and the wealth puts his sons in the top 2½ per cent. From the table it appears from the evidence that Revell's view could explain part of the change over the period 1924–60, when the top 1 per cent in England and Wales lost 23 per cent and the next 4 per cent of wealth-owners *gained* 5 per cent, although since 1960 the share of the next 4 per cent has remained broadly unchanged.[1]

Women and wealth Over the course of the century there has been an increase in wealth-holding among women. There have always been women of means, but in recent years there have been two factors which have increased the share of property owned by women:

[1]This interpretation is controversial; see Polanyi and Wood (1974) for a different view.

the tendency for married couples to hold property jointly and the increased longevity of women (the estimates of Revell show that the increase in wealth-holding is particularly marked among widows). The effect of married couples sharing ownership is rather like that of gifts. If husbands born in a post-Victorian era shared their wealth equally with their wives, then a single wealth holding of £50 000 might be replaced by two of £25 000, which would again have the effect of lowering the share of the top 1 per cent of individual wealth-holders while raising that of the next 4 per cent. The trends may in part, therefore, reflect a move towards sexual equality and not a re-distribution between rich and poor *families*.

Owner-occupation One of the most striking social changes since the beginning of this century has been the increase in owner-occupation. Between 1900 and 1970, the proportion of owner-occupied dwellings rose from around 10 per cent to 50 per cent. Coupled with the rise in house prices, this must have had a profound effect on the distribution: 'when one individual owned several houses which he let out as an investment, he had a good chance of appearing in the top 1 per cent, whereas the houses now appear in a number of smaller estates' (Revell, 1965, p. 381). The fact that a person owns a house does not, of course, imply that he has significant *net* worth, and if the increase in owner-occupation was largely made up of young couples with 90 per cent mortgages, then the quantitative effect would be small. However, the increase of house prices over the past two decades has meant that most owner-occupiers now own a substantial part of the value of their house. It is reasonable to suppose that the increase in owner-occupation has led to a definite reduction in the degree of concentration.

Share prices Given that assets take different forms at different levels of wealth-holding, changes in their relative prices may well affect the distribution. This is particularly important in the case of shares, quoted and unquoted, which are held disproportionately by the very rich, and which vary considerably in price. According to the estimate of Lydall and Tipping (1961), 96 per cent of *personally held* shares are in the hands of the top 5 per cent. The remaining shares are mainly held by institutions, such as insurance companies and pension funds; this means that changes in share prices are likely to affect other wealth-holders (e.g. via bonuses on with-profits insurance policies), but that this indirect effect operates more slowly. The main impact of short-term movements in stock exchange prices is likely therefore to be on the top wealth-owners. (Smith and Franklin (1974) show how in the United States the share of the top ½ per cent of the population has moved inversely with Standard and Poor's share price index.) Thus the fall in share prices in 1973/4 may be expected to have caused a reduction in concentration, although if the lower levels are maintained, the effect will filter through to small savers via insurance policies and pension rights.

The analysis of the four factors just described is not intended to cast doubt on the changes in the distribution; the spread of home ownership, for example, is clearly a genuine reduction in concentration. The main point is to bring out the need to understand the forces at work before one can make confident predictions *about the future*. It is not enough simply to characterize the process as one of 'spontaneous levelling-up', which can be extrapolated into the next century. To the extent that it is due to increased owner-occupation, the spreading of this effect through the whole population depends on a further growth in home ownership or a rise in house prices relative to other assets. To the extent that it is attributable to falls on the stock exchange, it must be borne in mind that these may be reversed in different economic and social conditions. To the extent that it reflects a family rearrangement or the increased longevity of widows, the lowest wealth groups may have derived little benefit.

7·4 Wealth in the United States

In the United States, *Fortune* magazine reported in 1968 a study of 'America's centi-millionaires', which identified 153 individuals whose wealth exceeded $100 million, including that owned by spouses, minor children and trusts. Some of the highlights of this list are shown in Table 7·4. At the very top were J. P. Getty and Howard Hughes. The wealth of the former was estimated as follows:

Getty's Visible Assets	Low valuation $ million	High valuation $ million
Getty Oil Company shares	899	1235
Art museum and collection	25	60
Other real property	30	40
Spartan Aircraft Company shares	3	3
	957	1338

Source: Fortune, May 1968, p. 157.

The major difference between the low and the high valuation is that the former was based on the market value of shares in Getty Oil Company, whereas the latter allowed for the value of control. The market value of a share was $82·50, but *Fortune* pointed out that since Getty controlled the company, he was in a position to liquidate, and the

TABLE 7·4
America's centi-millionaires, a selection 1968

$1 billion–$1·5 billion	J. P. Getty (oil)
	H. Hughes (aircraft, tools, real estate)
$500 million–$1 billion	H. L. Hunt (oil)
	E. H. Land (Polaroid)
	D. K. Ludwig (shipping)
	Mellons:
	Ailsa Mellon Bruce
	Paul Mellon
	Richard King Mellon
$300 million–$500 million	N. B. Hunt (oil)
	C. S. Mott (aged 92) (General Motors)
	J. D. MacArthur (insurance)
$200 million–$300 million	J. P. Kennedy (father of president)
	W. R. Hewlett
	D. Packard (electronic calculators)
	D. Wallace (*Reader's Digest*)
	Rockefellers:
	David Rockefeller
	John D. Rockefeller III
	Laurance Rockefeller
	Nelson Rockefeller
	Winthrop Rockefeller
$150 million–$200 million	C. Carlson (Xerox)
	Bob Hope
	H. B. du Pont
	R. W. Woodruff (Coca-Cola)
	Fords:
	Benson Ford
	Mrs. W. Buhl Ford II
	(Josephine Ford)
	William C. Ford

Source: Fortune, May 1968, p. 156.

estimated liquidation value, after capital gains tax, was over $110 a share. This illustrates the possibility referred to earlier that the value of shares may considerably exceed their market price.

The *Fortune* figures clearly involve a substantial amount of guess-work, and more complete estimates are needed. Although there have been a number of surveys of wealth-holding, they have in general been based on small samples and have excluded certain types of property. The main source of evidence is, therefore, as in Britain, the estate tax returns. Unlike the British Inland Revenue, the American tax authorities have only published estimates for a few years and there is no regular official series; there have, however, been important academic studies, notably those of Lampman (1962) and Smith (1974).

The method applied by Lampman was broadly similar to that described earlier: he applied mortality multipliers to the basic estate returns, and the multipliers were adjusted to apply to higher wealth classes. He distinguished between 'prime' wealth ('to which a person has full title and over which he has the power of disposal') and 'total' wealth, which is a broader concept, including private pension rights and property held in trust. These two definitions correspond in broad terms to the realization and going concern valuation used above. As in Britain, the estate returns cover only the larger wealth-holders, with the shortfall being even more serious in view of the relatively high exemption level ($60 000). Lampman concentrated on the group owning $60 000 or more, whom he referred to as 'top wealth-holders', although since the lower limit is less than one-ten-thousandth of the estimated wealth of J. P. Getty, the term 'top' may be rather misleading. In order to allow for the wealth of those not covered by the estate data, Lampman made use of independent estimates of the total holdings of different assets (the total personal holding of government bonds, for example, can be estimated from the issuing source). He also made adjustments for wealth missing from the estate returns.

Lampman found that in 1953 the top wealth-holders made up 1·6 per cent of the adult population and owned 30 per cent of prime wealth (it is interesting that the alternative definition, total wealth, gave the very similar figure of 32 per cent). For purposes of comparison, it is easier to take the share of the top 1 per cent of the adult population, which was 24 per cent in 1953. This may be compared with the estimate for Britain for 1950, of over 40 per cent belonging to the top 1 per cent. Lampman himself concluded that there was much greater concentration in England and Wales than in the United States.

The comparison just made, like that of Lydall and Lansing (1959) referred to in Chapter 2, relates to the early 1950s, and we have seen that since that date the share of the top 1 per cent has fallen in Britain. It is therefore interesting to examine how the distribution has been changing over time.

The long-term trends were examined by Lampman, who presented estimates going back to 1922. These showed that the share of the top 1 per cent of the adult population rose during the 1920s from 32 per cent to a peak of 36 per cent in 1929; that it fell with the great crash in 1929, and reached 28 per cent in 1933. It fell still further to 21 per cent in 1949, but after that date the trend appeared to have ceased.' Lampman also drew attention to the effect of taking the distribution among *families* rather than individuals. The share of the top 2 per cent of families was estimated very approximately to have fallen only from 33 per cent in 1922 to 29 per cent in 1953. Lampman concluded that 'a considerably greater amount of splitting of estates between spouses was being practised in 1953 than in 1922' and that 'the decline in inequality shown on the basis of individuals tends to be an over-statement of the decline which would be found on a family basis' (1959, p. 388).

The pattern just described closely resembles that in Britain. The effect of the Depression was greater, but there was the same fall in concentration over the Second World War, and the same apparent stability in the early 1950s. What is interesting is that the more recent trends in the United States, as brought out by Smith and Franklin (1974), suggest that since then the distribution has remained un-changed. Their estimates, designed to be consistent with those of Lampman, indicate that the share of the top ½ per cent of the total population was no lower in 1969 than in 1949. The conclusion reached by Smith and Franklin is that:

Wealth in the United States has become less concentrated in the last half century. The diminution has not been great, however, and it all occurred during periods when the market system was functioning under duress or was in administrative abeyance, specifically, the Great Depression and World War II (1974, p. 163).

This conclusion may need to be modified in the light of further refinements, but it has important implications for those who, like Polanyi and Wood (1974), believe that the United States experience is relevant to that in Britain.

7·5 Distribution of wealth and the individual life-cycle

Up to this point we have been concerned with the concentration of wealth-holding in the entire adult population at a particular date (the 'current distribution'), and this clearly needs careful interpretation before we can draw conclusions about the existence of inequality. In this section we examine one important consideration: the relationship between wealth-holding and the individual life-cycle. In the analysis of the distribution of income, it was recognized that annual income data may overstate the degree of lifetime inequality as a result of the systematic variation of income with age. In the same way, the current distribution of wealth may overstate the degree of inequality in a lifetime sense, as a result of age differences. Great importance has been attached to age differences by Polanyi and Wood (1974), who suggest that the observed distribution of wealth is not very different from 'the "10 per cent owns 30 per cent" which would reflect differences in wealth from savings accumulated through a lifetime, even if incomes and inheritance were equal'.

The extent of concentration of wealth in a hypothetical egalitarian society of this kind may be seen as follows. Suppose everyone is identical in every respect apart from age (having the same market opportunities and the same tastes) and inheritance and gifts are prohibited. Let us assume that after reaching the age of 25 all individuals live for a fixed period (50 years). They spend the first 40 years of this period working for a wage which is the same for everyone, and during this period they save for their retirement. They can borrow or lend freely at a constant interest rate (again the same for everyone). They are assumed to know for certain that they will live for 50 years and to plan for a constant stream of consumption. They leave no bequests and make no gifts. If we take a zero rate of interest and assume a constant population, the pattern of wealth-holding has the particularly straightforward form shown in Fig. 7·1. From this it can readily be calculated that the wealthiest 10 per cent of the adult population (those aged 62–6) account for 19 per cent of the total wealth.

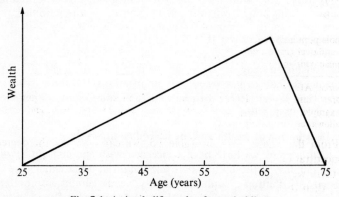

Fig. 7·1. A simple life-cycle of asset-holding

This model is highly simplified and does not take account of factors such as a positive rate of interest, a growing population, propertyless married women, and the existence of (equal) inheritance. If allowance is made for these factors, the results suggest that the share of the top 10 per cent could in this hypothetical egalitarian society reach 30 per cent of the total wealth (Atkinson, 1971), as assumed by Polanyi and Wood. At the same time, it should be noted that the share of the top 1 per cent in the hypothetical society would be some 3 per cent, which *is* very different from that observed in Britain. Polanyi and Wood do not refer to this.

What relevance have these hypothetical calculations to the distribution of wealth in Britain? In order to assess this, we may look at the actual pattern of wealth-holding by age. From the estate duty statistics in Britain it is possible to make estimates of the distribution of wealth within age (and sex) groups. By standardizing for age in this way, we should be able to eliminate the major life-cycle differences, and hence throw light on the importance of life-cycle factors in giving rise to 'apparent' inequality in the current distribution.

TABLE 7·5

Distribution by age and sex group, Great Britain 1963—67

	Male			Female		
	Proportion of wealth in that class owned by top					
Age	1%	5%	10%	1%	5%	10%
25—34	31·2	50·5	64·1	54·8	80·6	92·7
35—44	27·5	49·3	63·1	43·9	74·6	88·5
45—54	28·3	52·7	66·8	38·2	66·4	81·2
55—64	26·8	51·2	66·0	29·0	56·9	71·5
65—74	27·5	52·8	68·1	26·8	54·1	69·3
75—84	28·9	57·1	72·4	26·4	53·6	68·8
85—	30·4	60·1	74·7	27·5	56·8	72·2
Whole population aged 25 and over (male and female combined)	31·5	58·3	72·7	31·5	58·3	72·7

Source: Atkinson (1971), Table IV.
Note: these figures are not comparable with those in Tables 7·2 and 7·3: for example, they relate to the population aged 25 and over, and make no allowance for missing wealth.

From the results given in Table 7·5, we can compare the degree of concentration within age groups with that in the population as a whole. If there were significantly less concentration among people of the same age, then this would indicate that life-cycle factors were important. In fact this does not seem to be the case. For the whole population, the share of the top 1 per cent was 32 per cent. Considering men first, it is true that in all age groups the share is less than 32 per cent, but in no case is the difference very large: the lowest figure is 27 per cent for the age group 55—64. In the case of women, the share of the top 1 per cent is even greater in three age groups, and in no case does it fall below 26 per cent. These figures suggest that the degree of concentration within age groups is not markedly less than that in the population as a whole.

Contrary to what a number of writers have suggested, therefore, the observed distribution is not consistent with there being equal incomes and inheritance.[1] It remains conceivable that the concentration within age groups may be entirely explained by

[1] It is possible that part of the concentration within age groups could be explained by differences in the timing of inheritance, but it is unlikely that this is a major factor—see Atkinson (1971).

differences in earnings, and associated differences in savings, rather than inheritance. If the top 1 per cent of earnings are 3 times the average in after tax terms, and all interest income is assumed to be accumulated, then the percentage of earnings saved would have to be *ten times* that of the average earner in order to give the top 1 per cent a share of 30 per cent of the wealth of their age group. Polanyi and Wood (1974) quote evidence from the United States (Projector, 1968) for a ratio of ten, but the same source gives alternative figures as low as two, on which basis the share of the top 1 per cent would be only some 6 per cent.

While it is conceivable that dispersion of earnings, coupled with large differences in savings behaviour, could explain the distribution within age groups, it is hard to square this explanation with the evidence about the age composition of wealth-holders. If it were really true, then the rich would be primarily those in late middle age and retirement, and this should show up in the proportion of wealth held by different age groups. This is not, however, the case. If we look at those in Britain with wealth in excess of £125 000 in 1968 (broadly the top 0·1 per cent), then nearly one-third were aged under 45. This is scarcely consistent with the view that the concentration can be explained by steady accumulation out of earnings over the individual lifetime.

It appears that the distribution of wealth cannot be attributed simply to age differences, not is it simply a reflection of earnings differentials:

while life-cycle considerations together with earnings inequality may well account for a lot of inequality of wealth, they cannot account for its peak, nor for the distribution of estates, nor for the fact that wealth in each age group is distributed more like that of wealth in the population as a whole than like the distribution of earnings (Flemming and Little, 1974, p. 4).

There are forces leading to concentration at the top which need further explanation, and these are discussed in the next chapter.

8
WEALTH AND THE CAUSES OF CONCENTRATION

It costs a lot of money to die comfortably.

(Samuel Butler 1835–1902)

The last chapter described the degree of concentration of wealth-holding in Britain and the United States. We saw that the distribution, particularly the holding of the top 0·1 per cent, could not be explained entirely by age or as a result of the dispersion of earnings coupled with normal life-cycle saving. In this chapter we examine two main ways of joining the top 0·1 per cent: the accumulation of self-made fortunes and inheritance.

8·1 Accumulation of wealth

Let us begin by considering a simple process of accumulation. A person's total wealth increases on account of saving, which is a proportion of his earnings plus the accumulation of all the income from his capital, including capital gains. In the previous chapter we examined the effect of differences in earnings, and associated variations in the proportion saved. There may, however, be differences between individuals in their propensity to save: i.e. differences which are personal characteristics and not related to earnings. Some people may be more thrifty than others.

In order to see the force of thrift, let us take a concrete example. Suppose that Mr A has average earnings, which rise in real terms at an annual rate of 3 per cent, and that he saves 5 per cent of his earnings each year. He receives interest of 4½ per cent in real terms and all of this is reinvested. If he begins at age 25, he will have amassed capital of something like nine times his initial annual earnings (in real terms) by the time he retires at 65. This will clearly not put him in the top 1 per cent, let alone anywhere near the top 0·1 per cent. If the proportion of earnings saved were a quarter rather than 5 per cent, he would accumulate an amount equal to some forty-five times annual average earnings, and would be about half way to joining the top 0·1 per cent. Even to get this far would require a high degree of abstinence, and it is interesting to note in this context that Runciman's example, Mr Rowse, a London Transport driver who died in 1972 leaving £62 388, had no children, and was reported never to take a holiday and to have just the bare necessities (1974, p. 104). These conclusions do, however, depend on the rate of return that a person can get on his wealth, as can be seen from the following figures:

Return on wealth %	Amount accumulated at age 65 as multiple of initial earnings (in real terms)[a]
10	33
8	20
6	12
3	7

[a](Saving 5 per cent of earnings from age 25.) These figures may be compared with the amount required to enter the top 0·1 per cent, which is some 100 times average earnings.

Whether a small saver stands any chance of catching up with the top 0·1 per cent in his lifetime depends, therefore, on the yield he can expect on his wealth. If we base the predicted yield on the return to ordinary shares over the past fifty years, it is at first sight encouraging, amounting to around 10 per cent per annum. However, this leaves out two important factors: inflation and taxation. The return of 10 per cent in money terms made no allowance for the rise in prices, nor was it adjusted for the income tax and capital gains tax payable. The return after taxation and allowing for inflation was only some 5 per cent. This means that even investing in ordinary shares, which over the long term have performed better than many other assets, Mr A's return would have been towards the lower end of the range considered above. (Projecting these returns into the future is clearly dangerous, but it seems at present unlikely that the real return will be substantially higher in the years to come.)

This analysis suggests that the force of accumulation is unlikely to be sufficiently strong to allow a person with no inherited wealth to join the top 0·1 per cent purely on the basis of thrift. By judicious investment a person may put himself on the fringes of high wealth, but no more. For example, in the United States $10 000 invested in the Dow Jones index in 1925 would have accumulated to $62 000 by 1965, enough to put the person just in Lampman's class of top wealth-holders, but as we have seen in the previous chapter, this is not even the top 1 per cent. In Britain, Runciman (1972) has suggested that 'there are many vehicle-builders, dock-workers and printers, with council flats and two or three earners in the household, who could in theory afford to put [£4 a week] into a good unit trust'. Even assuming that they were to have two or three earners for the whole of 40 years, which is obviously very unlikely, saving £4 a week would allow them to amass some £24 000 at a real return of 5 per cent, so that they would scarcely qualify as 'rich'.

So far we have considered Mr A with average earnings. The combination of high earnings and exceptional thrift could well allow a person to save enough to join the top 0·1 per cent. However, at a return of 5 per cent he would no do so until late in life. A person with three times the average earnings, saving a quarter of his earnings, would not reach wealth of one hundred times national average earnings until nearly the age of 60. This cannot account for the substantial proportion of the top 0·1 per cent under this age.

If differences in thrift alone cannot provide the answer, the remaining factor explaining self-made fortunes is the return to wealth. We have seen that for Mr A to hope to catch up with the top 0·1 per cent in his lifetime, he must obtain a return considerably higher than that available to the average investor on the stock exchange. This is clearly not impossible, as has been demonstrated by many household names, but the main way in which it can be done is by becoming an active and successful entrepreneur. As described by *Fortune*, 'it is necessary to enter a business at or near the ground floor, to hold a major interest, and to resist selling during hard times' (May 1968). Not only is the return to the successful likely to be much higher than from armchair investment, but the process of accumulation is favoured by the tax system. A businessman can set the costs of expansion against taxable profits, and when he floats his company on the stock exchange, the resulting capital gains are taxed at a lower rate than investment income. It is as the result of this, according to Copeman and Rumble, that 'one can see really successful new business owners become millionaires or even multi-millionaires in 10 to 20 years, even in very highly taxed countries where top salaried men are very tightly pinched' (1972, p. 25).

The sources of self-made fortunes are very varied, as is illustrated by the *Fortune* list of American centi-millionaires, who range from the Rockefellers to Bob Hope. Some important routes to such wealth can be distinguished. The first is the invention or development of a new technique or product. The wealth of such men as Mr Chester Carlson (Xerox) Dr Land (Polaroid Camera) represents, in part, the monopoly rent which can be extracted by inventors or innovators. Invention, by itself, is not enough, there being many instances where the originator was not the person who obtained the monopoly rent, and the commercial exploitation of the idea is clearly of great importance. Commercial success depends to a large extent on an ability to forecast future consumer needs, and indeed this responsiveness to market trends is in itself a second major source of self-made fortunes. The success of many entrepreneurs derives not so much from inventing a new product or mode of production, as from being in a rapidly growing industry. This was probably true of the motor industry millionaires, of those who developed airline travel, of those who saw the prospects for electronics and computing after the Second World War (e.g. Hewlett and Packard in the *Fortune* list), and those who developed supermarket and chain trading (Sir Jack Cohen of Tesco and Charles Clore of British Shoe).

A third, rather different, element is the ownership of natural resources. The discovery of oil or other minerals has led to many self-made fortunes, often unrelated to any active entrepreneurial effort. The substantial increase in the value of building land has, on a smaller scale, had a rather similar effect. The ability to exploit natural resources depends in some cases on decisions by government bodies, particularly planning and zoning. This introduces a fourth element: the impact of government restrictions and the gains which can be made by those able to circumvent the restrictions. This has been apparent in the case of property development in Britain. On top of an acute shortage of office accommodation in London after the Second World War were imposed planning controls, which generated very substantial gains to those with the knowledge to exploit restrictions such as those on permitted floor-space. In the same way, the ban on office building in 1964 led to large capital gains on complete buildings. The fifth, and final, element is that of pure luck, of being in the right place at the right time, or of a gamble coming off. In this context it must be remembered that the generation of self-made fortunes very often involves a substantial element of risk-taking. Whether it arises from uncertainty concerning the outcome of an invention (Land worked for years perfecting the Polaroid camera) or of exploration for natural resources, whether it arises from uncertainty concerning the decisions of competitors or the government, there is an ever present risk of loss or outright failure. The successful entrepreneurs discussed here are only a small fraction of those who set out to make money this way. To quote Josiah Wedgwood (1929), himself the descendant of an archetypal self-made entrepreneur, they must 'take great risks and [have] exceptional luck or exceptional talent'.

The relative importance of these different elements can only be determined by taking a representative sample of self-made millionaires and examining in detail the role played in the origin of their fortunes by the five factors described above. An illustration is provided in the study by Rubinstein (1971) of the industrial origins of British fortunes (both self-made and inherited), which are classified as 'old' (agriculture, textiles, foreign trade, etc.), 'intermediate' (brewing, engineering, etc.) and 'new' (retail, newspapers, property development, etc.). Of the millionaires dying in the latter part of the last century, 81 per cent were classified as having wealth originating from old industries; by 1920–39, this proportion had gone down to 48 per cent and that of new industries had risen to 25 per cent; finally, by 1960–9, old and new industries were equally represented. This shows, as expected, a steady shift in the direction of industries which were growing more rapidly.

8·2 Inheritance and the transmission of wealth

In the last section we considered wealth acquired through accumulation, but it can also be acquired through inheritance, a term used here to denote all wealth receipts, including both bequests and gifts from living people. In this section we examine the transmission of wealth and the distribution of inherited wealth.

A stylized pattern of wealth transmission between generations is shown in Fig. 8·1. It begins with a self-made man, who through the

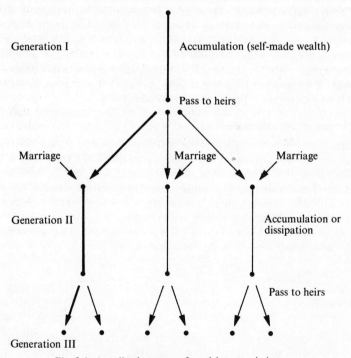

Fig. 8·1. A stylized pattern of wealth transmission

processes described in the previous section has accumulated a substantial fortune. This fortune is passed on to his heirs, who belong to
Generation II. The heirs may also inherit from other members of
Generation I (e.g. an uncle or aunt), and they may marry into money.
The total received through inheritance and marriage provides the 'start'
in life of the second generation. This wealth may be augmented through
further saving and indeed the heirs may become active entrepreneurs;
alternatively it may be dissipated. The resulting wealth then passes to
their heirs in Generation III and the process continues.

The pattern set out in Fig. 8·1 was described as 'stylized' because it
leaves out a number of elements. Transfers of wealth do not necessarily
pass from one generation to the next; they may pass from brother to
brother; they may pass from employer to chauffeur; they may skip a
generation (grandfather to grandchild). Wealth may be transferred to
charitable or other bodies. In Britain there is little evidence that
charitable bequests exercise an important equalizing influence, although
they are clearly much more common in the United States, as is
exemplified by the Ford, Rockefeller, Carnegie and other foundations.
Finally, transfers need not necessarily take place at death, and estate
taxation may provide a strong incentive for gifts before death.

The pattern of wealth transmission shown in Fig. 8·1 does, never-
theless, serve to bring out some of the important influences at work in
determining whether the wealth of this dynasty grows or dies away over
time. If Generation I made a million through his enterprise, how likely
is it that Generation III will still be millionaires?

The pattern of inheritance

Laws and customs regarding the division of wealth among heirs vary
greatly between societies. In some cases there are legal restrictions
placed on the disposal of estates at death. The law of *legitim* (or
reserved portion) found in some European countries entitles the heirs
to a certain proportion of the estate, depending on the degree of
relationship. Similar provisions apply in other countries when a person
dies without making a will. An example of such intestacy succession is
shown below (taken from the Ohio State Law):

Decedent with surviving spouse

No children	1 child	2 or more children
Spouse ¾	Spouse ½	Spouse $\frac{1}{3}$
Parents ¼	Child ½	Children share $\frac{2}{3}$

When there is no surviving spouse, the estate is divided equally among
all children, and if there are no surviving children, it goes to more
distant relations.

The broad effects of laws of *legitim* or intestacy for the transfer of wealth to the next generation are to divide estates equally among all children. This pattern of inheritance gives the greatest force for the equalization of wealth. If the average self-made millionaire (and spouse) has 2·4 children, and they in turn have 2·4 children, the amount inherited by Generation III under equal division would be £175 000 and by Generation V it would be down to £30 000 (assuming no new accumulation took place). This strong equalizing tendency may be modified by marriage, but it is clear that equal division could lead to a relatively rapid departure from the top 0·1 per cent.

Equal division is not, however, the only possible pattern of inheritance. At the other extreme is the custom of primogeniture, by which all wealth is passed on to the eldest child or eldest son. In terms of Fig. 8·1 this would mean that wealth followed the route marked with a heavy line; it would remain intact, leaving aside savings or dissaving, from generation to generation. This custom was associated in the past with landed estates, but appears to have been practised also in the case of other forms of wealth. Our knowledge about patterns of inheritance is very limited and in Britain there is little more recent evidence available than Wedgwood's study of 1929. At that time he found evidence of primogeniture, concluding that 'frequently the lion's share of the estate went to one particular son—usually, but not always, the eldest' (1929, p. 164). Between the extreme cases of primogeniture and equal division are various other patterns of division. Estates may be equally divided among male children; estates may be divided between sons and daughters in an unequal proportion. A pattern which is quite commonly observed is that all children receive a 'comfortable' amount and the remainder goes to the eldest child (a modified form of primogeniture).

Family size

Where wealth is shared among all children, the question of family size becomes important. If the wealthy tend to have larger-than-average families, then the tendency towards equality will be stronger. If wealthy families had three children, rather than 2·4, £1 million would be reduced to £12 500 each by Generation V. However, from the very limited evidence regarding the family size of the top 0·1 per cent, it seems unlikely that this is a major equalizing factor.

One aspect which is often overlooked is the relationship between family size, the sex of the children, and the pattern of division. There are reasons to expect primogeniture, in its pure or modified form, to be preferred in a large family. This is especially the case where primogeniture is linked with the control of a business enterprise or of an estate, and for this purpose the next generation must contain a son willing and able to take over. As Dr Johnson said of the Thrale brewing family, 'the desire of male heirs is not appendant only to feudal tenures. A son is almost necessary to the continuance of Thrale's fortune; for what can Misses do with a brewhouse?' Although these remarks may not apply with equal force in our more liberated age, the reasons for maintaining wealth intact via primogeniture are still likely to be less pressing where there is no heir to play an active role in management.

Marriage

In the examination of the effect of primogeniture and equal division, we referred to the influence of the patterns of intermarriage between families on the development of wealth-holding. If no property were vested in women, marriage as such would have little effect on the distribution: wealth would pass from father to son(s) in the way described above. However, there have always been wealthy heiresses and it has become increasingly common over this century for women to hold wealth in their own right. As a result, an heir may receive a substantial part of his fortune through his mother's side of the family.

The influence of marriage patterns where there is equal division and women inherit on equal terms with men can be seen in terms of the following example. Suppose that all families have two children (a boy and a girl) and that the whole of the wealth of the country is initially in the hands of the top 5 per cent. If people choose their marriage partners at random, most of the children of the top 5 per cent marry people with no wealth and the degree of concentration tends to fall over time. In practice, however, it seems unlikely that the pattern of marriage will take this form. The rich tend to marry the rich because they have the same social background and are quite simply more likely to meet each other. In the extreme case where the top 5 per cent intermarry completely and no new blood enters their ranks, the degree of concentration will not be reduced, even though estates are equally divided. Class marriage, where husband and wife come from families with the same level of wealth, leads to effectively the same situation as where all property is inherited by sons; it is equivalent, in this sense at least, to everyone marrying his sister.

The impact of these different elements is summarized in Table 8·1, which shows the outcome of the polar assumptions about the division of estates and the patterns of marriage. For simplicity, it is assumed that each family has an equal number of boys and girls, and that there is no new accumulation. With primogeniture and no population growth (each family having two children) the distribution remains unchanged

TABLE 8·1
Wealth transmission under polar assumptions

	Primogeniture	Equal division among sons	Equal division among all children
Each family has two children			
Marriage random	Stable distribution	Stable distribution (same as primogeniture)	Tendency to equalization
Class marriage			Same as equal division among sons
Each family has more than two children			
Marriage random	Tendency towards increased concentration	Stable distribution	Tendency to equalization
Class marriage			Same as equal division among sons

Note: it is assumed that each family has an equal number of boys and girls, and that there is no new saving.

over time, this conclusion holding irrespective of the pattern of marriage. Where the family size is greater than two, the distribution becomes more concentrated over time under primogeniture, the rich becoming a decreasing fraction of the growing population. (The same would also happen in the two-child case if we supposed that a quarter of families had only girls, and that some heiresses married heirs.) Where wealth is equally divided among male children, the distribution again remains stable, in the sense that the share of the top groups is unchanged. In the case of no population growth this is, of course, the same as primogeniture. Equal division among *all* children, on the other hand, brings marriage into importance; and where marriage is random, there is a tendency to equalization. Unless there is purely class marriage, the share of the top groups will be falling over time.

8·3 The distribution of wealth—inheritance and self-made fortunes

Earlier in this chapter, we saw that the average person starting from nothing is only likely to join the top 0·1 per cent of wealth-holders if he engages in active entrepreneurship or enjoys considerable good

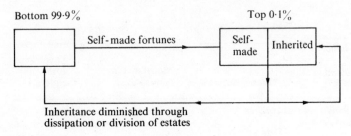

Fig. 8·2. The wealth process

fortune. In each generation a small number of self-made men, owing their success (in varying proportions) to ability, willingness to take risks, and luck, emerge from this process to join the propertied class—see Fig. 8·2. This wealth is then passed on to their heirs, and as a result may be consolidated or depleted, depending on the factors described in the previous section, and on the heirs' propensity to save.

In this section, we examine the balance between 'self-made' and inherited wealth in the top 0·1 per cent. This is a question of considerable importance, and one which has major implications for the conclusions we draw about inequality. We can imagine two polar situations. In the first, the top group consists entirely of self-made men, who have started from nothing, and whose wealth disappears at their death. This society would be very fluid. The top 0·1 per cent might own 10 per cent of total wealth, but they would be quite different families from those who made up this group in the previous generation, as in Schumpeter's description of the capitalist 'hotel', always full but with the guests always changing. At the other pole is the case where there is no 'new' wealth, and the top 0·1 per cent have all inherited. In this society the top group would belong to the same families as had constituted the top 0·1 per cent in the previous generation, and indeed for time immemorial. The difference between these two societies would not be apparent from examining the share of the top 0·1 per cent, but there is clearly a major difference from a 'dynastic' view of equity. In the first society, it could then be the case that everyone stood the same chance that he, or one of his descendants, entered the top 0·1 per cent, but this would not be true of the second case, where there would be clear dynastic inequality.

Some of the factors influencing the balance between self-made and inherited wealth have already been discussed. The analysis of the previous sections suggested that the persistence of inherited wealth depends on the patterns of inheritance and marriage, and on the savings behaviour of the children. If estates are divided equally among all children, if marriage is random and if heirs are given to riotous living, then the departure of a dynasty from the top 0·1 per cent will be relatively rapid. In such a situation we should observe self-made men at the top of the *Fortune* list, with inherited wealth taking up the lower ranks and disappearing after a number of generations. On the other hand, where there is primogeniture and the heirs add to their inheritance, then the descendants of the self-made man may remain in the top 0·1 per cent. Indeed, it will be the oldest fortunes which come at the top of the list, since they have been accumulating for the longest period. The addition of self-made wealth to the top 0·1 per cent then serves to dilute the inherited wealth and prevent its share in the total from growing over time, but the self-made will make up only a proportion of the total.

In order to go further, we need to look at the empirical evidence. In the case of the *Fortune* list of centi-millionaires given in the previous chapter, it is estimated that about half had inherited the bulk of their wealth, including such well known names as Mellon, Rockefeller, du Pont, and Ford. The article suggested that inheritance had been declining as a source of great wealth, although since the proportion of fortunes regarded as inherited was much the same in 1968 as in 1957, the basis for this conclusion was not clear. However, it did appear that the heirs of those appearing in the earlier *Fortune* list in general failed to retain their position: of the 22 people on the 1957 list who had died, only one placed an heir on the list of 1968.

The remaining half of the *Fortune* list were either self-made men or people who had considerably increased their inheritance. Examples of the second category were the two men at the very top, J. P. Getty and Howard Hughes, who both inherited substantial amounts but added very greatly to their inheritance. This illustrates the difficulty in distinguishing inherited from self-made wealth. Suppose that a person is now worth £200 000 and that he inherited £50 000 sixteen years ago. It would clearly not be correct to say that the difference of £150 000 represented accumulated wealth, since without the inheritance he would have been less well placed to accumulate. In order to make some allowance for this, we could postulate a certain rate of return on the inherited wealth: e.g. if the return were 7 per cent (in money terms), the inheritance would have trebled in sixteen years, so that the proportion of current wealth attributable to inheritance would be three-quarters rather than a quarter. On this basis, the *Fortune* definition probably understates the proportion of inherited wealth.

The *Fortune* approach is clearly subject to a great deal of error, and it is recognized in the article that many 'centi-millionaires' may be missing. This could well lead to a systematic bias. On the other hand, the alternative sources are far from ideal. The study by Barlow *et al.* (1966) of high income individuals in the United States found, for example, that 'gifts and inheritances accounted for a relatively small fraction of aggregate wealth'. However, the treatment of saving made possible by inheritance was very approximate, and the authors recognize that the sampling of individuals according to income may not adequately reflect those with high wealth, who may be more likely to have inherited. Indeed, of those with wealth in excess of $½ million, 28 per cent said that half or more of their assets reflected gifts or inheritance. This latter finding was supported by the Federal Reserve Board (1966) study, which showed that a third of this group had inherited a 'substantial' part of their wealth, although the definition was not made explicit.

In Britain the most recent evidence about the importance of inheritance has been provided by the investigations of Harbury and McMahon (1973) of those leaving wealth of £100 000 or more in 1956–7 and 1965. Taking a sample of male decedents, they traced the estates which had been left by the fathers, and thus examined the extent to which there were wealthy forebears. This method does not provide a fully adequate measure of the importance of inheritance. The *estates* left by the two generations are not necessarily a good indication of the total wealth transmitted, since they exclude wealth passed on in the form of gifts or settled in the form of trusts: e.g. there is one case in the sample where a person left £113 000 but is reported to have given away about £1 million during his lifetime. Some of those sons whose fathers apparently died leaving small estates may in fact have received from them substantial amounts in gifts or settled property. Moreover, while the father is the most likely person to have transmitted wealth, it may have come from other members of the family. Despite these problems, however, the evidence provided by Harbury and McMahon clearly throws some light on the role of inheritance, and is a very valuable source.

The results of the study are summarized in Table 8·2. This shows first that a very high proportion of those leaving more than £100 000 had fathers who themselves had been wealthy: over a quarter had left £250 000 or more (in real terms) and a half had left more than £100 000. If one regards as 'self-made' men whose fathers left less than £25 000, then they accounted for fewer than one-third. If there had been no connection between the wealth of fathers and sons, then one would expect—in contrast to those findings—that more than 99 per cent would have had fathers leaving £25 000 or less. This supports the earlier conclusion of Harbury that 'the chance of leaving an estate valued at over £100 000 . . . was outstandingly enhanced if one's father had been at least moderately well off' (1962, p. 867).

TABLE 8·2

Estates of fathers and sons, Britain 1956/7 and 1965

Percentage with father leaving at least[a]	Sons leaving estates of £100 000 or more in	
	1956−7	1965
£1 million	10	4
£250 000	34	26
£100 000	52	45
£50 000	58	58
£25 000	69	67
£10 000	76	77

Source: Harbury and McMahon (1973), Table II.
Note: [a]At constant 1956−7 prices.

The second conclusion drawn by Harbury and McMahon is that there appears to have been no significant change in the importance of inheritance over this century. Linking the results to the earlier study by Wedgwood (1929) for 1924−6, they found that 'the role of inheritance in the creation of the personal fortunes of top wealth leavers ... has not changed very much since the mid-twenties'. This finding has been disputed by Rubinstein (1974), who studied the occupation and social status of millionaires dying in Britain over the past century and a half. Men in his 'self-made' category rise from 12 per cent of the total over the period 1900−29 to 31 per cent in the 1960s. However, as he points out, the experience of millionaires may be rather different from that of wealth-holders in the range £100 000−£1 million, and it is interesting to note that Rubinstein's 'half-millionaire' group showed no such trend.

From this evidence it may be reasonable to conclude that around one-third of the top wealth-holders in Britain (broadly the top 0·1 per cent) are self-made men and that two-thirds have inherited substantial amounts. In the United States the importance of inheritance may be rather smaller, and the proportions could possibly be reversed. In neither country is there conclusive evidence of a trend towards the reduced importance of inherited wealth.

8·4 The redistribution of wealth

The analysis of this and the previous chapter suggests that inherited wealth provides a significantly unequal start in life for a small minority. The observed distribution of wealth cannot be explained away purely as the result of saving for retirement or earnings differentials, nor does the top 0·1 per cent consist solely of self-made men. Inheritance accounts for a sizeable fraction of the wealth of this top group, and in this respect there is undoubtedly inequality of opportunity.

In the light of this conclusion, we may briefly examine the redistribution of wealth through government policy. Many advanced countries, including Britain and the United States, employ a variety of measures designed to redistribute wealth: taxes on the ownership or on the transfer of wealth, measures to restrict the scope of property rights, and schemes to encourage wealth-holding at the lower end of the scale. In what follows, some of their main features are described, although the full implications clearly cannot be discussed in detail.

Taxes on the ownership of wealth

Taxes on the ownership of wealth may take two main forms. Firstly, there are annual taxes on the value of wealth, usually referred to as wealth taxes. Secondly, there are taxes on the income from wealth in the course of the tax year. In the first case, the relevant consideration would be that a person was worth £X, in the second that he received an income of £Y on his wealth.

Although at present neither Britain nor the United States imposes a wealth tax, such taxes have been used in a number of other countries. In western Europe they have a long history, going back to the thirteenth century in some Swiss cantons, and in recent years they have been in force in Luxembourg, Norway, West Germany, the Netherlands, Denmark, and Sweden. The taxes have in general been progressive, with wealth below a certain level exempted and, in some cases, rates which increase with the level of wealth. In Sweden, the tax starts at the equivalent of $45 000 or £19 000 and has rates rising from 1 per cent to 2½ per cent per annum. In Britain, the Labour government announced in 1974 its intention to introduce such an annual wealth tax. The illustrative scales of tax began at £100 000 and involved rates rising to 2½ per cent or 5 per cent on wealth of £5 million or over.

The alternative system, that of taxing the income from wealth, is rather different, in that the tax liability depends on the form in which the wealth is held. A person owning paintings or yachts would not be subject to tax, since these yield no taxable income. In Britain, investment income in excess of a certain amount is subject (in 1974) to additional tax at the rate of 10–15 per cent over and above that payable on earned income. On the other hand, there also exist a number of avenues for avoidance, which are particularly important in the case of unearned income. The relatively generous treatment of capital gains, for example, could reduce the effective rate of tax substantially. A person building up a successful business may obtain much of his financial reward in the form of capital gains when the company is floated publicly. In the United States, there is a similar surcharge on investment income above a certain amount, so that the top marginal rate is 70 per cent compared with 50 per cent for earned income. However, in addition to such loopholes as capital gains being charged at less than the full rate of income tax, there are further means of avoidance, such as tax-exempt bonds and depletion allowances, both of which may allow the wealthy to reduce their tax liabilities.[1] As a result, Fried *et al.* (1973) concluded that 'on the average, even extremely rich people—those with incomes over $1 million—pay less than a third of their income to the government in personal income tax'.

Taxation of the value of wealth, or the income from it, is directed at current ownership whatever its source. In terms of our earlier analysis, it may affect saving for lifecycle purposes, and it will fall on all those with substantial wealth, whether self-made or inherited. If the concern of the government is with inequality in inherited wealth, then the appropriate measures may be those linked to the transfer of wealth.

Taxes on the transfer of wealth

In Britain the main tax on the transfer of property was until 1974 the estate duty (it is to be replaced by the new capital transfer tax). The duty covers the transfer of property at death and is charged on the total amount transferred by the decedent, not on the amount received by individual heirs. The nominal rate schedule is highly progressive. A person in the top 0·1 per cent paying duty on the full value of his assets would be subject to a rate of around 50 per cent and the top rate is 75 per cent. Despite this, there are a number of reasons to doubt whether the estate duty has been very effective in reducing the concentration of wealth.

First of all, even if the nominal rates are paid, it may still be possible for a family to restore its position by new accumulation. Suppose that we consider a hypothetical family whose first generation died just as the 1894 budget took effect, leaving £500 000, which is equivalent to some £5 million today. The net estate was inherited by the eldest son who died in 1927, and then by his eldest son who died in 1960, in each case estate duty being paid at the full rates. Suppose also that they obtained a yield of 4½ per cent in real terms after taxation, which we have seen earlier in this chapter to have been about the average over the last fifty years, and that they saved one-third of this income. The

---

[1] It should be noted that the *incidence* of these concessions requires careful examination. In the case of tax-exempt government bonds, for example, the tax-exempt status may be reflected in a lower interest yield; however, this will be based on the tax rate relevant to the marginal holder, and the very rich may well face considerably higher tax rates.

present representative of the family would still be worth some £2 million, even though estate duty had been paid three times. Despite the high nominal rates, the effect of the wealth transfer tax may be offset by accumulation coupled with the passing on of the estate intact from generation to generation.

The weakness of the estate duty is further compounded when account is taken of avoidance, which is a more serious problem with this than with almost any other important tax. Avoidance is in fact so easy that 'whenever a particularly large estate is reported with the duty paid, representing between 60 per cent and 80 per cent of the value, the deceased is regarded as an eccentric' (Revell, 1967, p. 110). Each day the financial press carries advertisements for advice on reducing the burden of estate duty, by purchasing agricultural land, growing timber, taking out insurance, or establishing trusts. The most straightforward method of avoidance up to 1974, did not however require specialist advice; all that one needed to do was to pass one's wealth on in the form of gifts. Gifts made within seven years of death were treated as part of the estate, but providing sufficient foresight was exercised, it was possible to pass on wealth without any duty being paid. (The situation will be changed by the new capital transfer tax announced in 1974.)

This remarkable loophole is not found in the United States, where the federal estate tax is supplemented by a gift tax; the latter provides more generous treatment of transfers than the estate tax but not total exemption. Nonetheless, there remains considerable scope for reducing the effective tax liability: the use of trusts, the generous marital deductions, the establishment of charitable foundations. For example, John D. Rockefeller is reported to have paid virtually no estate tax when he died in 1960, since he had not only established trusts for his children earlier in life, but had also divided the final estate between a charitable foundation and his widow. Since the marital deduction permits half of the property of the deceased to be transferred to the surviving spouse tax-free, and since the transfer to the foundation is tax-exempt, he paid no tax. The establishment of a charitable foundation, such as the Rockefeller or Ford Foundation, means that the wealth does not pass to the heirs, but it may still allow them to enjoy considerable control over its use. The setting up of 'generation-skipping' trusts is another way of reducing the effective rate of tax. William Randolph Hearst Sr paid substantial estate tax in 1957, but it is estimated that no further tax will be payable until 2050 or later (Tuckman, 1973).

Estate taxes in Britain and the United States have the common feature that, apart from the provisions for the surviving spouse, tax liability is largely independent of the way in which the wealth is divided; they provide little inducement for donors to spread their wealth widely. It has therefore been proposed that the estate tax should be replaced by an inheritance tax levied on the amount received. In this way a million would bear less tax divided among ten heirs than if it was left intact to one person, and it would provide an incentive for, say, equal division to replace primogeniture.

The inheritance tax could take a variety of forms. It could be related to the individual bequest or gift, as is the case in a number of European countries. This, however, would provide no incentive for a person to leave wealth to those who had not previously inherited. The same tax would be payable if the money were left to J. P. Getty or to a person without a penny to his name. This would not accord with the objective of reducing inequality in the distribution of total inherited wealth. For this purpose, a much more effective alternative would be a tax based on the cumulated total of all wealth transfers, gifts, and bequests received by an individual over the course of his life in excess of a certain exemption level. The way in which such a tax would work has been described by Meade as follows:

Every gift or legacy received by any one individual would be recorded in a register against his name for tax purposes. He would then be taxed ... according to the size of the total amount which he had received over the whole of his life by way of gift or inheritance. The rate of tax would be on a progressive scale according to the total of gifts or bequests recorded against his name in the tax register (1964, p. 57).

Such a tax might appear at first sight like an administrative nightmare. The study by Sandford *et al.* (1973), however, showed that, although the administrative costs would be higher than with a straight estate tax, its operation was clearly feasible. The extra administrative burden may well be considered a small price for a tax which is explicitly directed at a major source of inequality of opportunity.

Other approaches

It is clear that there are many possible ways of making the taxation of wealth a more effective instrument for the redistribution of wealth. Fiscal measures are not, however, the only ones which can be adopted.

It would be possible to restrict the scope of private property. At present there are clearly limitations on the social and legal recognition of claims to ownership of property: one cannot, for example, claim a property right to a person, to the atmosphere, or to the sea. The scope of ownership could be further restricted in a variety of ways, ranging from relatively minor changes, such as the prohibition of certain types of trust set up largely to avoid tax, to the more radical measures which might be found in a socialist economy, such as an absolute limit on the amount of property which could be passed from one generation to the next.

A second approach would be to take 'countervailing' measures, designed to offset the impact of the concentration of wealth. These could again take many forms. It would be possible to extend state ownership of wealth, for example through nationalization or a capital levy to redeem the national debt. In Britain, nationalization has long been a leading aim of Labour party policy; but the motives for this have largely been concerned with control and the government's industrial objectives, rather than with redistribution. Indeed, with full compensation, nationalization would have no direct distributional effect. The state would acquire the physical assets, but would have to issue government bonds to the same value to pay the compensation, so that the net worth of the state would be unchanged. A capital levy, or a once-for-all tax on all wealth at rates comparable with those on estates, would lead to a substantial reduction in wealth at the top and, if the revenue were used to reduce the national debt, would change the balance between private and state capital. There are, however, a number of problems. The levy would catch saving for life-cycle reasons as well as inherited wealth. It would not provide a permanent solution, and fortunes accumulated after the levy would give rise to new inequality. The execution of the levy would be a major administrative task.

An alternative to the extension of state ownership is the increase of private wealth-holding by those who at present inherit nothing. Numerous measures have been proposed to encourage saving, but from the point of view of lifetime equity the important question is how far they serve to equalize the distribution of inherited wealth. This might be achieved through savings incentives, offering a return to small savers in excess of the market rate of interest: e.g. offering inflation-proofing of assets up to a certain sum per person. Many savings schemes in Britain, however, have tended to favour the higher income groups through their tax-exempt status. A more direct approach is the idea of the state providing a guaranteed minimum inheritance, either as a 'coming of age' bonus or as a capital element in the state pension, payable on retirement. This would be in effect a 'negative capital tax', parallel to the negative income tax proposals for the redistribution of income.

9
FACTOR SHARES

It has now become certain that the problem of distribution is much
more difficult than it was thought to be . . . and that no solution of it
which claims to be simple can be true.

(Alfred Marshall, 1890)

Inequality in the distribution of income depends on the distribution of
earned incomes, on the concentration of wealth, and on the relative
importance of income from earnings and capital. It is with this last
aspect that the present chapter is concerned. As pointed out in
Chapter 1, classical writing on the distribution of income was primarily
concerned with the distribution among classes. Ricardo, for example,
described 'the principal problem in Political Economy' as being to
determine how 'the produce of the earth . . . is divided among three
classes of the community, namely, the proprietor of the land, the
owner of the stock or capital necessary for its cultivation, and the
labourers by whose industry it is cultivated' (1821). At that time, it
may have been reasonable to suppose that these three classes
corresponded to different positions on the income scale. Today, the
relationship between the shares of factors of production and the
distribution of income among persons is more complicated, but factor
shares remain of considerable relevance. Although people may derive
income from more than one source—they may, for example, receive
interest on their savings in addition to their labour income—it is still
broadly true that income from property (capital and land) is of greater
importance at the top of the income scale. In this chapter we examine,
therefore, the shares of land, labour, and capital in total income and
how they are determined. Since fully adequate treatment of this
question would require more space than one chapter, and there have
been many books solely concerned with this subject, all that is
attempted here is a brief survey of the principal features which need
explanation and the theories which have been advanced.

9·1 The behaviour of aggregate factor shares
The share of wages or profits in national income may appear at first
sight straightforward to measure: the national income accounts contain
estimates of profits, rent, and wages, from which the required ratios
may be derived. It is not, however, as simple as that, since one cannot

readily allocate all income in a neat way between the three categories:

> the study of the trends in the functional distribution of income is handicapped by the fact ... that the nature of the components of income for which we have data has not been determined by the requirements of the economists but by the legal and institutional arrangements of our society (Kravis, 1959, p. 918).

The kinds of problems which arise may be illustrated by reference to the figures for the United Kingdom and the United States in Tables 9·1 and 9·2.[1]

Rent In the case where rent is paid in cash to the landlord, measurement is straightforward, and where the property takes the form of owner-occupied housing, an imputed rent can be estimated. The

TABLE 9·1
Percentage shares of gross national product,
United Kingdom 1860–1969

	Wages and forces' pay[a]	Salaries[a]	Self-employment income	Profits	Rents and property income from abroad	Adjusted share of labour[b]
1860–9	39	6	37		18	–
1870–9	39	6	37		18	–
1880–9	39	8	34		19	–
1890–9	39	9	33		19	–
1900–9	38	10	33		19	–
1910–14	37	11	16	17	19	55
1921–9	41	18	16	13	12	67
1930–8	40	19	14	14	13	68
1946–9	45	20	12	17	6	73
1950–9	44	22	10	18	6	73
1960–9	67		8		18	7	73

Sources: 1860–1959 calculated from Feinstein (1968), Tables 1, 2, and 5; 1960–9 from *National income and expenditure*, 1971, Tables 1 and 20.
Notes: [a]Including employers' contributions to pensions, etc.
    [b]Including estimated labour component of self-employment income.

[1]It may be noted that in the case of the United Kingdom the figures are presented as a percentage of gross national product, but that the United States figures are a proportion of national income (i.e. allowing for depreciation).

TABLE 9·2

Percentage shares of national income, United States 1900–65

	Employee compensation	Self-employment income	Profits and interest	Rent	Share of labour		
					Labour basis	Assets basis	Economy-wide basis
1900–9	55	24	12	9	77	63	72
1910–19	53	24	15	8	69	67	70
1920–9	60	18	14	8	78	68	71
1930–9	67	16	13	4	87	76	79
1940–9	65	17	15	3	78	74	78
1950–9	68	13	15	4	78	74	78
1960–5	71	11	15	3	80	76	80

Source: 1900–39 Kravis (1959), Table 1; 1940–65 from United States Department of Commerce. *Long-term economic growth*, US Government Printing Office.

Note: the figures have been rounded so that the shares add to 100 per cent.

main difficulties arise in the case of land and buildings occupied by companies, where it is almost impossible to separate the part of profit which represents a return to land from that which is the return to the capital employed. In view of this, many authors have chosen to discuss the distribution in terms of the twofold classification of labour and 'property', the latter including both profits and rents. This practice is followed in the final columns of both Table 9·1 and Table 9·2.

Self-employment income Problems of allocation arise even more acutely in the case of self-employment income, which represents a return both on the labour contributed by the self-employed and on their capital (or land). How is the income of the farmer, shop-keeper, or lawyer to be divided between 'wages' and 'property'? The method used by Feinstein in the estimates presented in Table 9·1 is to allocate to wages the income which the self-employed person would have received on average as a paid employee in the same sector of the economy and then to regard any residual as the return to capital. The United States estimates of Kravis in Table 9·2, on the other hand, employ a variety of methods. The first 'labour basis' is similar to that of Feinstein (although the earnings figure used was an average for the economy as a whole and was not broken down by sector). The second 'assets basis' is the reverse case, where the property employed by the self-employed is assumed to yield the same return as other property and the labour income is treated 'as the residual. The third method, the 'economy-wide' figures, assumes that the shares are the same as in the rest of the economy, so that the self-employed sector can in effect be ignored. The results from the three methods are rather different, particularly in the early part of the period, when self-employment accounted for nearly one-quarter of total income.

Government capital and housework The national income accounts relate mainly to cash income, the only major imputed income taken into account being the rents referred to above and farm produce for home production. The missing imputed income includes that accruing to the capital employed in the government sector and the capital employed in the home (consumer durables, cars, etc.) as well as the value of time spent on do-it-yourself, housework, etc. The last, for example, could make a very substantial difference. According to recent estimates, the value of housework performed by both men and women is of the order of 50 per cent of gross national product.

From Tables 9·1 and 9·2 it appears that in broad terms the share in national income of employee compensation (wages plus salaries) is around two-thirds, and that the share of labour, including the return to self-employment (but not that to home production), is more like three-quarters. The ratio of the shares of labour and capital is broadly 3:1. There also appears to have been a rise in the share of labour over time. In Britain the ratio was more like 1:1 before the First World War, and in the interwar period it was 2:1. In the United States the pattern is rather similar. The estimates given in Table 9·2 suggest that there has been a rise in the share of labour, if self-employment income is allocated on an 'assets' or an 'economy-wide' basis. The 'labour' basis estimates indicate that the share fell and then rose during the depression.

Constant shares?

The evidence just described casts doubt on the common belief that the share of labour is constant over time. As we saw in Chapter 2, attention was drawn to the apparent stability by Keynes and subsequent Cambridge economists have continued the tradition:

No hypothesis as regards the forces determining distributive shares could be intellectually satisfying unless it succeeds in accounting for the relative stability of these shares in the advanced economies over the last 100 years or so, despite the phenomenal changes in the techniques of production, in the accumulation of capital relative to labour and in real income per head (Kaldor, 1955ᵃ, p. 84).

The reference by Keynes to the statistical support for his statement was to the data for the share of wages in Britain. From Table 9·1 it can be seen that when he wrote, at the end of the 1930s, the share of wages was indeed at much the same level as it had been eighty years before; however, this ignores the secular increase which had taken place in *salaries*. The share of wages plus salaries had increased from 45 per cent to 59 per cent and this trend has continued, reaching 67 per cent in 1960–9.

A strong believer in the constancy of factor shares may still object to the evidence presented above by saying that he does not mean literal constancy and that the observed movements are still 'relatively small'. Kaldor, for example, referred not to constancy but to 'relative stability'. What does *relative* mean in this context? One interpretation might be in relation to the errors in the estimated components of national income; many of the figures are subject to quite considerable error and it could be that the observed changes lie within these margins of error. This question is discussed by Feinstein, who concludes that it is unlikely: 'If, as is probably *not* the case ... the whole of the understatement in GNP is in income from labour in the first period ... and in income from property in the latter period ... there would still be an increase of 7 percentage points in labour's share' (1968, p. 127).

Similarly, Kravis (1959) examines the effect of taking account of some of the deficiencies of the national accounting framework. The exclusion of the government sector (to overcome the fact that only the labour component is taken into account) does eliminate much of the increase in labour's share on an economy-wide basis. On the other hand, the use of replacement rather than original cost for the depreciation of capital[1] reverses this adjustment, and the economy-wide share of labour in privately produced income rose from 71 per cent in 1900–9 to 78 per cent in 1949–57. (Kravis also makes some rough calculations about the effect of allowing for the imputed services of consumer durables, and concludes that it would make little difference to the trend.) The final conclusion he reaches is that:

the notion of long-run constancy in relative shares is false . . . There has actually been a shift in the distribution of national income from property to labour . . . The size of the shift depends upon the particular assumptions used in allocating entrepreneurial income between its property and labour components, but there appears to be little doubt about the existence of the movement (1959, p. 917).

A second interpretation of relative stability has been advanced by Solow (1958): the relationship between the variation in the aggregate share of labour and the variation within individual industries. If the variation in the aggregate share is less than would be expected on the basis of the independent fluctuation of the shares in industrial sectors (food, textiles, chemicals, etc.) this suggests that a stabilizing force is operating at a macro-economic level. As Solow puts it, 'if the calorie content of breakfast, lunch and supper each varies widely, while the 24-hour total remains constant, we at once suspect a master hand at the control' (1958, p. 621). He tests this hypothesis using United States data and concludes that the variation in the aggregate share is in fact no less than would be expected on the basis of independent fluctuations of the sectoral shares, so that no special explanation of *aggregate* stability is required—what stability there is in the share of labour is attributable to the individual sectors of the economy.

The pattern of a general upward trend in the share of labour is found not only in the United Kingdom and the United States. The estimates presented in Table 9·3 for ten advanced economies show that in every case there was a rise in the share of employee compensation between 1938 and 1968. Employee compensation does not include self-

---

[1] With 'original cost', an asset, such as a piece of machinery, is depreciated at its original purchase price, but in times of rising prices this does not reflect the full cost of replacing it ('replacement cost').

TABLE 9·3
Percentage shares of employee compensation in different countries 1938–68

	1938	1948	1958	1968
Belgium	45	52	57	62
Canada	63	63	68	71
France	50	54[a]	59	63
W. Germany (A)	54	58[b]	60	64
Ireland	54	51	56	60
Japan	39	42[a]	52	54
Norway	55	58	65	68
Sweden (B)	52	61	66	72
UK	63	70	73	75
USA	67	64	71	72

Sources: 1938, 1948, 1958 from Heidensohn (1969), Table 1.
1968 from the International Labour Office, *Yearbook of labour statistics*, 1971, Table 24.
Notes: [a]1949
[b]1950
Estimates are for the share of employee compensation in national income except where indicated A (share in net domestic product) and B (share in gross national product).

employment income, and it may therefore overstate the increase in the total labour share, as can be seen from the earlier tables. Nonetheless the increase is clearly marked: in only two cases was the rise between 1948 and 1968 less than 8 percentage points.

The use of data for individual years as in Table 9·3, rather than averages over 5 or 10 years (as used in Tables 9·1 and 9·2) is subject to the criticism that it may not make adequate allowance for short-term cyclical movements in the relative shares. In broad terms, the share of wages tends to vary inversely with the level of activity, an extreme example being the rise in the share of labour in the US during the 1930s. (For discussion of short-term movements, see, for example, Neild (1963) and Kuh (1965).) This means that the choice of end-years may be important, as is illustrated by the recent British study of Glyn and Sutcliffe, who argued that between 1964 and 1970 the share of profits in company output had almost halved (1972, p. 58). (By taking company output, they avoided the problems of self-employment incomes and the government sector.) However, they ignored the fact that in 1964 the share of profits was higher than it had been in the preceding three years, and that 1970 was a relatively poor year for profits (by 1972 the share had risen again). From the short-term movements brought out in Fig. 9·1, it is clear that there has been a

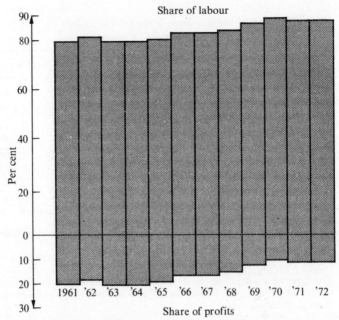

Fig. 9·1. The shares of profits and labour in the United Kingdom 1961–72
Source: Glyn and Sutcliffe (1972), Table C·1 and *National Income and Expenditure*; 1972 and 1973.

definite secular downward trend, but that the particular comparison made by Glyn and Sutcliffe overstated its magnitude.

To sum up, the empirical evidence suggests that in most advanced countries labour receives between two-thirds and three-quarters of national income and that its share has shown a long-run tendency to rise over time. In the rest of this chapter, we describe some of the main theories advanced to explain this pattern.

9·2 The orthodox competitive theory[1]

The determination of the share of wages and profits in national income is a difficult problem. The difficulty stems from a number of causes, but one of the most important is that it involves the whole economic system, and typically everything depends on everything else. In general, to determine the factor shares we need to be able to describe the whole state of the economy. Since a theory which can only make predictions

[1] This and the next section are more technical, and those with a limited appetite for economic theory may wish to go straight to the discussion, starting on p. 182 of the relationship between factor shares and the personal distribution.

about labour's share on the basis of assumptions sufficiently detailed to allow the determination of the wages paid to policemen in Cardiff or Chicago is likely to be too cumbersome to provide any insight, economists have commonly attempted to reduce the problem to a more manageable form. These attempts have taken two, not necessarily exclusive, routes:

(a) the formation of aggregate variables such as 'labour', 'capital', and 'output', which may be treated as homogeneous for the purposes at hand;

(b) the decomposition of the economic system, so that only a small number of the economic variables are considered as determinants of the factor shares.

In this section we examine the theory of factor shares presented in most textbooks; this is presented with varying degrees of qualification and caution, but can reasonably be described as the prevailing orthodoxy. (It is often referred to as the 'neoclassical' theory.) The theory is usually introduced as part of a general equilibrium analysis of the economy, the factor shares being determined as part of an overall explanation of the prices of factors and products: 'to build up a theory of distribution we thus need a theory of factor prices and quantities. Such a theory is a special case of the theory of price' (Lipsey, 1964, p. 407). This general formulation is then reduced to a simpler form, through the first of the two routes described in the previous paragraph: the assumption that the aggregate production possibilities of the economy can be aggregated into a single production function. This is the first of three key assumptions:

Assumption Output is determined by an aggregate function of total capital and total labour. This production function allows smooth substitutability between capital and labour with diminishing marginal returns to each factor, and exhibits constant returns to scale.

In this formulation, land is for simplicity ignored, so that the factor shares considered are those of labour and 'property'. The assumption of constant returns to scale means that if both capital and labour are increased by a given percentage, output will increase by the same amount. A second important assumption made in the orthodox theory is:

Assumption All firms and consumers act as perfect competitors, that is take prices, wages and the cost of capital as given (they cannot exercise any bargaining power) and all firms aim to maximize profits.

These assumptions, while commonly made in economics, have naturally been subject to criticism and these criticisms are discussed below.

Finally:

> *Assumption* The supplies of aggregate capital and labour are assumed to be given, a condition which may, for example, be secured by the full employment of a fixed stock of factors.

Given these assumptions, we can describe the equilibrium of the economy. If firms maximize profits at given product and factor prices, then this implies that they hire labour up to the point where the value marginal product of labour is equal to the cost of labour, and capital up to the point where its value marginal product is equal to the cost of capital.[1] (The total paid out to the factors is guaranteed to add up to the total value of output by the assumption of constant returns to scale.) Writing w for the wage rate, and r for the return to capital, we have the conditions:

w = value marginal product r = value marginal product of
    of labour   capital

This gives a relationship between the relative shares of capital and labour and the supply of the two factors (since the marginal products depend on the factor supplies):[2]

$$\frac{\text{Total profits}}{\text{Total wages}} = \frac{\text{Capital} \times r}{\text{Labour} \times w} = \frac{\text{Capital} \times \text{Marginal product of capital}}{\text{Labour} \times \text{Marginal product of labour}}$$

In general, therefore, to provide a long-run theory of factor shares we need to explain how the factor supplies change over time. There is, however, one special case in which this is not necessary, and which played a leading role in early investigations. Where the aggregate production function takes a particular form, known as the Cobb–Douglas function, the shares of labour and capital are independent of

---

[1] For this to be true, the assumption that capital and labour are smoothly substitutable is clearly necessary. If capital and labour were required in fixed proportions (one man could only work with one shovel), then the marginal products would not be defined. This problem worried Bertrand Russell: 'Consider a porter on a railway whose business it is to shunt goods trains: what proportion of the goods carried can be said to represent the produce of his own labour?' In part the answer here is that we are concerned with aggregate production and not with production functions for individual industries (e.g. the railways), and that at an aggregate level the scope for substitution is greater, since there may be substitution between the different products.

[2] Since the value marginal product = price x marginal product, the price term drops out (appearing on both top and bottom) when we substitute to obtain the final expression.

the factor supplies. The theory would then be decomposable in the sense defined earlier. This function was first employed by Douglas (1934) to explain the relationship between the growth of output and the growth of capital and labour: i.e. an investigation of the nature of the aggregate production function. He appreciated, nonetheless, that with the further assumptions described earlier, the coefficients of his estimated production function would yield predictions about the factor shares. Douglas compared the shares implied by his measurements with those actually observed, and found a broad degree of agreement. More recently, however, studies have cast doubt on this conclusion (see below). Moreover, the Cobb–Douglas function implies that the relative shares remain constant over time, a prediction which is clearly not borne out by the evidence, as we saw in the previous section. This particularly simple resolution of the problem is not, therefore, one which can be sustained.

Except in the special Cobb–Douglas case, the factor shares depend on the relative supplies of capital and labour. This dependence may be represented in terms of the elasticity of substitution (denoted by σ), defined as the proportionate change in the ratio of capital to labour associated with a proportionate change in the relative factor rewards (r/w). It measures the ease of substitution, so that if the elasticity is low a change in r/w is associated with a small change in the capital intensity of production (by assumption the capital–labour ratio falls as r/w rises). The relevance of the elasticity of substitution may be seen from the fact that the relative shares of capital and labour may be written

$$\frac{\text{Total profits}}{\text{Total wages}} = \left(\frac{r}{w}\right) \times \left(\frac{\text{capital}}{\text{labour}}\right)$$

If the capital/labour ratio rises by y per cent, then the relative share of capital rises or falls, depending on whether the associated fall in r/w is less than or greater than y per cent, and this depends in turn on the value of the elasticity of substitution (σ). If σ is less than 1, then the associated change in r/w is more than y per cent and the share of capital falls; if σ is greater than 1, then the share of capital rises; and if $\sigma = 1$, the relative shares are unchanged (this is the Cobb–Douglas case). The proportionate change in the share of capital can in fact be shown to be:

$$(1 - \text{share of capital}) \times (1 - {}^1\!/_\sigma) \times (y \text{ per cent})$$

The application of this analysis to the trends in factor shares over time is illustrated by an example given by Solow (1958). He estimated that in broad terms the ratio of capital to labour in the United States had increased by 60 per cent over the first half of the twentieth century. If $\sigma = \frac{2}{3}$, which would be in line with some (but not all) empirical studies, and the initial share of capital were 30 per cent, then the proportionate change in the share of capital would have been:

$$0.7 \text{ times } (1 - 3/2) \text{ times } 60 \text{ per cent} = 21 \text{ per cent}$$

In other words, the share of capital would have gone down by about one-fifth, or from 30 per cent to 24 per cent, and as Solow says 'this is just the order of magnitude observed'. He does not, of course, mean by this that the issue is settled, but that the orthodox theory could at least be consistent with the evidence.[1]

The orthodox theory has been the subject of considerable criticism. It is not possible here to cover all the issues which have been raised in a long, and often bad-tempered, debate, and we focus on two areas which relate to the basic assumptions: the absence of perfect competition and the problems which arise in trying to derive an aggregate production function.

The assumption of perfect competition is one of analytical convenience, but it does not accord with the market imperfections which appear to characterize most advanced economies. One way in which this assumption can be relaxed is through the straightforward introduction of a degree of monopoly. If a firm possesses monopoly power, it does not hire labour up to the point where the wage equals the value marginal product, but only to the point where the wage equals the marginal *revenue* product:

$$w = (1 - m) \times \text{Value marginal product of labour.}$$

where m represents the degree of monopoly.[2] In this way, if the monopoly profit is assumed to accrue to the owners of capital, the relative share of labour is reduced to only $(1 - m)$ times its previous value. (This explanation has some similarity with that put forward by Kalecki and discussed in the next section.)

An empirical test of this variation on the orthodox theory can be made simply by comparing the observed wage share with that predicted

---

[1] In order to conclude that it is consistent, we need of course to take into account the impact of technical progress, since technology clearly changed between 1900 and 1949. If technical progress is assumed to be labour- or capital-'augmenting', then the relevant consideration becomes the 'effective' capital–labour ratio, taking account of the increasing efficiency of the inputs over time. If labour- and capital-saving innovations had tended to balance each other, then the calculation described above would remain valid.

[2] The degree of monopoly is the reciprocal of the elasticity of demand.

from the production function. As we have seen, Douglas claimed that the competitive case ($m = 0$) provided a good fit with the evidence, but more recent studies cast doubt on this conclusion. Thurow (1968) has estimated a production relationship which is similar to that described earlier but allows for technical progress and unemployment, and from this obtained an estimate of the ratio between the wage and the value marginal product. In 1929 this ratio was 58 per cent and by 1965 it had risen to 63 per cent. Taken at its face value, this suggests that the share of labour may be reduced by the monopoly power of employers, although there are other factors which need to be taken into account, such as the impact of taxes. In the next section, the role of bargaining power, exercised both by employers and by trade unions, is discussed in greater detail.

The second set of difficulties, those associated with the aggregate production function, have greatly occupied theoretical economists during the past twenty years, and they provide a basis for the most sustained attack on the orthodox theory. In some cases this attack has been rather indiscriminate, and it is necessary to isolate the issues involved. Most importantly, it is the *aggregate* nature of the theory of factor shares which is at stake, not the whole of orthodox theory. Hahn and Matthews sum up the situation as follows: 'As far as pure theory is concerned the "measurement of capital" is no problem at all because we never have to face it if we do not choose to. With our armchair omniscience we can take account of each machine separately' (1965, p. 110).

They go on, however, to point out that this is 'of little comfort to the empirically inclined', and this is well illustrated by the present case. The general neoclassical theory is too complex to allow straightforward statements to be made about the determinants of factor shares. For this purpose, short cuts have to be taken, and this is the role of the assumption of an aggregate production function; it is also, however, the source of serious objections to the orthodox approach. We have seen that the main predictions of the theory concerned the relationship between the factor shares and the supply of factors, and the link between the increase in the capital–labour ratio and the fall in the ratio (r/w), via the elasticity of substitution. This assumed that r/w fell as the capital–labour ratio rose, but in fact there is no need why this should necessarily happen in a more general model of production. As was demonstrated in early contributions by Robinson (1953) and Champernowne (1953), it is possible for a higher ratio r/w to be associated with a rise in an index of capital per worker and subsequent work has shown that this cannot be ruled out as an unlikely event.

What are the implications of this demonstration? Quite simply they mean that there is little theoretical foundation for the aggregate production function used as a short-hand earlier in this section. The only justification that can be given is the *ad hoc* one 'that it works in practice'. If one does not accept this argument there is no alternative way of predicting the behaviour of factors shares, other than by solving the whole general equilibrium system. This is possible, but it means that no straightforward results can be obtained. In this form the theory is harder to refute but less useful at a global level.

Before leaving the orthodox theory, it should be noted that it is often referred to as the 'marginal productivity' theory. This term has been avoided here, since it is wrong to suggest, as some authors do, that the 'share of labour is *determined* by its marginal product'. First, the relationships between factor prices and marginal products are *derived* from more basic assumptions and are not themselves the primary postulates. Secondly, these relationships are consistent with a variety of assumptions about other aspects of the model. As we have seen, in the general case the orthodox theory only relates the relative shares to the factor supplies; it does not complete the explanation of the long-run behaviour of the economy. This closure of the model could indeed involve assumptions similar to some of the alternative approaches described in the next section.

9·3 Alternative approaches

In this section we examine some of the alternative approaches to the determination of factor shares. For this purpose, they are grouped together under three headings.

Bargaining power theories

The bargaining power theories may be divided into those concerned with the monopoly power of firms and those concerned with collective bargaining and union power. The former are represented by the work of Kalecki, who argued that the share of labour depends inversely on the degree of monopoly. As Kalecki described it in 1939, the analysis begins at the level of the individual enterprise, where prices are set by equating marginal revenue and marginal cost. Marginal cost is assumed constant and taken here to include only wage costs. (Kalecki laid considerable stress on raw material costs, but these are omitted for ease of exposition.) Aggregating across enterprises, Kalecki concluded that the share of labour is equal to $(1 - \bar{m})$ where $\bar{m}$ is the average degree of monopoly.[1] In assuming that the latter can be regarded as a

---

[1] If we write p for the output price and α for the labour requirement per unit of output, the marginal revenue = marginal cost condition gives $p(1 - m) = w\alpha$, where m is the inverse of the elasticity of demand and represents the degree of monopoly. The labour share $w\alpha/p$ equals $1 - m$. It may be noted that this differs from the earlier formulation, in that $m = 0$ implies that the labour share is 100 per cent.

macro-economic concept, the Kalecki theory is in effect making the same leap as the orthodox theory from the micro-economic level to an aggregate representation. Just as in the orthodox case, there are problems with such a move; the aggregate degree of monopoly depends, for example, on the relative importance of different industries.

The prediction of the Kalecki model, that the share of wages depends inversely on the degree of monopoly, may be tested by examining whether the share has tended historically to fall when monopoly power increased. This approach has been taken by Phelps Brown (1968), who examines the experiences of the United Kingdom, United States, Sweden, and Germany from 1860 to 1965. As he points out, there are difficulties in observing the degree of monopoly. Kalecki refers to the increasing concentration of industry, and there are statistical indices of concentration covering, for example, the shares in total output of the top three firms. These indices may not, however, reflect the actual degree of monopoly, which could well depend on factors other than market shares.

The evidence from the four countries leads Phelps Brown to conclude that 'there is little to suggest that [the monopolistic pricing] theory has seized on a dominant factor in distribution' (1968, p. 27). For example, he points to the higher share of industrial profits in the United States in the latter part of the nineteenth century, but suggests that there were few grounds for holding that there was a higher degree of monopoly than in Germany or the United Kingdom. It is important to note, however, that he treats changes in international competition as an alternative to the Kalecki explanation, whereas these may well influence the monopoly power of domestic firms, an aspect which has been stressed in recent contributions (see the discussion of the radical approach below).

The theories concerned with collective bargaining have been less precisely formulated, but in general lead to the not unexpected prediction that the share of wages increases with trade union strength. As in the case of the degree of monopoly, there are problems in observing union power. It may be measured by trade union membership or by more subjective measures: Phelps Brown and Hart (1952), for example, refer to the fall in the labour share in Britain following the Taff Vale court decision, which seriously restricted the scope for strikes, and in 1926–8 after the collapse of the General Strike.

The relationship between union membership and the share of labour is discussed by Fleisher (1970). He suggests that the level and growth of membership lead one to expect that the share would be relatively high and/or growing rapidly in 1910–19, 1930–9 and 1939–48, but that this is only borne out in the 1930s. He concludes that 'if one ignores the basic upward trend in both union membership and labour's share over the past sixty years, there is no observable stable relationship between the two series' (1970, p. 186). Rather similar conclusions are reached by Phelps Brown (1968), who points to the failure of the share of labour to rise in the twenty years before the First World War, despite the increased strength of trade unions, but draws atention to the successful resistance to wage cuts during 1921–2 and during the 1930s in the United States, which led to a rise in labour's share. The general conclusion drawn by him was that 'trade unions have taken little effect to narrow the share of profits when they have acted as the hammer' (1968, p. 21), although they have at least once had a permanent effect on labour's share by resisting wage cuts. The validity of these conclusions has been questioned by radical economists, who have suggested that one cannot ignore the general upward trend in union membership and the labour share, and have argued that increased union militancy in recent years has led to a fall in the share of profits.

Accumulation and the Kaldorian theory

Associated with the names of Kaldor and other Cambridge (England) economists is a rather different theory of the determination of factor shares. This theory makes assumptions that permit both aggregation and decomposition of the economic system, in such a way as to allow a straightforward explanation of relative shares.

The main assumptions of this model, as set out in Kaldor (1955^a), are described below:

Assumption It is assumed that the aggregate production relationship may be summarized by a constant ratio of investment to incremental output denoted by v.

This assumption plays the same role as that of the aggregate production function in the orthodox theory. The second assumption is that usually regarded as central to the theory:

Assumption Planned savings are a constant fraction (s_p) of profits and a constant fraction (s_w) of wages, where s_p is greater than s_w.

This has been described as a 'classical' savings hypothesis, in view of the link with classical economists, notably Ricardo, although it did not play a major role in their thinking. The extreme case where s_w is zero corresponds to the Marxian assumption that all accumulation is carried out by capitalists. Finally the theory assumes:

Assumption The economy is on a long-run growth path with an exogenous rate of growth of output fixed in proportional terms.

This can most simply be interpreted in terms of a full employment constraint on output, with the effective labour force growing at a constant proportional rate (the only qualification being that the wage should be above the subsistence level).

For purposes of exposition, let us take the extreme case where s_w is zero. Planned savings are then s_p times profits, and if they are equal to planned investment, we have

$$s_p \times \text{Profits} = \text{Investment} = v \times (\text{Increase in output})$$

so that the share of profits is given by:[1]

$$\frac{\text{Profits}}{\text{Output}} = \frac{v}{s_p} \times (\text{Proportional growth rate of output})$$

We arrive therefore at the conclusion that the share of profits is determined by the propensity to save out of profits, the exogenous rate of growth and the investment-incremental output ratio.

This 'widow's cruse' theory, as it is sometimes called,[2] allows the factor shares to be determined from the equilibrium of planned savings and investment, without regard to the rest of the economic system. In this sense it is decomposable. This decomposition of the economic system is attractive, since it allows definite predictions about the share of profits to be derived from consideration of only a few elements of the economy. The share of profits is, other things being equal, higher when there is a higher ratio of investment to output, and if we compare countries with different propensities to accumulate out of profits (s_p) the share of profits is greater where the rate of savings is lower. The question is, however, whether this model is a plausible representation of the economy.

Two elements play a central role in allowing the decomposition of the economy: the assumption that the ratio v is constant and the assumption of given savings propensities. These are considered in turn. According to Johnson, 'the crucial weakness in the Kaldor theory is that the [ratio v] is assumed not to be influenced by the rate of profit' (1973, p. 202). If we ask what difference it would make if the capital–output ratio became an endogenous variable, it can be shown that the ratio of profits to capital (the rate of profit) is determined by

---

[1] Where workers save, the share of profits is given by the slightly more complicated relationship $(nv - s_w)/(s_p - s_w)$ where n is the rate of growth of output.

[2] So called because any reduction in the savings of capitalists has to be offset by a corresponding rise in profits if equilibrium is to be maintained (if s_p is halved then profits must double): to quote Kaldor 'capitalists earn what they spend, and workers spend what they earn' (1955a, p. 96).

s_p and the rate of growth, independently of the level of v.[1] The assumption is therefore crucial for the determination of the *share* of profit, but not for the *rate* of profit on capital. The importance of distinguishing between these two concepts is demonstrated by the fact that we can link the Kaldorian savings assumption to the earlier orthodox theory. With the assumption of competition made there, the equality of the marginal product of capital with this exogenous rate of profit determines the capital–labour ratio. The share of profits then depends on the properties of the production function: for example, if it is Cobb–Douglas in form then the shares remain constant over time. Although Kaldor would not accept the assumption of perfect competition, this shows how the classical savings function could be used to 'close' the orthodox system.

The assumption of an exogenous investment-incremental output ratio may be seen, therefore, as an alternative to the orthodox aggregate production function. Let us turn now to the second key assumption: the classical savings hypothesis. The plausibility of this assumption has been the subject of debate. The supporters argue that it captures an important feature of growth in capitalist economies–the role of capital accumulation out of profits–and reference has already been made to the classical antecedents. The critics, on the other hand, have asked why savings propensities should differ between classes of income.

In an early contribution, Pasineti (1961) pointed to the need to distinguish between differential savings propensities according to source of income and different propensities by social classes. Where workers save, it becomes important to know whether they save a fraction s_p of the profits paid to them or whether they save the same fraction s_w as they save out of wages. Kaldor inclines to the former view, on the grounds that 'the high savings propensity out of profits attaches to the nature of business income, and not to the wealth (or other peculiarities) of the individuals who own property' (1966, p. 310). This raises the issue as to how far corporate behaviour can be viewed independently of personal savings decisions:

the addition to the real assets of corporations made possible by corporate savings must affect share values, and in the long run it is difficult to see how share values can diverge widely from the value of real assets. Change in share values is likely to have an influence on the saving behaviour of the owners of the shares (Hahn and Matthews, 1965, p. 23).

Where corporate saving leads to a rise in share values of an equal amount, and where this capital gain is regarded by share-holders as fully

---

[1] Profits divided by capital equal $(^1/s_p)$ × (investment/capital).

equivalent to personal savings, the higher corporate saving is exactly offset by a corresponding reduction of personal saving. The firms are simply saving on behalf of the share-holders. This takes a rather extreme view of the behaviour of share-holders and the stock market, but it may not be inappropriate in a long-run context and points to an important difficulty with the Kaldorian version.

The Pasinetti interpretation is based firmly on individual decisions, but here too the plausibility of the differential savings assumptions has been questioned. Some writers have asked why the savings propensities should differ between classes, pointing out that labour could always increase its share of national income by saving more (the converse of the footnote on p. 177). Others have suggested that it is not appropriate to a modern capitalist economy.

One can imagine an economy divided into two quite different distinct social classes . . . The labourers may be imagined . . . to have no need to save for the reason of making provision for old age . . . The capitalist class consists of those who are wealthy, interested in the accumulation of property and in passing it on to their offspring . . . This model, as stylized economic models go, may not be too bad as a representation of the state of England in the eighteenth or the early nineteenth century, but as an even stylized representation of a modern economy it is simply not adequate (Bliss, 1975, Ch. 6).

Similarly, there are objections to the assumption that the savings propensity is uninfluenced by economic variables: 'why is it not influenced by the growth rate, or the rate of interest, or the price of champagne?' (Bliss, 1975, Ch. 6). The capitalist class may possibly accumulate without regard to the return, but if working-class saving is interpreted in life-cycle terms, then it is very likely to be influenced by the rate of interest. The incorporation of such considerations is clearly a major requirement before the class savings theory can be accepted.

At an empirical level, the Kaldorian theory can be tested in a variety of ways. It is possible to investigate the evidence concerning particular assumptions, especially the classical saving hypothesis; alternatively the predictions of the theory may be tested directly, by examining the relationship between the share of profits and the ratio of investment to total output (using the first equation on p. 177, or a modified version allowing for savings by workers). Since we observe actual rather than planned magnitudes, such a test is of limited value, but it may give some indication whether the theory is at least consistent with the historical record. In the United States Reder showed that the evidence for full employment periods was 'not inconsistent with the acceptance of Kaldor's theory' (1959, p. 190) after 1921, but not in the period 1909–14. Phelps Brown (1968) has similarly pointed out that the shifts through the years of the First World War cast doubt on the theory, although he recognizes that the share of profits moved in parallel with the proportion of output invested at other times.

Marxian and radical theories

Since the mid-1960s there has been a great growth of interest in radical economics. This growth was to a considerable extent stimulated by political events, but at an academic level its achievements include the establishment in the USA of the Union for Radical Political Economics and the introduction of radical economics curricula at many universities. The radical view had in fact by 1971 reached a state of recognition where it was described by Samuelson as 'an important movement in the history of ideas' (Foreword to Lindbeck, 1971).

What is the radical alternative view of the determination of the distribution of income? In part this is defined negatively as being in opposition to the prevailing orthodoxy; as Samuelson pointed out, it 'represents a growing discontent on the part of students with what they are being taught in the universities'. More positively, radical economists have tended to emphasize the role of economic and political power and the exploitation of labour by capital:

radical interpretations of profit and wages emphasize the sociological facts that the capitalist class owns all of the productive facilities and resources, while the working class owns only its own labor power . . . the capitalists . . . receive a large share of national income while putting forth no effort (or, as Marx phrased it, under these conditions, they are able to extract, or 'exploit', this profit from the workers' product) (Hunt and Sherman, 1972, pp. 226–7).

The influence of Marxist analysis is clearly illustrated by this statement (although it should be noted that in other areas radical economists have been much less subject to this influence). There is not sufficient space here to describe the Marxian scheme of analysis in full or to consider the whole range of possible interpretations. The central concept for our purpose, however, is the rate of exploitation,[1] or the ratio of surplus value to variable capital. This ratio is often expressed in terms of the division of the working day into the time which a person

[1] For a discussion of the suggestive nature of this terminology, see Robinson (1966, p. 21), where she compares it with the alternative use of the term 'exploitation' by Pigou to denote the difference between wages under perfect competition and under imperfect competition, and argues that by the latter 'the reader is unconsciously lulled into the conclusion that, as long as competition prevails, labour receives all that it can rightly claim'. (Pigovian exploitation is measured by the term m on p. 172.)

works for himself and the time which he works for the capitalist: a ratio equal to 1 means, for example, that half the working day is 'paid' labour and the other half 'unpaid'.

The distribution of income depends on the rate of exploitation, but there is no straightforward way in which this concept can be related to actual changes in money profits and wages.[1] The application by modern radical economists of Marxian analysis to the behaviour of observed factor shares has, therefore, tended not to work within the formal theoretical framework but to take over qualitative elements stressed by Marx, in particular the relative bargaining power of capital and labour: 'as radical economists see it, the shares of national income going to workers and to property owners are largely determined by the relative power of the two groups' (Gurley, 1971, p. 59).

One important example of this approach is the study of Britain in the 1950s and 1960s by Glyn and Sutcliffe, referred to earlier in this chapter, which attributes the rise in the share of wages in recent years to a change in bargaining power. They argue that there has been an intensification of international competition with the reduction in trade barriers and spread of multinational companies. This has more than offset the reduction in domestic competition arising from increasing concentration of British industry, so that the monopoly power of firms has diminished:

as the period went on increases in money wages came to have a bigger and bigger effect in reducing the profit share. Our explanation is that in the early fifties, when international competition was weak, increases in money wages could be easily passed on in higher prices, whereas by the middle and late sixties only a much smaller proportion of wage increases could be passed on (1972, pp. 60–1).

At the same time, they argue that recent years have seen an increase in union militancy and in the ability of workers to secure wage increases. They conclude that 'the basic reason for the decline in the profit share was the squeezing of profit margins between money wage increases on the one hand and progressively more severe international competition on the other' (p. 65).

This analysis, although not necessarily its conclusions, has been challenged by a number of writers. As we saw at the beginning of the chapter, Glyn and Sutcliffe's choice of end-years tended to exaggerate the magnitude of the long-run downward trend, although from Fig. 9·1 it can be seen that the direction clearly remains downward, even if one

[1] Desai, for example, argues that 'a Marxian analysis cannot rely on data on wages . . . to prove exploitation' (1974, p. 57).

takes years which are comparable. They were primarily concerned with profits before tax, whereas profits after tax show a less marked decline, reflecting the reduced burden of company taxation. More generally, there are statistical difficulties in trying to explain one part of the economic system in isolation from other, simultaneously determined elements. To take one example, changes in wages and profits affect prices, and the rate of price increase may in turn influence wage demands and levels of profitability. The simple equations used to explain changes in profits may well not adequately account for such inter-relationships. For this kind of reason, the analysis of Glyn and Sutcliffe, while suggestive, cannot be regarded as definitive.

The radical explanation of relative shares in terms of the power of labour and capital offers little as yet that is new at a theoretical level; indeed the Glyn and Sutcliffe interpretation does no more than combine the two elements of bargaining power discussed at the beginning of this section—monopoly and union strength. Radical economists have not as yet provided a more explicit analysis of relative power which would depart from existing theories.[1] Solow (comment on Gurley, 1971) pointed out that there have been no studies by radical economists relating changes in distributive shares to independent measures of the distribution of power in society, and this led him to conclude that the contribution of radical economics had been negligible'. A more sympathetic view would conclude that, while at present radical economics has not as yet led to any major departures, it may bring about a shift in emphasis and lead to more thorough investigation of the considerations missing from the orthodox theory.

9·4 Factor shares and the personal distribution of income

After struggling with the preceding sections, the reader will probably agree with Marshall's pronouncement about the problem of distribution with which we began this chapter. We have seen that alternative theories have attempted to simplify the economic system so as to throw light on the determinants of the shares of wages and profits, but that this distillation brought with it many problems. The theories all emphasize aspects of the real world which are clearly important—the role of technology, the contribution of accumulation to growth, the strength of unions and employers, and the class interests of workers and capitalists—but none seems by itself fully adequate as an explanation of the observed pattern. In view of this, no attempt is made here at any

[1] Similarly, they do not deny the role played by factor supplies. The quotation from Gurley (1971) continues by pointing out that 'relative factor supplies set limits within which the power exerts itself'.

kind of conclusion; instead, this final section considers briefly the relationship between factor shares and the personal distribution which is the main concern of the book.

At the beginning of this chapter, reference was made to the Ricardian identification of factor income with the three main classes of society:

Labour income ⟶ workers
Capital income ⟶ capitalists
Rent ⟶ landlords

While this class identification may still have relevance today, account must be taken of changes in the economic and social structure of society which have taken place since Ricardo wrote.

The first change concerns the ownership of capital. The Ricardian classification is based on the assumption that the working class owns no capital, but in a present day advanced economy most workers have accumulated some savings for life-cycle reasons. The fact that people save for old age, either contractually or on their own account, means that part of the income from capital accrues to pensioners or members of the working population. Part of the profits of General Motors may be paid in dividends to an elderly widow with a few hundred dollars of saving or may go to a pension fund which in turn pays benefits to pensioners with low incomes. A closely related phenomenon is the spread of home ownership, which means that part of the share of rents accrues to occupiers rather than landlords.

The second change concerns the development of institutions which stand between the productive sector of the economy and the household sector. We referred just now to pension funds. These funds act as intermediaries, owning assets but having liabilities to the household sector, so that part of the income from capital is channelled through their hands. The entire company sector is indeed of this form. Profits accrue to companies, and they make decisions about their disposition, either paying them out as dividends or retaining them for investment in the company. In the latter case they do not immediately form part of personal income. On the other hand, as we have seen in the discussion of the Kaldor model, the share-holders may nonetheless benefit as a result of capital gains, these forming the counterpart in personal income of the retained profits which appear as part of national income.

A third major change has been the increase in the role of the state, which also acts as an intermediary between the productive sector and household incomes. Part of the wealth of the personal sector is held in the form of government bonds and other government liabilities. The interest paid on this national debt is a component of personal income, even though it has no counterpart in a return to a productive factor. While government taxes and transfers may be seen as redistributing a given pre-tax income, some transfers are commonly treated as 'original' income: for example, the *Blue Book* figures discussed in early chapters included state pensions as 'pre-tax' income. Taxes on companies must also be taken into account. As noted earlier, the share of profits in before tax terms has fallen more sharply than profits after tax. Before tax profits have received most attention in the literature, but it is profits after tax that are relevant to the personal distribution.

These considerations mean that total *national* income does not match up directly with the total *personal* income, as will be clear to anyone who has tried to do it from the national accounts. In broad terms, to go from gross national product to personal income as defined in earlier chapters, we have to take the following steps:

	Gross national product
−	Depreciation
=	National income
−	Retained company profits
−	Taxes on companies (e.g. corporation tax)
−	Profits accruing to government
+	Government transfers to persons (e.g. pensions)
+	Interest paid by government
+	Capital gains
+	Missing imputed income (e.g. home production)
=	Personal income before tax

In order to relate the distribution by factor shares to that by persons we have, therefore, to trace through these links and to take account of classes of income, such as government transfers, which did not appear in our earlier discussion.

The second consequence of the changes since the time of Ricardo is that the interests of different classes have become somewhat blurred. The worker may also be receiving profit income via his rights to a pension fund and may also benefit from (imputed) rent via the ownership of his house. It does not necessarily follow that a rise in the share of property is to the benefit of those at the top of the income distribution. At the same time, the concentration of wealth remains such that in general it is the rich for whom income from profits is important and the rest of the population who depend primarily on wage income or state benefits. If we regard earnings and transfers as 'labour' income, and the remainder as 'property' income, we may use the simple formula given by Meade (1964): if the top 5 per cent in the income distribution receive a per cent of the income from earnings and b per cent of the income from property, then their share in total income is given by

$$(a \times \text{Share of earnings}) + (b \times \text{share of property})$$

If a were 15 per cent and b were 55 per cent (Meade takes rather higher figures for 1959), then the overall share in total income of the top 5 per cent would rise from 17 per cent, if the share of property were 5 per cent, to 25 per cent, if the share of property were 25 per cent. Changes in the share of earnings and property income may therefore still have a significant effect on the share of the top income groups.

10
POVERTY

A decent provision for the poor is the true test of civilisation

(Samuel Johnson, 1770)

In earlier chapters we have examined the distribution of income among the population as a whole; we now focus attention on the lower part of the income scale and the problem of poverty in Britain and the United States.

10·1 The definition of poverty

What exactly do we mean by poverty in countries such as Britain and the United States? This question has generated a great deal of controversy. Indeed there are those who would argue that it is absurd to talk about poverty in present day advanced countries, since those considered poor in the United States today have an income greater than the *average per capita* income of a hundred years ago, to say nothing of their being many times better off than the average Indian today. While it is true that low income families in Britain and the United States would rank high on a world income scale, or in relation to the past, it is misleading to suggest that poverty may be seen in terms of an absolute standard which can be applied to all countries and at all times, independent of the social structure and level of development. A poverty line is necessarily defined in relation to social conventions and the contemporary living standards of a particular society, and in this way somebody in the United States may be adjudged poor even though he has a higher income than the average person in India.

In order to bring out the reasons why poverty cannot be meaningfully defined in an absolute way, it may be useful to consider the work of Rowntree in Britain and of Orshansky in the United States. Rowntree, in his study of poverty in York in 1899, was the first to consider in any detail the problems involved in defining poverty, and clearly saw his approach as being based on absolute lines: a family was considered to be living in poverty if its total earnings were 'insufficient to obtain the minimum necessaries for the maintenance of merely physical efficiency' (1901, p. 117). For this purpose he used estimates by the American nutritionist Atwater to calculate the minimum requirements of protein and calories. These requirements were translated into 'a diet containing the necessary nutrients at the lowest cost compatible with a certain amount of variety' (p. 129). The resulting menus were not ones that made the mouth water, as is shown in that for Tuesdays:

Breakfast	porridge and skim milk
lunch	bread and cheese
Dinner	vegetable broth, bread, cheese, dumpling
Supper	bread and porridge

To the expenditure on food were added certain minimum amounts for clothing, fuel and household sundries. This gave a poverty standard in 1899 of 5s 6d for a single person, 9s 2d for a couple and £1 0s 6d for a couple with four children, with the addition in each case of the rent paid.[1] This treatment of rent was based on the assumption that it was outside the control of the household.

The work of Orshansky, which provided the basis for much of the recent research on poverty in the United States, was similar to that of Rowntree, in that she took as her starting point estimates of minimum food expenditures. These were developed by the United States Department of Agriculture and were based on judgements regarding an acceptable trade-off between nutritional standards and consumption patterns. The calculation of total income requirements took a rather different form. On the basis of household budget data, Orshansky (1965) estimated the proportion of income spent on food in families of different sizes, and multiplied the minimum cost diet by the reciprocal of this proportion. If the cost of food requirements for a family of four was $1000 per annum and the proportion of income spent on food was ⅓, this would give a poverty standard of $3000. The resulting poverty standard in 1962 ranged from $1900 for a couple with no children to $3130 for a family with two, and to over $5000 for a family of five children.

Attractive as this absolute poverty approach may be at first sight, it involves a number of serious conceptual difficulties, as has been pointed out by Townsend (1954), Rein (1970), and others. Most importantly, there is no single 'subsistence' level which can be used as a basis for the poverty line. Even in the case of food, which might appear to provide the firmest foundation, it is difficult to determine requirements with any precision. There is no one level of food intake required for subsistence, but rather a broad range where physical efficiency declines with a falling intake of calories and proteins. Moreover, an individual's nutritional needs depend on his level of activity, the office worker requiring less than a miner or a farm worker. Where precisely the line is

[1] Equivalent to 27½p, 46p and £1·02½p in decimal currency. All amounts referred to subsequently have been converted to decimals.

drawn depends, therefore, on the judgement of the investigator and the idea of a purely physiological basis for the poverty criterion is lost.

Even if nutritional requirements could be determined in terms of calories, protein, etc., there would still be problems arising from the disparity between expert judgement and actual consumption behaviour. This disparity is highlighted by calculations like those of Stigler (1945), who showed that the minimum cost of a nutritively adequate diet for an adult male was some $100 a year (in current prices). Not only do housewives lack the dietary knowledge required to calculate the least cost foods, not only are poor families forced to purchase food in uneconomical ways,[1] but also eating habits are profoundly influenced by social conventions. This was recognized by Rowntree in his inclusion of items such as tea, which has little or no nutritional value, but which people will not go without (in this context he refers to the riot which took place in Bradford workhouse when they tried to replace tea by a more nutritive gruel). Orshansky stated explicitly that 'social conscience and custom dictate that there be not only sufficient quantity but sufficient variety to meet recommended nutritional goals and conform to customary eating patterns. Calories alone are not enough' (1965, p. 5).

In the case of non-food items, there is an even greater degree of arbitrariness. Rowntree's 1950 standard included 2p a week for wireless, 3p for a daily newspaper and 34p for beer, tobacco, presents, holidays and books. It is hard to justify the inclusion of these items on an absolute subsistence definition. As Townsend (1962) has pointed out, 'a family might maintain its physical efficiency just as well in a caravan . . . as in a three-bedroom house. It could go to bed early and spend nothing on electricity.' The approach adopted by Orshansky avoided this kind of judgement, but has been criticized on other grounds. Friedman (1965) has argued that the proportion of income spent on food was under-estimated, and hence the allowance for non-food needs *over*-estimated. (In terms of the example given earlier, if the proportion of income spent on food were 40 per cent rather than $\frac{1}{3}$, this would give a poverty standard of $2500 rather than $3000.)

All these considerations point to the fact that the Rowntree/Orshansky approach conveys a misleading impression of concreteness, and that any meaningful poverty line is inevitably influenced by the contemporary living standards. A poverty line cannot be defined in a vacuum, but only in relation to a particular society at a particular date.

[1] For example, through being unable to exploit the economies of bulk buying. For discussion of whether in general 'the poor pay more', see Caplovitz (1963), Alcaly and Klevorick (1971) and Piachaud (1974).

Poverty must be seen not in *absolute* but in *relative* terms:

People are 'poor' because they are deprived of the opportunities, comforts, and self-respect regarded as normal in the community to which they belong. It is, therefore, the continually moving *average* standards of that community that are the starting points for an assessment of its poverty, and the poor are those who fall sufficiently far below these average standards. (Social Science Research Council, 1968).

The relative nature of poverty has long been recognized. Adam Smith, for example, said in widely quoted passage:

By necessaries, I understand not only the commodities which are indispensably necessary for the support of life but whatever the custom of the country renders it indecent for creditable people, even of the lowest order, to be without. A linen shirt, for example, is strictly speaking not a necessity of life. The Greeks and Romans lived, I suppose, very comfortably though they had no linen. But in the present time . . . a creditable day-labourer would be ashamed to appear in public without a linen shirt, the want of which would be supposed to denote that disgraceful state of poverty (1776, p. 691).

In the same way, Marx referred to the fact that for the worker 'the number and extent of his so-called necessary wants . . . are themselves the product of historical development and depend, therefore, to a great extent on the degree of civilization of a country' (quoted by Coates and Silburn, 1970, p. 24).

Poverty has, therefore, to be interpreted in relation to the living standards of the society in question, and in this sense it is reasonable to regard some people in the United States as poor even though, as Harrington (1962) put it, they live better than medieval knights or Asian peasants.

It is, however, important to clear up two possible misconceptions. First, it should be emphasized that the adoption of a relative poverty standard does *not* mean that the poor are necessarily always with us. It is sometimes suggested that if, for example, we define the poverty line as half the average income, moving up with the general standard of living, then poverty cannot be abolished. On the contrary, it is quite possible to imagine a society in which no one has less than half the average income—in which there is no poverty according to this definition. The adoption of a relative concept of poverty does not prejudge the issue as to its extent. Secondly, the fact that the poverty line may rise with the general level of incomes is not simply a matter of 'keeping up with the Joneses'. It is a reflection of the interdependence of standards of living, as is well described by Jencks:

The goods and services that made it possible to live on $15 a week during the Depression were no longer available to a family with the same 'real' income in 1964 . . . many cheap foods had disappeared from the stores. Most people had enough money to buy an automobile, so public transportation had atrophied, and families without automobiles were much worse off than during the Depression . . . a person without a telephone could not get or keep many jobs . . . During the depression, many people could not afford indoor plumbing and 'got by' with a privy. By the 1960s, privies were illegal in most places. Those who could not afford an indoor toilet ended up in buildings which had broken toilets. (1972, p. 5).

Official poverty standards

This concept of relative poverty may be translated into hard cash in a variety of ways. Indeed, as soon as we recognize the relative nature of poverty, we must accept that there can be no single definition. The choice of a poverty standard is a political decision and, as the Social Science Research Council (1968) put it, 'views on the subject are as varied and conflicting as the social philosophies from which they spring'.

In Britain, nearly all postwar investigations of the extent of poverty have taken as their definition the scale of eligibility for the means-tested social security scheme of Supplementary Benefits (previously National Assistance). In other words, a family is considered to be in poverty if its income is below the level at which it would qualify for Supplementary Benefits. This approach has a number of shortcomings, but the level does represent an 'official' view of the minimum standard of income at a certain date—it is the floor set by the government to the social security system. To quote Abel-Smith and Townsend, who used this definition in their study *The poor and the poorest* :

Whatever may be said about the adequacy of the National Assistance Board level of living as a just or publicly approved measure of 'poverty', it has at least the advantage of being in a sense the 'official' operational definition of the minimum level of living at any particular time (1965, p. 17).

Or, as it was put by the National Board for Prices and Incomes (1971), in their report on low pay: 'Parliament has approved scales of supplementary benefits . . . with the result that it has *de facto* expressed a view as to the level of income below which families are in need.' In the United States, an official government poverty standard was set explicitly by the Council of Economic Advisers, who felt that it represented 'a concensus on an approximate standard'.

In what follows, we shall rely heavily on these official definitions of poverty, since much of the available evidence is presented in this form, but it should be stressed that they are open to objections. Social concensus is not necessarily the right way to define a poverty standard, and even if it is accepted, it is not clear that the Council of Economic Advisers have set the appropriate level. While the Supplementary Benefit scale has been approved by the British parliament as a minimum income level, it does not necessarily enjoy widespread social approval as a national minimum and may well not provide the resources required to participate in the customary activities of the society in which people live. An attempt to get closer to the latter conception has been made, for example, by Townsend in his 1968—9 survey of poverty in Britain, which investigated whether below a certain income level a significant number of families reduce their participation in the community's style of living. As he recognizes, there is no unitary and clearcut national 'style of living', but he suggests that there are types of consumption and customs which may be indicative: for example, in operational terms, owning a refrigerator, having had a holiday away from home in the past year, having sole use of an indoor WC, having parties on children's birthdays.

An important objection to the use of the official poverty standards is that they are based purely on money income and ignore other aspects of deprivation. No account is taken of poor quality housing, schools or health care, which may or may not be associated with low money incomes. No account is taken of the limited availability of community facilities, parks, playgrounds, transport, and of other environmental inequalities. Moreover, poverty may represent only one aspect of a more general powerlessness, an inability to influence one's environment. As described by Kincaid, 'lack of money is only one element in a complex of deprivations which make up the experience of poverty' (1973, p. 172).

10·2 The extent of poverty in Britain

In this section we describe the evidence about poverty in Britain, as measured by the official Supplementary Benefit scale. Before doing so, we should note certain implications of adopting this poverty standard. Firstly, it means that poverty is being measured in terms of current money income defined on a weekly basis. As we saw in Chapter 3, such a short assessment period may indeed be considered appropriate when we are concerned with the extent of poverty. Secondly, Supplementary Benefits are assessed for a family unit. The payment is based on the income of an adult, dependent spouse and children, but not on that of non-dependent members of the same household, such as a grown-up son or daughter. This means that all intra-household transfers (e.g. contributions to the housekeeping) should in theory be taken into account. Thirdly, the Supplementary Benefit scale rates for families of different sizes embody equivalence scales, the rate for a single person being some 60 per cent of that for a couple, and so on. The rationale of these equivalence scales is not very clear, and it has been suggested by some writers, notably Wynn (1970), that they make inadequate allowance for the needs of older children. A further feature of the Supplementary Benefit scale is that, like the Rowntree scale, it is defined exclusive of housing costs. The poverty standard consists therefore of a fixed scale—so much per adult, child, etc.—plus the rent or other housing outlay. In this way, the scale makes an approximate allowance for variations in the cost of living, housing costs being the element with the greatest regional variation.

TABLE 10·1

British Supplementary Benefit scale in relation to average earnings and expenditure[a]

| | Supplementary Benefit scale (1972) as % of | |
	Earnings of average employee[b]	Average expenditure of household of that type
Single pensioner	24	75
Pensioner couple	34	55
Married couple with:		
1 child (aged 7)	41	42
2 children (aged 4, 7)	45	37
4 children (aged 4, 7, 10, 12)	59	c
Fatherless family with		
2 children (aged 4, 7)	34	c

Notes: [a]The Supplementary Benefit scale includes an allowance for average housing outlay.
[b]This is the overall average earnings figure, not that for a particular household type.
[c]Not available.

The Supplementary Benefit scale is set out in Table 10·1, where it is expressed as a proportion of the general level of average earnings, as well as average expenditure, for a household of a given type. In broad terms, the poverty standard ranges from three-quarters to well under half of the average expenditure, so that it can scarcely be described as generous. When Rowntree drew up his poverty standard, he stressed that:

the standards adopted ... err on the side of stringency rather than extravagance ... as I have pursued my investigation, I have been increasingly impressed by the fact that to keep a family of five in health on [£2·65] a week (in 1936) ... needs constant watchfulness and a high degree of skill on the part of the housewife (1941, p. 29).

Today the government do not publish the breakdown of how they expect the Supplementary Benefit to be budgeted, but the position is well illustrated in the study by Lister (1972) of eighteen families living below the Supplementary Benefit scale. Their standard of living was clearly higher than that of Rowntree's families, as indicated by the high proportion with television sets. but in some respects the picture was depressingly similar: the children had no pocket money and 'the occasional cigarette was the greatest luxury many enjoyed'.

The main sources of evidence about poverty in Britain are official statistics. In Chapter 4 we examined the Inland Revenue's estimates of the distribution of income, based on tax returns, and these have been used by Gough and Stark (1968) to measure the extent of poverty. The Inland Revenue surveys, as published, provide inadequate coverage of those with low incomes; in particular, many old people do not appear in the statistics. Moreover, the figures leave out most social security benefits and hence understate the incomes of those who are un-employed or sick. The modified version of the statistics published (until 1967) in *National income and expenditure* makes corrections for these problems, but these estimates are not classified by family size, so that one cannot relate income to needs. As a result, the income tax source can only be used if it is adjusted in a number of important respects.

The estimates of Gough and Stark make allowance for some of these shortcomings, although they have had to make assumptions about the ages of children and about average rent. The results for 1954, 1959, and 1963 are shown in the upper part of Table 10·2 and indicate that around 10 per cent of the population had incomes below the poverty scale—or five million people. It should be emphasized that these figures relate to incomes including all social security benefits in payment; so that five million people appeared to be in poverty even after allowing for the impact of social policy.

The second main official source is the *Family expenditure survey*, which was used by Abel-Smith and Townsend in their influential study *The poor and the poorest* (1965). They had access to the raw returns from the surveys of 1953—4 and 1960, and used these to estimate the proportion of households below the National Assistance scale (in

TABLE 10·2

Summary of recent poverty studies in the United Kingdom

Year	Study	Source	Percentage of population below National Assistance/ Supplementary Benefit scale	Approximate number of persons (millions)
1954	Gough and Stark	IR	12·3	6·3
1959	Gough and Stark	IR	8·8	4·6
1963	Gough and Stark	IR	9·4	5·1
1953–4	Abel-Smith and Townsend	FES	1·2	0·6
1960	Abel-Smith and Townsend	FES	3·8	2·0
1967	Atkinson	FES	3·5	2·0
1969	Atkinson	FES	3·4	2·0
1972	Government	FES	3·2	1·8

Sources: Gough and Stark (1968, Table IV), Abel-Smith and Townsend (1965, Table 25), Atkinson (1969, Table 2·2 and 1974), *The Times*, (8 July 1974).

Notes: IR = Inland Revenue survey
FES = Family expenditure survey

1953—4 this was assessed in terms of expenditure and in 1960 in terms of income). The *Family expenditure survey* avoids a number of the problems inherent in the Inland Revenue survey. Its definition of income includes social security benefits; there are no problems about double-counting; fewer units are excluded[1] and it provides more information about needs. It is, however, based on an extremely small sample (covering about 1 person in 2500); there are problems due to non-response and possible under-reporting of income; there are difficulties in 'blowing up' the results to cover the whole population; and the basic unit in the published tabulations is the household, rather than the family unit relevant to assessing eligibility for assistance.

The poverty standard adopted by Abel-Smith and Townsend was the National Assistance scale (including rent) plus 40 per cent. The purpose of the 40 per cent addition was to allow for the fact that the incomes of persons receiving assistance could be higher than the basic scale because of additional allowances (e.g. for heating, special diets, etc.) or items of income disregarded by the National Assistance Board (e.g. the first part of a disability pension). However, for comparability with the other studies, Table 10·2 focuses attention on the population below the basic scale. As can be seen from the table, they found in 1960 that 3·8 per cent of the population had incomes below the National Assistance scale. This figure is considerably less than the estimate by Gough and Stark for 1959, but nonetheless indicates that a substantial number of people—two million—were at or below the poverty line (the reasons for the differences between the two estimates are discussed below). A further 5½ million had incomes within 40 per cent of the assistance scale:

	Percentage of population	Numbers (approx.)
below 80% scale	0·9	½ million
below NA scale	3·8	2 million
below 140% scale	14·2	7½ million

The basic returns of the *Family expenditure survey* have not been made available to subsequent investigators for this purpose, but it is possible to make approximate estimates from the published tabulations. Lines 6 and 7 of Table 10·2 show estimates made for the late 1960s. Since these involve assumptions about the housing costs of each family and about the ages of children, they must be regarded with considerable caution. At the same time, they are in the same broad

[1] The exclusions are, however, important. The survey, being concerned only with households, leaves out the homeless and those living in institutions.

range as the Abel-Smith and Townsend estimates, and suggest that the extent of poverty did not decline dramatically during the 1960s. This is supported by the last line of Table 10·2, which shows the results of official estimates made using the basic *Family expenditure survey* returns for 1972.

From Table 10·2 it is clear that the two sources, the Inland Revenue survey and the *Family expenditure survey*, lead to rather different results. The discrepancy may in part be explained by differences in the methods adopted. As we have seen, the Supplementary Benefit scale is based on the family unit. Abel-Smith—Townsend, and Atkinson, however, were forced by the unavailability of data to use a household unit, and this leads to an understatement of the incidence of poverty. For example, a substantial number of pensioners live in households containing other adults. Unless these other members of the households also had incomes below or close to the poverty line, the pensioners would not have appeared to have been poor in the Abel-Smith—Townsend and Atkinson estimates, even though they might have had incomes (including any intra-household transfers) below the assistance scale.

Secondly, use of the *Family expenditure survey* is likely to lead to an understatement of the extent of poverty because it is based on normal income rather than current income. Those people who have been out of work for less than three months are recorded as continuing to receive their normal earnings, although they may well be receiving considerably less. The evidence of the Ministry of Social Security (1967) enquiry into families with two or more children showed that in the case of low income families where the father was sick or unemployed, about a third of the men had been off work for less than three months and would have appeared in the *Family expenditure survey* as being above the Supplementary Benefit scale, when in fact, their current incomes were below it. Further support for believing that the estimates of Abel-Smith—Townsend and Atkinson are too low is provided by a 'minimum' estimate made for 1966 on the basis of the surveys of the incomes of retirement pensioners (Ministry of Pensions and National Insurance, 1966), and families receiving family allowances (Ministry of Social Security, 1967), which gave a figure of 3·7 per cent for the two groups alone. (These surveys took a family unit and current income.)

Thirdly, in the case of the Inland Revenue survey, the use of annual income leads to an understatement of the number with incomes below the Supplementary Benefits scale in a given week. Moreover, no allowance is made for any income tax or National Insurance contributions paid, so that take-home pay may be lower than suggested by their figures. On the other hand, the needs of an income unit may be overstated (where children are born in the course of the year or married persons die); there is some overstatement as a result of the assumptions about family composition; and spurious extra income units may appear (e.g. children or students with earnings). As a result, there may be an overstatement of the numbers below the poverty line.

Finally, it is important to distinguish between people *at* the Supplementary Benefit level and those who are strictly below it, and the different studies have made this distinction with varying degrees of accuracy. The estimates of Gough—Stark and Atkinson, because of the assumptions made about needs and the aggregated form of the income data, probably included some people at the Supplementary Benefit level and hence overstate the numbers strictly below. This is likely to be particularly important in the case of the annual Inland Revenue data, and could well make a sizeable difference. On the other hand, the official estimate for 1972 excluded all those receiving Supplementary Benefit, and this gives an underestimate, since some of those receiving benefit are actually below the scale as a result of the 'wage stop'.[1]

In broad terms, it appears that the number of people living below the poverty line in Britain lies somewhere between the *Family expenditure survey* based estimates of 3½ per cent of the population and the Inland Revenue survey based estimates of around 9 per cent. The former figure is too low and the latter is probably too high. Exactly where between these two estimates the true figure lies cannot be determined on the basis of the information now available. It is also important to remember that it is not just the *number* of people beneath the poverty line that is important, but also the *extent* to which they fall below. We should clearly be more concerned if the poverty gap were £5 than if it were a few pence. A full analysis again requires better data than exist at present.

The fact that a significant minority of the population in Britain today lives below the Supplementary Benefit level is widely accepted; much more controversial is the question whether the incidence of poverty is declining over time. In 1970, for example, there was a long debate about whether the poor had become poorer under the Labour government. Such questions are clearly difficult to setle. First, there is the change in the poverty standard to allow for rising prices and incomes. Although the general trend in the Supplementary Benefit scale has been in line with average earnings, there have been considerable year-to-year variations. In the 1953—60 period considered by Abel-Smith and Townsend, the real value of the National Assistance scale for

---

[1] The wage stop is a regulation which means that if a person has normal earnings below the assistance scale he will not receive the full level of benefit if he is out of work.

a single pensioner rose by 11 per cent, whereas the average real disposable income per person increased by 24 per cent. This means that the poverty standard applied by Abel-Smith and Townsend rose less rapidly than the incomes of the general population, so that if all incomes had risen proportionately, we should have expected the measured extent of poverty to decline. Secondly, there are demgraphic changes. These were discussed by Abel-Smith and Townsend, who pointed to the rise between 1953 and 1960 in the proportion of the population over 65 and in the number of families with six or more children. To this extent the increase in poverty shown by their figures can be attributed to an increase in the population at risk, rather than to a worsening of the position of old people and large families. Thirdly, there are changes in the form in which the data are available: for example, Abel-Smith and Townsend's 1953 results related to expenditure, but those of 1960 related to income.

These qualifications should be borne in mind when considering the fragmentary evidence about the trends in the incidence of poverty provided by the studies listed in Table 10·2. The only broad conclusion which can be drawn is that there is no clear indication in recent years of a trend towards the elimination of poverty, defined in terms of the official Supplementary Benefit scale. In these terms, poverty in Britain has remained a problem of considerable magnitude throughout the past twenty years.

10·3 The causes of poverty

The evidence about the immediate causes of poverty in Britain, and the changes which have taken place over this century, is summarized in Table 10·3. The figures for 1953–4, 1960, and 1972 have been estimated from the studies described in the previous section; those for 1899 and 1936 come from the investigations by Rowntree of poverty in York. The differences between York and other parts of the country, and the major social changes which have taken place since 1899, mean that comparisons between the earlier and the later figures must be made with considerable caution. At the same time, it should be noted that the definitions of poverty employed are broadly comparable, since there is a direct line of descent from the Rowntree standard to the Supplementary Benefit scale. (The Beveridge proposals for National Assistance were based on similar calculations to those by Rowntree for his 1936 study.)

The broad trends may therefore be accurately reflected. In particular, it seems safe to conclude that there has been a substantial rise in the importance of old age as a cause of poverty, reflecting demographic changes and the trend towards earlier retirement. Similarly, there has been a decline in the importance of large families (those with 5 or more children), which in 1960 accounted for only one-fifth of the families in poverty where the father was in regular work.

In Rowntree's original 1899 survey, he found that 'the life of a labourer is marked by five alternating periods of want and comparative plenty'. The periods of want were those of childhood, when he himself had children and when he was too old to work. The evidence shown in Table 10·3 suggests that, despite the changes in the relative importance of different causes of poverty, it remains true that poverty is associated with these three stages in a person's life-cycle.

The present day relevance of Rowntree's description may be seen from the experience of a man whose earnings throughout his life are the lowest decile for his age group,[1] and who has the following life history:

Age		
22	One child aged 1	Wife not working
27	Two children aged 3, 6	Wife not working
34	Three children aged 5, 10, 13	Wife not working
44	One dependent child aged 15	Wife at work part-time
54	–	Wife at work part-time
62	–	Wife retired
65	Retired	

The pattern of family income is shown by the solid line in the upper part of Fig. 10·1. Typically, the earnings of low paid workers reach a peak early in their lives and then decline, and this pattern is shown in the diagram, where earnings are at their highest in the 30s. In terms of the lowest decile of the overall distribution, earnings are above this level between the ages of 25 and 49 and he falls below in his 50s. The variation of earnings with age has to be viewed in the light of family needs at different stages of the life-cycle. For this purpose, needs have been assessed on the basis of the Supplementary Benefit scale plus 40 per cent (and rent), following the approach of Abel-Smith and Townsend. The dashed line in the upper part of the diagram shows the earnings that the man would have to make for his family to reach this standard. The variation of need with age has much the same pattern as earnings but is rather more accentuated. As a result, earnings at the lowest decile are less than sufficient to meet the Supplementary Benefit plus 40 per cent standard in earlier years; they are also insufficient as the man nears retirement, when his earnings drop and his wife's

[1] As we saw in Chapter 6, the lowest decile was taken as a definition of low pay by the Prices and Incomes Board. It is not, of course, likely that any one person would remain at the lowest decile throughout his life; the person considered here would undoubtedly be below the lowest decile of *lifetime* earnings.

TABLE 10·3
Immediate causes of poverty, Britain 1899–1972

| | Proportion of people in poverty (%) | | | | |
	1899	1936	1953–4[a]	1960[a]	1972[b]
Old age	}10	15	49	33	55
Sickness		4	7	10	11
Unemployment	2	29	5	7	11
Family with man in work:					
4 or fewer children	55[c]	37	}38	32	}14
5 or more children	22[c]	5		8	
Single-parent family	11	10		10	–

Sources: 1899 estimated from Rowntree (1901) by permission Rowntree
Charitable Trust.
1936 estimated from Rowntree (1941) by permission Rowntree
Charitable Trust.
1953–4 and 1960 estimated from Abel-Smith and Townsend (1965)
1972 *The Times*, 8 July 1974.

Notes: [a]The figures for 1953–4 and 1960 are based on the Abel-Smith/Townsend
poverty line.
[b]In 1972, the sickness and unemployment categories exclude those off
work for less than 3 months. Single parent families were not distinguished separately in the source. (There is a further unclassified group.)
[c]In 1899 families with 5 or more children who would have been below the
poverty line even if they had had 4 or fewer children were allocated by
Rowntree to the '4 or fewer' category (he referred to it as 'low wages').

earnings cease. The lower part of Fig. 10·1 shows the gap between
earnings and needs, measured in £ in 1972, and provides a modern
version of the diagram used by Rowntree to illustrate the life-cycle of
poverty.

An alternative way of viewing the causes of poverty is in terms of the
distinction drawn by Jackson (1972) between poverty caused by
unforeseen interruptions of income, as a result of unemployment,
illness, or the absence of one parent; and poverty related to the
foreseeable life-cycle of need, such as that examined above. One may
have reservations about Jackson's particular classification: for example,
unemployment may be quite foreseeable for many unskilled workers.
Nonetheless, it is interesting to ask how far poverty is associated with
exceptional circumstances and how far it is the normal expectation of
many people at certain stages in their life.

Table 10·3 shows that 'exceptional circumstances' (on Jackson's
classification) accounted for only 27 per cent of those below the
poverty line in 1960. The needs of these households may be very acute,
but they are only a minority of those with incomes below the poverty
line. This situation has not changed very much over the years, leaving
aside the effects of the depression of the 1930s, since in 1899 the

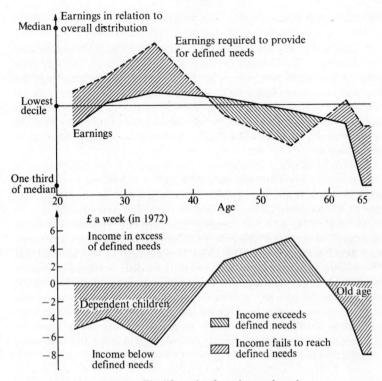

Fig. 10·1. The life-cycle of earnings and need

corresponding figure was 16 per cent. After the social security legislation of the past seventy years, one might have expected to see a considerable decline in the number of those for whom poverty was a normal expectation, and that it would remain only a problem for those with exceptional needs, but this has not happened.

If poverty is the normal expectation for many people at certain ages, it is clearly important to ask whether it is the same people who suffer poverty at these stages of the life-cycle, as was assumed in Fig. 10·1. Was the old age pensioner in poverty in 1960 also unemployed in 1936; and did he grow up in a low wage family of 1899? For this purpose, the figures in Table 10·3 are less helpful, since they represent a 'snapshot' at one point in time and tell us nothing about individual life histories. As we have seen in earlier chapters, very little is in fact known about the lifetime patern of incomes. There is inadequate evidence to measure the continuity of poverty throughout lifetimes or its persistence across generations. At the same time, there is indirect evidence which suggests that this may be a marked feature of our society.

In Chapters 5 and 6 we saw that there are a number of reasons why the children of low wage families are themselves likely to have poor earnings prospects. Not only is there a direct link between earnings and parental socio-economic background, but there is an indirect link via education. There is a relationship between stress conditions at home and poor school performance; and children of poor parents are likely to be encouraged to leave school early, so that they can supplement the family income.

There is similarly a link between low wages at work and poverty in retirement. In Fig. 10·1 the low paid worker was assumed to retire on a state National Insurance pension, but this is less than enough to raise him to the bare Supplementary Benefit level. The state pension may be supplemented by an occupational pension scheme. However, although two-thirds of the male labour force belong to such schemes, fewer low paid workers are covered. The 1970 'New earnings survey' showed that 78 per cent of non-manual male full-time workers belonged to private pension schemes, whereas the corresponding proportion for manual workers was 50 per cent, and for unskilled manual workers 38 per cent. In the same way, the margin for the low paid worker to save on his own account is small and, combined with poor investment opportunities, this means that savings can scarcely be expected to make any significant contribution to incomes in old age.

10·4 Poverty in the United States

Poverty in the United States differs in a number of respects from poverty in Britain: in the nature of the problem, in the way it had been analysed, and in the policies adopted in the hope of securing its elimination. This reflects the dissimilarities in social and economic backgrounds, the variations in the institutions of social policy, and differences in the concerns of people and governments. At the same time, the problems in the two countries have much in common, not the least being the re-awakening of interest in the early 1960s.

The official study of poverty in the United States which marked the opening of the War on Poverty was published in the *Economic report of the President* for 1964. The Council of Economic Advisers, which was responsible for the report, began by making clear that they were concerned with a relative standard of poverty:

society does not have a clear and unvarying concept of an acceptable minimum. By the standards of contemporary American society most of the population of the world is poor; and most Americans were poor a century ago. But for our society today a concensus on an approximate standard can be found (1964, p. 57).

The 'concensus' standard adopted by the CEA for the poverty line was a figure of $3000 per family in 1962 prices. This was based on estimates by the Social Security Administration of budgets for a non-farm family of four persons. The only allowance for differences in family size was that the poverty line for single persons was set at $1500. It may be noted that since in 1962 the median income was $6220, the poverty scale was broadly comparable with the Supplementary Benefit standard in Britain (see the entries for a single person and for a couple with two children in the first column of Table 10·1).

On the basis of this poverty line, the Council estimated that of the 47 million families in the United States, one-fifth were living in poverty in 1962. These families contained 30 million persons, of whom over 11 million were children. Moreover, over 10 per cent of families had total incomes below $2000. This led President Johnson to declare that 'there are millions of Americans—one-fifth of our people—who have not shared the abundance which has been granted to most of us, and on whom the gates of opportunity have been closed'.

The definition of poverty employed by the Council of Economic Advisers was recognized by them as being very crude. The index did not, for example, make adequate allowance for variation of need with family size. The fact that the $3000 standard was applied both to a childless couple and to a family with six children led to biased estimates of the composition of the poor, large families being relatively under-represented. Since that time, the poverty criterion has been refined, following the work of Orshansky referred to earlier, and it now takes account of factors such as family size, the age of the head of the household, and income in kind for farm families (the poverty standard for farm families is some 15 per cent lower).

A further important feature of the official poverty definition is the way in which it is adjusted over time. The Council of Economic Advisers claimed in 1964 that there had been 'substantial progress made since World War II in eliminating poverty', and its estimates showed that the proportion of families living in poverty had declined from 32 per cent in 1947 to 20 per cent in 1962: According to more recent figures, the proportion fell further, to 12 per cent, in 1972. This conclusion depends crucially, however, on the poverty definition. In contrast to the definition used when discussing poverty in Britain, the Council standard only increased over time to allow for rising prices and took no account of the rise in real incomes. As was pointed out in the

Manpower report of the President 1970:

The poverty index makes no allowance for an improvement in living standards, like that enjoyed by the population as a whole during the past decade. Between 1959 and 1968, the median income for all four-person families in the country rose by about one-third in real terms ... But the poverty index for an average family of four was less than $600 higher in 1968 than 1959 ... an increase just large enough to allow for rising prices (US Department of Labor, 1970, p. 120).

If the Council poverty standard were extended back to 1935, rather than 1947, then over 50 per cent would have been below this level: the poverty line would be above the median income.

A different approach, one closer to the British method, is that suggested by Fuchs (1969), who defined the poverty standard as half of the median income. This gives a figure for 1962 very close to the Council of Economic Advisers' definition ($3110), but quite different results for the trends over time: the proportion in poverty was 19 per cent in 1947 and exactly the same in 1970. Fuchs stresses that there is nothing inherent in his approach which leads to the proportions necessarily remaining stable: 'The stability is not due to some mathematical property of the measure, or to some law of nature. It reflects the failure of twenty years of unprecedented prosperity and rapid economic growth to produce any significant change in the distribution of income, at least at the lower end' (1969, p. 202). On this basis, in the United States as in Britain, poverty appears to be an enduring problem.

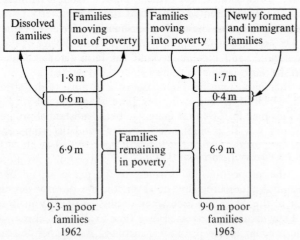

Fig. 10·2. Changes in poverty, United States 1962–63

Stability is important in terms not simply of aggregate numbers, but also of individual life-histories. The United States data throw some light on the continuities discussed in the previous section, at least with regard to year-to-year changes. Fig. 10·2 shows the number of families (in millions) who remained in poverty, according to the Council definition, in both 1962 and 1963. Of the 9·3 million families below the poverty line in 1962, a very substantial number (74 per cent) remained below. Only 1·8 million families moved out of poverty, even though the total fell. Thurow and Lucas (1972) concluded that this data indicated 'a low degree of economic mobility among the poverty population'. More recent evidence quoted by Barth *et al.* (1974) gives a rather different picture for a longer period (1967–71). Of the families in poverty in 1967, only about a third remained poor throughout the next four years; on the other hand, a further 42 per cent showed no consistent tendency to escape from poverty levels of income.

The Council of Economic Advisers devoted considerable attention to the composition of the low income population:

Some believe that most of the poor are found in the slums of the central city, while others believe that they are concentrated in areas of rural blight. Some have been impressed by poverty among the elderly, while others are convinced that it is primarily a problem of minority racial and ethnic groups. But objective evidence indicates that poverty is pervasive ... the poor are found among all major groups in the population and in all parts of the country (1964, pp. 61–2).

TABLE 10·4
Poverty in the United States 1972

Persons	Percentage of total poor in group	Percentage of group below poverty line
Aged 65 and over	15	19
Negro	31	33
In family with female head	33	38
Farm resident	8	21
Resident inside central city	35	14
		(All families 12 per cent)

Source: US Bureau of the Census (1973).

The first column of Table 10·4 confirms that in 1972 the 'high risk' groups identified by the Council did not account for the majority of those below the poverty line. Those aged 65 and over made up only 15 per cent of the total in poverty; there were nearly two whites in

poverty for every black; two out of three people in poverty did not live
in central cities. The figures are not based on exclusive categories, and
one person may appear in two or more rows of the table: for example,
a black woman aged 65 living in New York. For this reason, we cannot
add the figures in the first column. It can, however, be calculated from
the Bureau of the Census source figures that the total number of
persons in poverty who came into one or more of the three categories
(aged, black, or in a family headed by a female) was 14·4 million out of
a total in poverty of 24·5 million in 1972. There was a large number of
people outside these high risk categories who were in poverty—indeed
they accounted for 40 per cent of the total.

The Council of Economic Advisers were right, therefore, to stress
that poverty is found among all major groups. Just as in Britain,
poverty cannot be explained as 'exceptional', and this has important
policy implications. At the same time, certain groups are clearly at
much greater risk. This is brought out by the second column in Table
10·4. In 1972, 12 per cent of the total population were in poverty, but
the proportion for those aged 65 and over was 19 per cent, and for
blacks it was nearly three times. It is on this last aspect that the
remainder of this section is focused.

Racial discrimination
The relationship between poverty and racial discrimination is one of the
major differences between Britain and the United States. The dispro-
portionate number of blacks below the poverty line is of course only
part of a wider picture of racial disparities: 'in every sphere of
American life the economic condition of the Negro minority is inferior
to that of the White majority' (Kain, 1969, p. 2).

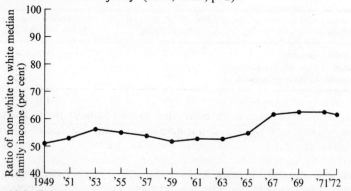

Fig. 10·3. Relative incomes of white and non-white families, United States
1949–72.
Source: US Department of Labor (1971) and sources given there.

The very substantial gap in terms of incomes in general is shown in Fig. 10·3. In 1972, median family incomes of non-white families were less than two-thirds of those of white families. In examining the difference between the incomes of whites and non-whites, we may (as in Chapter 6) distinguish between that part attributable to observed characteristics, such as age, education, geographical location, unemployment, and that part due to 'pure' discrimination. Is the higher proportion of blacks in poverty explained by their higher unemployment (the non-white unemployment rate has typically been over twice that for whites), lower education, or the larger proportion living in the south? Or is it the case that people in the same place, with the same qualifications, get paid less on account of discrimination? This is not to suggest that differences in observed characteristics are unaffected by discrimination—the higher unemployment rate of non-whites may well reflect discriminatory hiring practices and young blacks expecting to face labour market discrimination may well be less interested in education—but the distinction does help to isolate the influences at work.

This question has been examined by Thurow (1969), who used data from the 1960 census for the incidence of poverty in different states to estimate the contribution of different factors to the explanation of poverty, measured according to the Council of Economic Advisers' definition. At that time, the proportion of white families in poverty was 18·6 per cent, compared with 47·9 per cent for non-white families, so that the gap to be explained was 29·3 per cent:

Sources of gap	Contribution (%)
Families living on farms	− 0·3
Families with no one in labour force	1·3
Family heads with less than 8 years of education	12·7
Population aged 14 or over who worked 50−2 weeks per year	3·6
Index of industrial structure	0·8
Families headed by non-white	11·3

From these results it is clear that other factors are important, particularly education and unemployment, but that 'pure' discrimination appears to be responsible for over one-third of the gap. It is interesting to note that Thurow's analysis, based on aggregate data for states, is supported in this respect by the study of Duncan (1968), using quite different data for individual incomes. He concluded that around one-third of the difference in average income arose because 'Negro and white men in the same line of work with the same amount of formal schooling with equal ability, from families ... of the same socio-economic level, simply do not draw the same wages and salaries'.

The analysis in the previous paragraph brings out the importance of education and of pure discrimination. In both cases, there are some reasons to believe that the degree of difference has declined in recent years. The gap between the number of school years completed by whites and non-whites has been narrowing; there has been some equalization of resources in education;[1] and under the War on Poverty, there was a rapid increase in compensatory education programmes. The civil rights legislation of the 1960s may similarly have reduced the degree of pure discrimination. Employers can no longer legally discriminate against black employees: there are affirmative action programmes providing for minimum quotas of black employees; unions can no longer restrict entry to blacks (the Brotherhood of Railroad Trainmen, for example, had a 'Caucasian only' clause until 1959). How far such changes have affected racial differences in income is less clear. It is true that Fig. 10·3 shows a rise in the median income of non-white families relative to whites over the period 1949–72. In the first part of the period there was no apparent trend, and a comparison of 1949 and 1959 shows little alteration as far as overall family income was concerned. The main part of the improvement took place in the 1960s. This picture has, however, to be interpreted carefully, and we need to look more closely at the changes that have taken place.

The movement of overall family income conceals the fact that the pattern was quite different for men and women. For women, the ratio of median incomes improved substantially over the period, reflecting in part an increase in full-time employment among non-white women. For men, on the other hand, the ratio fell between 1949 and 1959, and by 1965 had only returned to its previous level. In more recent years, the ratio has risen, but the improvement for male incomes is considerably less than for overall family income. Secondly, within the male group, the experience differed markedly by age. In the youngest age groups, there was a substantially larger rise in the relative position of non-whites over the period 1959–69. Insofar as this may be attributed to the particular cohort—young blacks entering the labour force in the 1960s—it suggests the possibility of a continuing improvement. All the same, older cohorts showed relatively little change: the group aged

---

[1] Freeman (1973) has traced the development of state school provision. Before 1890 the estimated expenditure per head was roughly equal between races; with the disenfranchisement of blacks under the new state constitutions of that era, the ratio changed to 5:1 in favour of whites. He argues that in recent years the position of blacks has improved.

45–54 in 1969 were in the same relative position as those aged 35–44 in 1959. Farley and Hermalin (1972) concluded that:

> a primary reason why Black men improved their income in the 1960s was that young men entering the labor market obtained incomes more nearly equal to those of young White men. Apparently, even during the prosperous 1960s, there was not much relative improvement in income for Black men who were 25 and over in 1960.

One consequence of this may be increased disparities of income *within* black America. It is interesting to note that blacks form an increasing proportion of those in poverty, and this is true even if a relative definition is adopted. It may be that young adult blacks and the black middle class are gaining, but the poor are standing still or getting poorer.

Thirdly, in examining the long-run trend in relative incomes, it is important to abstract from cyclical influences, since the position of non-whites tends to improve as unemployment falls, as may be seen from Fig. 10·3. In 1958, unemployment was nearly 7 per cent, whereas by 1967 it had fallen to 4 per cent; during this period the relative income of black males rose from 50 per cent to over 60 per cent. This is a very substantial gain, but it represents a once-for-all effect: 'as the economy moves toward full employment, non-white incomes rise more than proportionately, but the equalization does not continue once unemployment stops falling' (Thurow, 1969, p. 61). According to the estimates of Rasmussen (1970), a 3 per cent reduction in the employment rate would be expected to raise the relative income of black males by 8 per cent; when this is taken into account, the upward trend works out at about $\frac{1}{3}$ per cent per annum. At this rate, the gap would not be closed for over a hundred years.

Finally, it is important to bear in mind the effects of the migration from the south. Between 1940 and 1966, a net total of 3·7 million blacks left the south for other regions, and the proportion of total blacks in the metropolitan areas of the north and west rose from 20 per cent to nearly 40 per cent. There is marked regional variation in relative incomes: in 1959 the median income of black men in the south was 47 per cent of the white median income, compared with over 70 per cent in other regions. To the extent that this is due to regional differences in discrimination, rather than to individual characteristics, the movement of blacks out of the south would tend to raise the national ratio. This point was examined by Batchelder (1964), using data covering the period 1949–59. During this period the national ratio remained broadly constant, so that within each of the four main regions the relative position of black men (but not women) actually declined. In the following decade, 1959–69, the relative position of black men improved in all regions, but the rise was less marked regionally than in the country as a whole—with the interesting exception of the south, where it rose from 47 per cent to 54 per cent. As Batchelder recognizes, this regional pattern may be explained by the individual characteristics of the migrants, but the extent to which the rise in the overall average can be attributed to such structural shifts in American society warrants close investigation.

For the reasons just described, statements such as that by Moynihan, adviser to successive Presidents, that 'the 1960s saw the great breakthrough for blacks' must be treated with caution. There are signs that the extent of discrimination may be declining over time, but it is important to ask how far it is due to the prosperity of the 1960s, or to structural changes that will not be repeated. It seems in fact, from the experience of the past two decades, that the elimination of racial differences in income will be a slow process.

10·5 The future of concern

In many countries it was widely believed in the 1950s that poverty was no longer a problem. The impact of social legislation, Keynesian measures to maintain near-to-full employment, and rising wages, had, it was believed, ensured the abolition of poverty. In the early 1960s this was to change. In Britain the work of Wedderburn, Abel-Smith and Townsend demonstrated the existence of a substantial minority living at or below the National Assistance standard. In the United States, the writings of Galbraith and Harrington and the experiences of President Kennedy while campaigning in West Virginia contributed to the re-awakening of interest and to the War on Poverty.

The same pattern emerged in other countries. In Australia, the first ever survey of the extent of poverty was carried out in 1966. Applying a poverty standard which was broadly comparable, in terms of average earnings, with that employed in Britain and the United States, the study showed that at least 4 per cent of the population were living in poverty. In Canada, the Economic Council estimated that the proportion of the population living in poverty was similar to that in the US, and in 1965 the government announced a war on poverty. In Sweden a Royal Commission on Low Income Groups was established in 1966. In France, the publication of De La Gorce's book, *La France pauvre*, greatly influenced by Harrington, led to renewed concern about poverty. On the basis of data given in this study, it was estimated that about 20 per cent of the population could be considered to be in poverty, including a large number of old people, agricultural workers, and immigrants.

Whether the revival of concern will prove to be short-lived, reflecting a coincidence of political expediency and academic fashion, has yet to be seen. The analysis in this chapter suggests, however, that poverty as it has concerned governments in recent years is unlikely to pass rapidly away, and that it cannot be regarded as simply a problem of exceptional circumstances or minority groups. If poverty in advanced countries is to be eliminated, then far-reaching and broadly based measures are necessary and it is to these that we now turn.

11
POLICIES FOR
INCOME MAINTENANCE

Our task of reconstruction does not require the creation of new and strange values. It is rather the finding of the way once more to known, but to some degree forgotten, ideals and values.

(Message to US Congress by President Roosevelt, preceding passage of Social Security Act, 1935)

This chapter examines the present policies for income maintenance in Britain and the United States, the reasons why they have failed to guarantee a minimum income to all according to the official poverty standard, and the reforms which could be introduced.

11·1 Social Insurance and after

The social security system in Britain owes much of its present form to the Beveridge Plan, conceived during the Second World War and translated into legislation by the Labour government in the immediate postwar years. The fundamental aim of the Plan was 'to abolish want by ensuring that every citizen willing to serve according to his powers has at all times an income sufficient to meet his responsibilities' (Beveridge, 1942, p. 165). This 'national minimum' was to be guaranteed as of right, through social insurance covering retirement and all major risks of loss or interruption of earnings, and through family allowances. The scheme was to cover everyone irrespective of income, and the benefits were to be paid at the same flat rate for all.

The evidence of the previous chapter has demonstrated that the intentions of the Beveridge Plan have not been fulfilled. Despite the introduction of National Insurance, there are still some two million people in Britain below what the government considers to represent a minimum standard of living. Similarly, in the United States, the social insurance system introduced under the Act of 1935 has not prevented many people from falling below the official poverty line. In this section we examine the reasons for this failure of social insurance.

Poverty in old age
Old people are the single largest group living in poverty in Britain today. They are also the group whose needs have been most intensively studied; nonetheless, there is very little up-to-date information about

the financial position of old people and for the most part we have to rely on a study by the Ministry of Pensions and National Insurance (1966) carried out some ten years ago.

The primary social security provision for old age is the National Insurance retirement pension and virtually everyone aged 65 or over (60 for women) who has retired from full-time work receives such basic pensions (there are a few exceptions, such as a small number of very old people past retirement in 1948 and not insured under earlier schemes). The basic rate of pension for a single person has averaged some 20 per cent of average gross earnings, and approximately one-third for a married couple, although there have been year-to-year variations. The total pension may be higher than this, on account of increments for deferred retirement, the graduated pension, and the age addition for those aged 80 or over, but many people receive little more than the basic rate.

The fundamental principle of the Beveridge Plan was that the social insurance benefits should be sufficient to guarantee subsistence, so that people should not have to resort to means-tested supplementation because of the inadequacy of the insurance benefits. In this respect, the postwar legislation departed from the Beveridge principles. The basic National Insurance benefits were consistently below the minimum standard set for National Assistance and later Supplementary Benefits. In 1948, the National Insurance benefit for a married couple was £2·10, whereas the National Assistance scale was £2 plus housing expenditure, so that a pensioner couple with rent of more than 10p a week would have been below the poverty line if they had relied on National Insurance alone. In 1974, the corresponding rates were a National Insurance pension of £16·00 for a couple and a Supplementary Benefit scale of £16·35, so that even without any housing costs the couple would have been below the poverty line. There has, therefore, been a consistent failure to provide basic state pensions which meet the government's own standards of adequacy.

Successive governments have put forward proposals for new state pension schemes. The Labour government of 1964–70 had plans for an earnings-related pension; the Conservative government of 1970–4 favoured a new 'second-tier' pension, under which those people not covered by private pensions would also receive a state reserve pension, again earnings-related. Neither scheme, however, would have had an immediate effect. The Labour scheme had a twenty-year transition period, and the Conservative state reserve pensions would not have reached maturity until the year 2019. These schemes would have done little, therefore, to help the pensioners of this century. The state reserve scheme had the further drawback that it offered limited protection against inflation and relatively poor benefits for low paid workers, particularly women. This latter point reflects the fundamental problem with earnings-related benefits, that differences in earnings are preserved in old age although these can be mitigated by a 'progressive' formula, such as that employed in the Labour scheme, providing for a pension of 60 per cent of earnings up to half the national average and 25 per cent beyond. Without such progression, an earnings-related scheme may not ensure adequate pensions for the low paid.

The inadequacy of the National Insurance pension would be less serious if old people could rely on alternative sources of income. However, a significant number have *no income at all* from anything other than state sources. This very surprising fact was brought out by the government survey of 1965, which showed that one in five of all pensioners had no other income. Single women were particularly badly off in this respect, a third having no other income. The proportion with no other income was also very much higher for the older age groups, reaching 44 per cent for the group aged 85 and over. The very old were much less likely to be able to supplement their incomes by earnings and many had exhausted their savings.

For those who do have other income, the principal sources are occupational pensions, interest on savings, and earnings. The 1965 survey showed that for married couples and single men, pensions from previous employment were received in about half the cases and on average supplemented the National Insurance pension by 50–70 per cent. Only 14 per cent of single women, however, were receiving occupational pensions. Occupational schemes have in the past granted relatively few pensions to the widows of deceased employees and the proportion of women employees covered by occupational schemes is lower than that of men. Savings provided an additional source of cash income for over half the pensioners, but for most the amounts involved were fairly small. About 30 per cent had no savings at all in 1965, and only a quarter had more than £600. But it should be noted that these amounts did not include the value of any owner-occupied property, and about one-third owned their own homes free of mortgage commitments. For these pensioners, housing costs were lower on average than for those in rented accommodation. The retirement condition for pensioners between 65 and 70 (60 and 65 for women) and the associated 'earnings rule' restricting the amount they can earn before the pension is reduced, means that they are effectively limited to part-time work. Even so, the opportunity to work may make a substantial difference to a pensioner's income, but the proportion with such earnings was low.

This evidence demonstrates the widely differing economic circumstances of old people. At all stages in the life-cycle there are wide differences between people in their access to economic resources, but this is even more marked in old age. Since 1965 the spread of occupational pensions will have narrowed the gap, but factors such as accelerated inflation and reduced employment prospects for the elderly may have worked in the opposite direction, and there can be little doubt that the differences in old age remain important. The professional person retired on half his final salary, with the opportunity for part-time work and living in his own house, is in a quite different position from the person with only the National Insurance pension who is living in rented accommodation. It was this kind of situation that Titmuss described as 'two nations in old age'. For the less privileged of these classes, the only recourse is to Supplementary Benefits, and the shortcomings of this means-tested scheme are described in Section 11·2.

In the United States, the main social insurance provision for old age is the Old Age, Survivers, Disability, and Health Insurance (OASDHI). This programme has evolved more gradually than National Insurance, its coverage being extended over the years (the 'H' for example was added in 1966). The scheme now covers more than 90 per cent of those aged 65 and over. The pension depends on the age at retirement, the eligibility of the spouse for benefit, and the level of earnings before retirement. The pension is, therefore, earnings-related in contrast to the flat-rate National Insurance pension in Britain. In 1972 a single person with average earnings in manufacturing would have retired at the age of 65 with a pension equal to 34 per cent of gross earnings (Henle, 1972), which is more favourable than the corresponding ratio in Britain and is sufficient to bring him comfortably above the official poverty line. On the other hand, a worker who had earned no more than the minimum wage throughout his working career would have been entitled to an amount which represented only 87 per cent of the poverty line. Moreover, if he had been forced to retire early at 62, through losing his job or ill health, the pension would have been less that 70 per cent of the poverty standard. It should also be stressed that these figures relate to the pension paid *at retirement*; after retirement, the purchasing power is maintained, but the pension does not necessarily rise with rising incomes elsewhere in the economy. The average OASDHI pension paid to all retired persons in 1972 was, in fact, less than the poverty line.

As in Britain, pensioners may supplement their income from a variety of sources. Private pension plans may provide substantial benefits on retirement, but they cover only part of the labour force; moreover, in many cases the benefits are not augmented after retirement to allow for rising prices and incomes. A relatively small proportion of people over 65 continue to work and, for this group, earnings provide a substantial fraction of their income. A larger number, around half, have income from savings, but this provides on average considerably less in the way of income. The picture is, in fact, very similar to that in Britain. Those who continue to work or are able to retire with a generous company pension (for example, a person covered by the Detroit Edison plan, with a total pension of 55–65 per cent of previous earnings) are unlikely to find themselves below the poverty line; those who have only the OASDHI pension are much more likely to find themselves dependent on means-tested welfare payments.

Family poverty

In Britain many writers have referred to the 'rediscovery' of family poverty during the 1960s, but perhaps more important was the growing realization that family poverty was not solely due to family size. The Sunday newspaper supplement image of family poverty is typically of families with six or more children and has no doubt affected attitudes to family policy. This was, of course, very much the view Beveridge took of the problem.

The social surveys of Britain between the two wars show that in the first thirty years of this century real wages rose by almost one-third without reducing want to insignificance, and that the want which remained was almost always due to two causes—interruption or loss of earnings power and large families (Beveridge, 1942, p. 154).

This belief led him to propose family allowances to provide for the subsistence needs of children, but to exclude the first child on the ground that 'very few men's wages are insufficient to cover at least two adults and one child' (p. 155).

In this respect Beveridge was wrong. The evidence in the previous chapter has demonstrated that large families, those with five or more children, account for only a small proportion. The special government enquiry in 1966 into the circumstances of families confirmed this picture. Of the total number of families receiving family allowances (i.e. with two or more children), with an income below the poverty line even though the father was in full-time work, fewer than half had four or more children:

families with	% of total families in poverty (with 2 or more children)
2 children	33
3 children	24
4 children	17
5 or more children	27

Source: Atkinson, 1969, Table 5·2.

There are, therefore, many families with three or fewer children who are living below the poverty line. The reasons for this are twofold. Firstly, Beveridge was wrong to assume that low wages would not be a problem. The Supplementary Benefit scale for a man, wife, and one child aged 11 came to £11·90 in January 1972, plus housing costs of (say) £2·50 a week. To reach that level of take-home pay, a man would have had to earn £16·50 a week (allowing for work expenses), and at that time an estimated 250 000 full-time adult male workers were in fact below this level. These workers did not necessarily have dependent children, but the calculation demonstrates that earnings may be too low to support even a one child family.

The second cause of family poverty is the low level of family benefits. In the calculation described in the previous paragraph, account was taken of the child tax allowances provided for all children. These allowances have a long history, going back to the original income tax introduced by Pitt in 1799, and allow deduction for tax purposes of an amount which varies with the age of the child. The value of the allowances increases with the income of the family, since it depends on the marginal tax rate,[1] and they provide no benefit to the poorest families who would in any event be below the tax threshold. For families with two or more children, there are also family allowances as proposed by Beveridge. As in the case of the social insurance benefits, however, the level of the payment is below that which he recommended. Indeed in 1966 the rate for the second child was the same in *cash* terms as that proposed by Beveridge in 1942, though prices had more than doubled. Increases in the rates of family allowances have been very infrequent. During the Conservative government of 1970–4, the allowances remained unchanged while prices rose by 40 per cent. The only important change in family benefits during this period was, in fact, the introduction of the means-tested Family Income Supplement, which is discussed in Section 11·2.

Poverty and exceptional circumstances
In the previous chapter, we distinguished between poverty related to the foreseeable life-cycle of need, as discussed so far, and poverty associated with the interruption of income in exceptional circumstances.

The interruption of earnings through unemployment or sickness does not necessarily lead to poverty. In Britain, the National Insurance

---

1 The marginal tax rate is the proportion of extra income which goes in tax. If a man with a marginal tax rate of 40 per cent earns an extra £1, he pays 40p in tax. A child allowance reduces the amount of his income which is subject to tax, so its value in tax saved would be 40 per cent of the allowance.

scheme as originally enacted provided a flat-rate benefit and this has since been modified to include an earnings-related supplement. However, where the interruption is lengthy or repeated, it is possible for workers to exhaust their entitlement to the earnings-related supplement or, in the case of unemployment, to the flat-rate benefit (which is only paid for 12 months). At the end of 1972, under half of all unemployed men were receiving flat-rate benefit and only about 10 per cent the earnings-related supplement. There is in fact a 'hierarchy' of benefits in unemployment, ranging from the company executive with a generous 'handshake', through the short-term unemployed with the earnings-related supplement, to the long-term unemployed dependent solely on Supplementary Benefits. In the case of sickness absence, the employer may provide sick pay. In 1970 three-quarters of adult male workers were covered by sick-pay schemes, although the proportion for unskilled manual workers was lower. Moreover, the benefits provided for manual workers are in many cases much lower than for non-manual workers: 'normally in the case of men manual workers, the "full wages" paid during sickness would be distinctly less than total earnings' (Ministry of Labour, 1964, p. 29). Low paid workers are, therefore, less likely both to be covered by a scheme and to receive full pay for the period of sickness. As a result they are more dependent on National Insurance and Supplementary Benefits.

The position is rather different for single parent families, a group which includes widows and widowers, unmarried mothers, and mothers (and fathers) who are separated or divorced. With the exception of widows, this group is not at present eligible under the National Insurance scheme for any benefit as of right (apart from family allowances). A widow who has children receives a flat-rate insurance benefit for as long as they are dependent on her, and in certain cases this may be supplemented by a widow's pension paid by her husband's former employer. As a result, widows are less likely to fall below the poverty line than other single parents. They accounted, however, for only around a quarter of the 500 000 fatherless families in Britain in 1971. Of the remainder, 240 000 were women divorced or separated from their husbands. In these cases maintenance might be payable, but this depends on the ability and willingness of the father to pay. Many single parent families are therefore dependent on Supplementary Benefit, and this was true of half the fatherless families (apart from those of widows) in 1971 (Finer, 1974, Appendix 10). Of the remainder, 19 per cent were living on incomes below the Supplementary Benefit level.

In the United States the status of family benefits and programmes for unsupported families is almost the reverse of that in Britain. It is one of the few advanced countries without a general family allowance scheme. On the other hand, it has had since 1935 a means-tested programme for unsupported families with dependent children (AFDC). Moreover, this programme has been extended over time. Since 1961 it can, for example, cover families where the father is unemployed, and there have been suggestions for widening its coverage still further, to provide a means-tested benefit for all families. In this way, it would arrive by a different route at the same kind of scheme as the Family Income Supplement in Britain. The possibilities of such an approach are discussed in the next section.

11·2 The rise and failure of means-testing

Means-tested programmes are the oldest in the social security system; indeed the Supplementary Benefit scheme in Britain can be traced back to the Elizabethan *Acte for the Reliefe of the Poore* of 1598. In more recent times, they have, however, increased greatly in importance. Whereas Beveridge envisaged that 'the scope of assistance will be narrowed from the beginning and diminish throughout the transition period for pensions' (1942, p. 12), the number dependent on assistance has grown from 1 million in 1948 to nearly 3 million in 1973. New means-tested benefits have been introduced: for example, rate rebates in 1966, prescription charge exemptions in 1968, Family Income Supplement in 1971. In 1973 there were over forty national means-tested schemes and many more under the control of local authorities. Moreover, the scope of the means-tested programmes has been extended. In the case of rent rebates, a national scheme for all tenants has replaced the previous schemes covering council tenants in certain local authorities. The early rate rebate scheme, which largely benefited pensioners, has been replaced by one with wider eligibility.

The main feature of means-testing is that eligibility is determined by a family's income, in relation to its needs as defined for the purposes of the particular scheme.[1] In some cases, a family is eligible either for full benefits or for none at all: for example, a family qualifies for free school meals if its income is below a certain level, but if its income rises above this level, eligibility is lost completely. In most cases, the withdrawal of the benefit is tapered as income rises. Under the Family Income Supplement (FIS), a family receives, in addition to family

---

[1] Not only the definition of needs but also the definition of income varies from scheme to scheme. For Family Income Supplement, it is gross income which is relevant (i.e. before tax and National Insurance contributions); for exemption from prescription charges, on the other hand, a person may deduct not only tax and insurance contributions, but also working expenses, mortgage repayments, and hire purchase commitments.

allowances, a payment equal to half the gap between its income and a prescribed income level. In 1974, the prescribed income level for a family with two children was £28 a week, so that if its income was £24 a week, a FIS payment of £2 a week was made, but if the income rose to £26, then the supplement would be cut to £1. In this way, the benefit falls to nothing as the family's income reaches the prescribed income level. In the case of FIS, the definition of needs relates only to family size; in other schemes, the definition involves other elements. For example, rent rebates depend on (*i*) income, (*ii*) family size and (*iii*) rent, according to a formula such as the following:

Rebate = 60 per cent of rent − 17 per cent of excess of income over
needs allowance

where the needs allowance depends on the number of dependants (the full formula is more complex). One consequence of this is that these schemes have become extremely complicated, as is illustrated by Fig. 11·1, showing some of the questions which have to be answered on the application form for the relatively simple Family Income Supplement.

In the United States there has been a similar growth in the importance of the means-tested welfare system. As described by Aaron (1973, p. 5):

Until the late sixties low-income Americans receiving federal, state, or local assistance were a small minority . . . only 7·1 million received public assistance, roughly 2 million lived in low-rent public housing . . . and 4·3 million received surplus agricultural commodities. Few households benefited from more than one of these programs.

By the early 1970s, this had changed:

The number of public assistance beneficiaries almost doubled to 13·8 million . . . Food and surplus agricultural commodities were used by more than 10 million persons . . . medicaid was providing largely free medical care for 18·2 million persons . . . a growing number of families received benefits under two, three or more programs.

These programmes all involved tests of income to determine eligibility and were in large part administered by separate authorities.

The growth of means-testing stems from an understandable desire to focus benefits on those considered to be in need. Faced with the inadequacy of social insurance and other benefits, successive governments in Britain and the United States have turned increasingly to income-related schemes as a low-cost means of helping low income groups. This approach has not, however, succeeded in solving the problem of poverty, and means-tested schemes have been subject to two important criticisms: that they fail to reach all who are eligible, and that they involve high marginal rates of tax.

The first of these shortcomings was well recognized by Beveridge, who regarded 'the strength of popular objection to any kind of means test' as one of the main reasons for requiring that the social insurance benefits should be adequate in themselves and that people should not be forced to rely on means-tested assistance. The experience with Supplementary Benefit bears out his misgivings. The enquiry by the Ministry of Pensions and National Insurance in 1965 showed that 47 per cent of pensioners had incomes below the National Assistance scale (before taking account of the assistance in payment)—see the first line of Table 11·1. Of these, slightly over half were actually receiving National Assistance (second line of Table 11·1). Of the others, some were disqualified because they had savings in excess of the allowed limit, but nearly one-third were apparently entitled to benefit but not claiming. Checks by the Ministry on the accuracy of the information led to some reduction in the estimate but they still concluded that 'rather more than 700 000 pensioner households (about 850 000 pensioners) could have received assistance if they had applied for it' (1966, p. 83). This confirmed the earlier findings of Cole and Utting (1962), and Abel-Smith and Townsend (1965). In its enquiry the Ministry explored the reasons why people did not claim. One clear reason was that people were ignorant or misinformed about the

TABLE 11·1
*Take-Up of National Assistance by
retirement pensioners, Britain June 1965*

	Number of pensioners (million)	% of total pensioners
Income (before National Assistance) below National Assistance scale	2·9	47
Receiving National Assistance	1·5	25
Not entitled on account of savings	0·4	6
Apparently entitled to National Assistance but not receiving it	1·0	16

Source: Atkinson (1969), Table 3·6 (rounded).

CLAIM FOR FAMILY INCOME SUPPLEMENT

● Claim only if you have one or more dependent children and you are in full-time paid work and are normally so employed

● In the case of a couple living together as man and wife, whether married or not, it is the man who must be in full-time work; both columns headed 'Man' and Woman' should be completed and both should sign the declaration overleaf

● Please use BLOCK CAPITALS throughout and answer all sections after reading the leaflet.

1.

	Surname	Other Names	Date of Birth	National insurance no.
Man				
Woman Mrs/Miss*				

*Delete as appropriate.

2. ADDRESS

_____

Town _____ County (including postcode) _____

3. Do you already have a Family Income Supplement order book?   (YES OR NO)........

4. State in the spaces below your GROSS earnings (before deductions for income tax, national insurance, etc.) from your present FULL-TIME employment for each of the last 5 weeks. If your present job began in the last 5 weeks, please state here when your job started..19.....
If you are not paid weekly, give details of your earnings over the last 2 months, amending the form as necessary. If paid monthly, state whether you are paid 4 weekly or the calendar month.

Employer's name and address	What is your job?	Pay week ended (Enter date)	Hours worked in this week	Gross Earnings Man (If NONE write "NONE")	Woman
		1 : :197		£ ·	£ ·
		2 : :197		£ ·	£ ·
		3 : :197		£ ·	£ ·
		4 : :197		£ ·	£ ·
		5 : :197		£ ·	£ ·

HOW MANY HOURS DO YOU NORMALLY WORK IN THIS EMPLOYMENT?................a week.
Please enclose the pay slips or other evidence of your pay as detailed above.
If any payment includes an addition which you do not normally receive, eg holiday pay, please give details.

_____

5. If you are self-employed please state the nature of your business and your latest trading profit showing the period covered. Please enclose your latest profit and loss account if available.

_____

HOW MANY HOURS DO YOU NORMALLY WORK IN THIS EMPLOYMENT?................a week.

6. Have you had any regular earnings from PART-TIME work in the last 5 weeks? (Answer "YES" or "NO" in the boxes alongside)

	Man	Woman

If "YES" state below the GROSS amount for each week.

Employer's name and address (if working on own account enter 'self-employed')	Pay-week ended (enter date)	Earnings Man	Woman
		£ ·	£ ·
		£ ·	£ ·
		£ ·	£ ·
		£ ·	£ ·
		£ ·	£ ·

DECLARATION   **WARNING:** TO GIVE FALSE INFORMATION MAY RESULT IN PROSECUTION
I/We declare that I/we have read the instructions on the form and to the best of my/our knowledge and belief the information given on this claim is true and complete. I/We claim family income supplement.

Date _____   Signature (Man) _____
If anyone who signs this form is not living at the address in Section 2 the second
address should be given in Section 11.   Signature (Woman) _____

POST OFFICE OF PAYMENT
Please state in full the official name and   _____
address of the Post Office where you wish   _____
to draw any supplement which may be
payable.   _____

Fig. 11·1 Extracts from application form for British Family Income Supplement
Source: Department of Health and Social Security.

provisions. This was not, however, the only factor, and between a quarter and a third said they did not apply because they disliked charity or the National Assistance Board, or because their pride would not let them ask for help.

The Ministry enquiry was carried out before the replacement of National Assistance by Supplementary Benefits, which had the aim of ensuring that 'the elderly will have no hesitation in claiming the new benefit to which they are entitled'. To this end, the Ministry of Social Security Act 1966 provided a specific *entitlement* to benefit, simplified the procedure for claiming and made a number of other changes designed to increase the 'take-up' rate. The introduction of Supplementary Benefits was claimed by the ministers concerned as a 'remarkable success' (Mr Houghton) and 'a tremendous social change' (Mr Crossman). These claims were based on the undoubted increase in the number of old people receiving assistance; however, they did not allow for the fact that a substantial part of the increase was attributable to the rise in the assistance scale, which increased the number eligible. On the basis of an analysis of the relationship between the scale and the number claiming over the period 1951–65, it may be estimated that the increase in the proportion of retirement pensioner households receiving assistance attributable to the new scheme was only some 1½ to 2½ per cent.[1] This figure is small in comparison with the number of pensioner households found to have been eligible but not claiming in 1965: 13 per cent on the Ministry's adjusted figures. It can only be concluded that the introduction of Supplementary Benefits has failed to provide an adequate solution.

The experience of low 'take-up' rates has been repeated with more recent means-tested schemes. The enquiry into the circumstances of families (Ministry of Social Security, 1967) drew attention to the fact that only 10 per cent of ratepayers with incomes below the National Assistance level had applied for rate rebates, although the great majority were eligible. Subsequent studies (e.g. Meacher, 1973) have found a low take-up for rate rebates and concluded that, while an intensive advertising campaign improved the response, the problem of non-claiming still remained a major one. When the Family Income Supplement scheme was announced, the minister stated that a high take-up was vital for its success and the programme was budgeted on the basis of a take-up rate of 85 per cent. The new scheme was widely advertised on television and in newspapers, and its administration was designed with a great deal of care. Nonetheless, the take-up rate has

[1] Atkinson (1969), Ch. 4. The most straightforward estimate was that a 10 per cent rise in the ratio (NA/RP) of the National Assistance scale to the retirement pension would lead to a 2·4 per cent increase in the number of pensioner households receiving assistance. With the introduction of Supplementary Benefits, the ratio (NA/RP) rose from 0·95 to 1·13, predicting an increase of 4·4 per cent. The actual increase was 5·8 per cent, giving a residual attributable to the introduction of the scheme of 1·4 per cent. Other methods of estimation gave somewhat higher figures.

fallen considerably short of 85 per cent, and in 1973 the government admitted that on their estimates 'only about one-half the total numbers eligible were actually receiving payments under FIS' (Select Committee on Tax-Credit, 1973, p. 16).

The problem of low take-up has received less attention in the United States, but its existence is clearly demonstrated in the analysis by Steiner (1971) of the food stamp programme. This scheme allows low income families to purchase food vouchers with a face value in excess of the purchase price, with eligibility for the programme and the size of the subsidy depending on income. Although the scheme was strongly supported by the Kennedy administration, it became clear after it had been in operation for less than five years that the stamps were not being taken up. A 1969 Senate report concluded that: 'nationally only 21·6 per cent of the poor people living in counties with food stamp programs participate in the program . . . Seven states have programs that reach less than 15 per cent of the poor' (quoted by Steiner (1971), p. 213). According to the Brookings Institution study of the 1974 budget, 'presumably all of the 25·6 million persons officially below the poverty line in 1971 are eligible to purchase stamps, but fewer than half are participating' (Fried *et al.* 1973, p. 109). Although this may well be an over-estimate of the size of the eligible population, there does seem to be strong evidence that the food stamp programme has not reached all those entitled. The reasons for this failure are numerous, but the main conclusion reached by Steiner was that 'the truth about food stamps is that it is . . . a demeaning program'.

The second objection to means-tested benefits is that they often involve high effective marginal rates of tax. As income rises benefits are withdrawn, and this has the same effect on disposable income as the taxation of income. A man receiving rebates for rent and rates might as a result of earning an extra £1 in 1974 pay 33p in income tax and 5½p in social security contributions, lose 17p off his rent rebate and 6p off his rate rebate, leaving him only 38½p better off. The effective marginal tax rate in this case would have been 61½ per cent. In certain cases he might actually have been worse off, the marginal tax rate exceeding 100 per cent, as would happen if his children had previously been receiving free school meals. In 1973 the effective marginal tax rate on a permanent £1 increase in earnings for a three child family varied between 38 per cent and 97 per cent at the lower levels, and was then 52 per cent over a wide band.[1] Over a considerable range of earnings, therefore, a family claiming all the benefits to which it was entitled would have derived less than 50p benefit from a permanent £1 increase in income. This situation has been described as 'the poverty trap', since a family below the poverty line could raise itself above only with aid of a substantial increase in gross pay: a family £1 below might have to earn £4 a week more.

At the top end of the income scale, high marginal rates of tax are often assumed to have adverse effects on the incentives to work and to save; and the existence of marginal rates as high, or even higher, at the lower end of the scale might be expected to have a similar effect. (Although the disincentive effect may be lessened by the fact that benefits may only be re-assessed some months later and that people may have only very limited knowledge of the marginal tax arising from the withdrawal of benefits.) A rather different aspect of high marginal tax rates which has only recently received much attention is their effect on wage negotiations. In the Wilberforce enquiry into miners' pay in 1972, M. Meacher, MP, pointed to the combined effect of the failure to raise the income tax threshold in line with rising earnings and of the growth of means-tested benefits. As a result, 'it is only large increases [in earnings] which can give any net gain at all' (Hughes and Moore, 1972, p. 101). The same point has been examined at length by Turner and Wilkinson, who argue that 'only by insisting on wage increases which are necessarily inflationary can wage earners secure a "moderate" gain in real living standards' (Jackson *et al.*, 1972, p. 98). The strength of this argument depends on how the standards for eligibility for means-tested benefits are adjusted over time, and there have in practice been regular increases, but this aspect of the poverty trap probably influenced the decision of the Conservative government in Britain to propose the alternative tax credit scheme examined in the next section.

The high marginal tax rates arising from the overlap of means-tested programmes in the United States have been identified by Aaron as one of the principal factors leading to the failure of welfare reform during the Nixon administration. As described by the Chairman of the Senate Finance Commitee, the President's family assistance plan:

finds it necessary to sharply curtail the amount of earnings that a person can retain when he goes to work . . . In many cases, after one considers the increase in social security taxes paid, the loss of medicaid benefits, and especially if the family is enjoying the benefit of subsidized public housing, the family income would be reduced by more than 100 per cent of every dollar that a father or mother proceeded to earn (quoted in Aaron 1973, p. 3).

The substantial marginal tax rates involved in the existing welfare system are illustrated by Fig. 11·2. The upper part of the diagram

1 It should be noted that benefit payments are not necessarily adjusted at once: the Family Income Supplement, for example, is not re-assessed for a year. This means that high marginal rates need not apply to temporary changes in earnings.

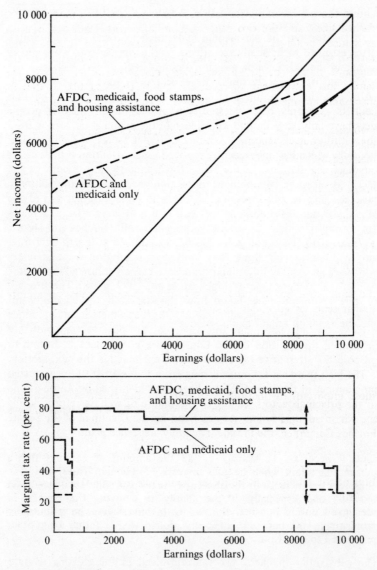

Fig. 11·2. Disposable resources and marginal rates of tax for a family of four, United States 1972.

Source: Aaron (1973). © 1973 by the Brookings Institution.

Note: Income tax and social security tax is taken into account and AFDC allows for work expenses.

shows the net income after cash assistance (AFDC) and medicaid (the dashed line), and the two schemes combined with food and housing assistance (solid line). The loss of benefits per extra dollar earned, or the marginal tax rate, is shown in the lower part of the diagram. It may be noted that where earnings reached $8390, the family lost entitlement to medicaid and to food stamps, so that its disposable income dropped by $1288. At this 'notch' the marginal tax rate is considerably in excess of 100 per cent. Proposals for reform involving an increased marginal rate of tax, such as the family assistance plan, would have exacerbated the problem, and this was one of the main reasons for their failure to pass Congress.

Increasing recognition of the failure of means-tested benefits to reach many of those in need and of the problems of the poverty trap has brought with it pressure for a new approach to income maintenance through a negative income tax.

11·3 Negative income taxation and tax credits

The debate about negative income taxation has been confusing in many respects. A variety of schemes have been proposed, some of which have the same name but appear to have little in common, while apparently similar schemes go under different titles. What exactly does negative income taxation entail, and how does it differ from a social dividend or a tax credit scheme? Why is it that in 1972 negative income taxation was espoused both by a liberal Democratic candidate for the American presidency and by a Conservative government in Britain?

The schemes could be classified in a variety of ways, but one of the most important distinctions is in terms of the extent to which they would replace the present income maintenance system. In what follows, we describe three of the principal possibilities.

Social dividend or demogrant

The most far-reaching change would be the complete replacement of all present social security benefits, of the income tax and of social security contributions, by a single social dividend or demogrant scheme. In its simplest form, this scheme would involve the payment of a social dividend to everyone, dependent only on their family status; the revenue required to finance the scheme, and to replace the present income tax, would be raised by a proportional tax on all income. The effect of this kind of scheme is illustrated in the top part of Fig. 11·3. The heavy line shows the income after allowing for tax and the social dividend. The point where the dividend is exactly offset by the tax payable is shown as the 'break-even' point. Those with low incomes would be net gainers and better off than with the existing income tax.

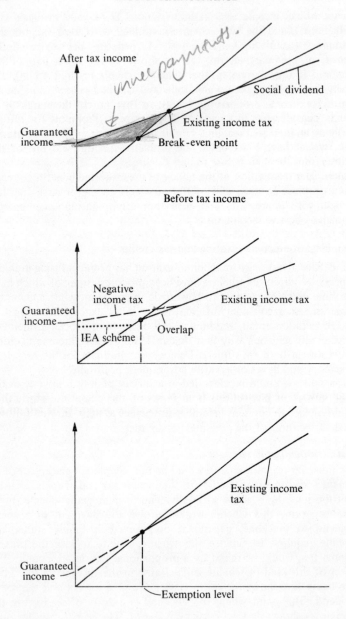

Fig. 11·3. Negative income tax schemes

Such a scheme was first proposed in Britain by Lady Rhys Williams in 1942, and has been taken up by a succession of authors, a recent example being Meade (1972). In the United States, the scheme was espoused by George McGovern in his presidential campaign, and he proposed a $1000 average *per capita* demogrant to be financed by a broad-based income tax (i.e. with fewer loopholes) at a rate of $33\frac{1}{3}$ per cent. This would have given a family of four a guaranteed income of $4000, with a break-even level of $12 000.

ıhe attractions of this approach are clear. If the demogrant were set at a level sufficient to raise a family with no other income up to the poverty line, then it would be much more effective than the present system. There would be no gaps in the programme and the problem of take-up would be eliminated. However, the main reason why this kind of scheme has failed to make progress was brought out in the McGovern campaign—that to pay an adequate demogrant (in terms of the poverty standard) would involve a substantial increase in taxation. The levels of payment proposed by McGovern were designed to meet the poverty line needs of a family of four; but critics soon pointed out that the proposed tax of $33\frac{1}{3}$ per cent was inadequate to raise the required revenue. Moreover, even at that rate of tax, the scheme would have involved substantial increases in taxation for those in the middle income ranges. In the same way, the straightforward social dividend proposed by Meade in Britain involved a tax rate of 53 per cent.

The essence of the problem may be seen quite simply from the following arithmetic. Suppose that the guaranteed minimum is set, for an average family, at *x* per cent of average incomes, and that the requirements of government revenue are such that the tax has to raise a further *y* per cent. This then determines the proportional rate of tax *x+y* per cent. For any likely values of *x* and *y*, for example, *x* = 30 per cent and *y* = 15 per cent, the tax will be substantially closer to 50 per cent than to $33\frac{1}{3}$ per cent.

Separate negative income tax schemes

The high rates of tax associated with the extreme social dividend approach and the fear that they would be politically unacceptable have led to alternatives being proposed which would retain the main elements of the present income tax and social security schemes. In particular, they would retain the progressively increasing rates of tax of the present income tax, allowing greater flexibility than a simple proportional rate, and most of the present social security benefits, allowing the negative tax payment to be set at a lower level. In the United States, the case for a negative income tax as a supplement to the existing provisions has been put in particular by Tobin: 'the merit of the negative income tax approach is that a workable and equitable system of aiding the poor can be introduced within the framework of present federal income taxation' (1968, p. 118).

These proposals have appeared in a variety of forms, but basically involve a guaranteed payment and then the withdrawal of payment at a rate of $33\frac{1}{3}$ per cent or 50 per cent—see the dashed line in the middle part of Fig. 11·3. As shown in the diagram, this leads to an overlap with the present income tax, and the negative tax rate would continue to apply until the after tax income is the same as under the present 'positive' tax schedule. Some people, therefore, would be both receiving negative tax supplements and paying ordinary income tax.

Negative income tax schemes of this type have been put forward as a means of channelling help to low income families without the disadvantages associated with means-tested benefits. They would be universal, the coverage not being limited to people satisfying certain conditions, and Tobin, Pechman, and Mieszkowski (1967) have argued that an automatic system of payment would be possible, avoiding the need for people to apply and hence the problem of low take-up. It has similarly been claimed that the negative income tax would reduce the marginal rates of tax, and proponents have stressed the difference between the proposed tax rates and that implicit in welfare programmes ($66\frac{2}{3}$ per cent).

The impact of the introduction of negative income tax on marginal rates of tax depends, however, on its relation to other means-tested benefits. As originally conceived, the negative income tax would have replaced public assistance and all benefits in kind, such as housing assistance and food stamps, but this would have meant setting the negative income tax payment at a considerably higher rate, to ensure that no families close to the poverty line would lose from the introduction of the scheme. (It is sometimes suggested that it is the necessary consequence of any reform that some people near the poverty line are made worse off, but, even apart from the equity considerations involved, such cases provide powerful ammunition for the opponents of reform.) The family shown in Fig. 11·2, for example, benefited from cash assistance, food stamps, housing and medicaid to the extent of $5860 in 1972, which means that the negative tax payment would have had to average nearly $1500 per person, or substantially more than currently envisaged. As a result, Tobin *et al.* (1967) see the housing, food stamp and medicaid programmes as continuing, with only public assistance being replaced by the negative income tax. The contribution to reducing the marginal rates of tax would therefore be smaller. If a person pays an extra 20 per cent of additional income in payroll and income taxes, while losing 25 per cent in housing assistance, and 20 per cent in medical assistance, then the marginal tax rate is only reduced from 84 per cent under the welfare system to 68 per cent under the negative income tax, with a tax rate of $33\frac{1}{3}$ per cent.[1] The continuance of other means-tested benefits blunts the effectiveness of negative income tax in reducing marginal rates: 'no matter how far Congress moves to build work incentives into cash assistance, the effort will fail unless in-kind assistance is also reformed' (Aaron, 1973, p. 52).

In Britain, the 'reverse income tax' scheme proposed by the Institute of Economic Affairs (1970) would have two important differences. The first is that the rate of tax would be 100 per cent, rather than 50 per cent or $33\frac{1}{3}$ per cent. The scheme would guarantee to all households a minimum income at the Supplementary Benefit level, but would not provide any further payments above that level—see the dotted line in the middle part of Fig. 11·3. The choice of a 100 per cent tax rate was dictated by a desire to minimize the cost of the scheme; it means, however, that the proposal can do litle to alleviate the problem of the poverty trap. The best that can be claimed is that the marginal tax rate would not exceed 100 per cent.

The second difference is in the method of administration. Recognizing that the income tax system does not cover many of those in poverty, and that for these people the income tax procedure would not allow benefits to be paid until the end of the tax year, the Institute suggests that 'the agency administering a RIT may have to use separate procedures for assessment of means from those now used for income tax'. This would represent, however, a major departure from the principle of using the income tax machinery to eliminate the stigma attached to present means-tested programmes. If a separate application has to be made, then it seems likely that at least some of those eligible would not apply for the reverse income tax. It would be a benefit designed for the poor, and it has yet to be demonstrated that it could be administered more successfully than present means-tested benefits.

The tax credit scheme—an integrated negative income tax
The third type of scheme is that closest to what the man in the street might expect the term 'negative taxation' to mean: simply setting the present income tax machinery in reverse and paying benefits to those below the tax threshold. The early versions of the scheme, notably that

---

[1] The disposable income retained = $(1 - 0·2)(1 - 0·25)(1 - 0·2)(1 - \frac{2}{3})$ of every $1 earned under the welfare system, giving a figure of 16 per cent; with a negative income tax, the last term becomes $(1 - \frac{1}{3})$ and the proportion of income retained rises to 32 per cent. The marginal tax rate is 100 per cent minus the proportion retained.

of Friedman (1962), were of this form. The scheme would operate through the existing tax machinery, the main new departure being that everyone would be required to file a tax return. On the basis of the information provided, a person would either pay tax as now or receive a negative tax supplement. In this way, it is hoped that the payment would be automatic and that the problems of take-up would be avoided. The operation of the scheme is illustrated in the bottom part of Fig. 11·3. The level of benefit, shown by the dashed line, is determined by the income tax exemption level and the rate applied. The negative tax would be fully integrated into the positive tax, and there would be no overlap.

In the United States this variant has received less attention than the Tobin scheme discussed above; in Britain, however, an integrated negative income tax was proposed by the Conservative government under the title of a 'tax credit', and if they had been returned to power in the general election of February 1974, the scheme would have been in force by the end of the decade. Its main feature was the abolition of income tax allowances and their replacement by a weekly tax credit payable to all. This would have had the effect of helping those below the tax threshold who do not at present obtain full benefit from the tax allowances. At the same time, tax would have been payable at the basic rate from the first £1 of income.

The way in which the scheme would have worked may be illustrated by reference to the position of a married couple. The illustrative credit for a couple in 1972 would have been £6 a week and the basic rate of tax 30 per cent. If the couple's income was £12 a week, the net payment to them would have been

$$£6 - (30 \text{ per cent} \times £12) = £2·40$$

If their income had risen to £20, then the tax credit would have been exactly offset by the tax due; and with an income above £20 they would have been net payers of tax.

In the case of children, the tax credit would have replaced not only the income tax allowances but also family allowances and the Family Income Supplement. As we have seen, the tax allowances provide no benefit to the poorest families; family allowances are inadequate to meet the needs of children; and the Family Income Supplement has only reached about half of all low income families. Their replacement by a single child benefit of equal value to all is therefore a step forward. With the exception of the child benefits, the existing provisions would have remained unchanged (in contrast to the proposal of Friedman to replace a wide variety of programmes). For adults, the levels of credit would have provided too low a guaranteed minimum income, and the government stated quite clearly that 'tax credits have not been designed with the intention of guaranteeing . . . that a family with no further help from the State would have enough to live on.' The social security system, including Supplementary Benefits, would therefore have remained largely intact.

The enactment of the tax credit scheme would have provided definite help to certain low income groups, who at present derive less than full benefit from the tax allowances. This is especially true of those now eligible for, but not claiming, Supplementary Benefit and Family Income Supplement. A family with two children where the father earned only half the average earnings would have gained to the extent of nearly £4 a week; a single pensioner dependent solely on the National Insurance pension would have been better off by £2 a week. There were, however, serious problems with the scheme as proposed by the Conservative government. It excluded some 10 per cent of the population: the self-employed, those unemployed, sick or disabled with no entitlement to National Insurance, and single parent families with low earnings. The needs of these groups are likely to be particularly pressing. Even in the case of those covered by the scheme, the benefit depended a great deal on individual circumstances. While the very poorest pensioners would have gained, the benefit would have fallen with income and pensioners at or only just above the Supplementary Benefit level would have been made worse off. Those receiving National Insurance sickness or unemployment benefit would have become subject to tax and the tax credit could well have been more than offset by the increased tax. It would have made only a very limited contribution to reducing marginal rates of tax. Finally, the problem of financing the scheme was inadequately considered. If the cost were to have been met by a rise in VAT, then the real gain in terms of purchasing power would have been considerably reduced.

11·4 Alternative strategies

In the preceding sections we have described the inadequacies of existing social insurance systems in Britain and the United States, the failure of means-tested welfare programmes, and some of the problems with negative income taxation. What then should be done?

If it is accepted that the means-testing strategy of recent years has failed to provide a solution, then the choice lies between the replacement of means-tested benefits by some form of negative income tax and their displacement by the expansion of social insurance and other categorical programmes. Various types of negative income tax have been described earlier, but the social insurance alternative requires elaboration. Its main features would be the extension of social insurance to groups not at present covered and the raising of benefits to provide a guaranteed minimum income at a desired level. In the United States, this approach would be typified by the introduction of child allowances payable to all families irrespective of income (although if the allowances were taxable, the net benefit would be less for higher income families). Within the existing social insurance programmes, the approach would involve, for example, the up-rating of OASDHI benefits and the extension of coverage. In Britain, the social insurance approach would involve a substantial increase in National Insurance benefits to bring them up to the average Supplementary Benefit payment, the replacement of the present child benefits by a uniform child endowment, and the extension of social insurance to provide complete coverage of groups such as single parent families and the disabled.

Opinion on the choice between these two approaches is often presented in polar terms, but this may well be misleading. Distinctions which appear clearcut, such as that between people who favour negative income taxation and those who do not, become less so in the face of the wide variety of schemes coming under this general label. The schemes favoured by the Conservative government in Britain and the McGovern campaign in the United States were, in fact, very different. Moreover, it is important to remember that the case for one type of approach may rest heavily on the institutional framework of a particular country. Given the differences between the existing income maintenance systems in Britain and the United States, it is not really surprising that the same policy may be espoused by Conservatives in one country and liberal Democrats in the other.

We can nonetheless distinguish certain differences in emphasis:

Pattern of benefits Both approaches are concerned with guaranteeing adequate minimum income, but they differ in the extent to which they seek to *concentrate* benefit on those at the lowest income levels. Under the negative income tax proposals, benefits would be withdrawn at a rate of $33\frac{1}{3}$ per cent or more as income rose; under the social insurance approach there would be less scope for such withdrawal, the main tapering of benefit being from their taxation under the income tax. The concentration of benefit on the lowest income groups is seen as a major advantage of negative income taxation, and Tobin has claimed that in the case of the alternative child allowance scheme, 'of the net benefits, nearly 80 per cent would go to families above the poverty line ... the end result would be a modest but dubious redistribution from childless taxpayers to large families, and very little redistribution from rich to poor' (1968, p. 110). If we felt fully confident about the adequacy of the poverty standard and that no one above this level was in need, then the sharp cut-off of benefits at the poverty line might well be acceptable. However, it may be doubted whether we can be *that* confident about the choice of a poverty line and we may feel that income redistribution towards those people not far above the poverty line may still be desirable. Moreover, the poverty line is defined for the purposes of analysis in terms of averages, and there may be people with incomes above the minimum who are, in fact, still in poverty because of individual variation in need.

Marginal tax rates and work incentives Associated with a particular benefit schedule is a pattern of marginal tax rates. The evidence concerning the effect of such differences in marginal rates on work incentives is limited, although more is becoming known, as the result of the negative income tax experiments in New Jersey and elsewhere. However, as Marmor has stressed, 'the absence of information about work incentives is no bar to the issue being politically important' (1971, p. 42). At a political level, concern about marginal rates is likely to focus on two issues: incentives for the poor not to work and the increase in taxation for the middle classes. The negative income tax with a high rate of withdrawal of benefit will have high marginal tax rates at the lower end (although lower than the welfare programme it would replace), and to this extent it is likely to be less attractive on the former count.[1] On the other hand, it provides benefits to those in work as well as to the unemployed, in contrast to the social insurance approach which only pays allowances for adults when they are not working. Moreover, to the extent that the negative income tax has a lower cost, it will involve less increase in taxation for the middle income ranges.

Measures to change pre-redistribution income A third difference concerns the relative importance of income maintenance as opposed to measures designed to change pre-redistributon incomes. Since the social insurance approach can provide no solution for the working man with no children, such measures must be accompanied by changes in labour market policy. The supporters of the social insurance approach typically favour the introduction of more effective minimum wage legislation, coupled with active steps to improve the employment prospects of the poor (such as the government acting as an employer of

---

[1] The effect on work incentives could be varied by relating the payment to the hourly wage rather than total earnings: see, for example, the wage subsidy proposals of Zeckhauser (1971) and Kesselman (1973).

last resort). On the other hand, many of the proponents of negative income taxation see it as a means of eliminating government interferences in the working of the market and envisage the abolition of minimum wage legislation.

Take-up and stigma The supporters of the social insurance approach attach great importance to securing 100 per cent take-up, and to the fact that 'our insurance type programs have worked better and gained greater acceptance than either our public assistance programs or those designed to aid the working poor' (US Department of Health, Education, and Welfare, 1969, p. 48). It seems safe to say that the social insurance approach would not encounter serious problems of incomplete take-up. On the other hand, with the negative income tax this is an open question, and it remains to be demonstrated that the scheme can be administered in a way which avoids the stigma of existing means-tested programmes.

Finally, whichever approach is adopted, it is widely agreed that new initiatives in the field of income maintenance are required. There is no reason to suppose that economic development and macro-economic policy can by themselves eliminate poverty, as was recognized by the Council of Economic Advisers: 'we cannot leave the further [reduction] of poverty to the general progress of the economy' (1964, p. 60). Such new initiatives are likely to involve a considerable cost. The original Tobin proposals for a negative income tax would have cost $14 billion in 1962, or 2½ per cent of the total gross national product. The British tax credit scheme had an estimated net cost of £1300 million, or almost the same percentage of gross national product. The cost of a social insurance alternative would be broadly similar. The elimination of poverty, as it has concerned government in recent years, requires a substantial transfer of resources.

12
WORLD DISTRIBUTION OF INCOME

In our circumstances an increase in the amount of goods produced and available for social services, for distribution, and for investment, is a socialist purpose ... An increase in production must have a very high priority in our social plans, it is the cornerstone for all our ambitions. It is necessary to stress this because the production of wealth for its own sake is not a socialist purpose. The purpose of production must always be the greater well-being of man.

(Julius Nyerere)

When the poverty line in the United States was $1000 per person, the *World Bank atlas* showed that the average *per capita* income in Brazil was under half that figure and that that in India was around one-tenth The differences between countries in terms of average *per capita* incomes, referred to here as the *international* distribution of income, appear on this basis to be very great. When we allow for the inequality within countries, then the distribution of income among all people of the world, referred to here as the *world* distribution, is extremely concentrated. In this chapter we examine the extent of such differences in income—whether they are as great as the figures suggest—and the scope for the world redistribution of income through foreign aid.

The international distribution is usually represented in terms of *per capita* incomes expressed in a common currency, here taken as the US dollar, using international exchange rates as a basis for the conversion. Although there are a number of serious drawbacks to such a measure, and these are discussed further below, it provides a first indication of the distribution between countries. Table 12·1 shows the *per capita* incomes of selected countries in 1970. It brings out the magnitude of the gap, measured in this way, between the United States at the top and the African and Asian countries at the bottom. In 1970 the ratio of *per capita* income in the United States to that in Tanzania was nearly 50:1, a difference which is some five times as large as that between the earnings of the prime minister and the average worker in Britain.

The second feature illustrated by the table is the continuous gradation in incomes between countries. One tends to think of advanced and developing countries in polar terms, but in fact no such sharp distinction can be drawn. If the ratio between the United States

TABLE 12·1
National Per capita incomes 1970

	US dollars
USA	4760
Sweden	4040
Canada	3700
Switzerland	3320
France	3100
Australia	2820
Netherlands	2430
United Kingdom	2270
Israel	1960
Japan	1920
Italy	1760
Greece	1090
Spain	1020
Venezuela	980
Chile	720
Mexico	670
Peru	450
Brazil	420
Iraq	320
Ghana	310
Egypt	210
Thailand	200
Bolivia	180
China	160[a]
Kenya	150
Uganda	130
Nigeria	120
Sudan	120
Sri Lanka	110
Haiti	110
India	110
Pakistan and Bangladesh	100
Tanzania	100
Indonesia	80[a]

Source: International Monetary Fund, *Finance and development*, March 1973, p. 27.

Notes: [a]Tentative estimate

The figures relate to gross national product *per capita* calculated at market prices and converted at an average exchange rate. They are rounded to the nearest $10.

and Tanzania in 1970 were 50:1, it would also be (in approximate terms):

40:1 Nigeria
37:1 Uganda
30:1 China
20:1 Egypt
15:1 Ghana
10:1 Peru
5:1 Greece

Nor can a straightforward geographical criterion be used to classify developing countries; there is no simple hierarchy (in ascending order) of Africa, Asia, Middle East, Latin America, and southern Europe. Within Africa, *per capita* income was $100 in Tanzania but three times that amount in Ghana; within Latin America, it ranged from $110 in Haiti to $980 in Venezuela. There is clearly a great heterogeneity of income levels, reflecting differences in history and social structure, as well as differences in natural endowments.

The figures for *per capita* income give equal weight to large and small countries and do not bring out the absolute numbers involved. It should be stressed, for example, that in 1970 half the world's population lived in countries with a *per capita* income of less than $175—all the countries below the horizontal line in Table 12·1. This feature is brought out more clearly using the Lorenz curve representation. The Lorenz curves for the distribution of *per capita* income in 1970 and 1949 are shown in Fig. 12·1, together with that for the distribution within the United States in 1970. This shows much greater concentration in the international distribution than that found within a single country: the share of the bottom 60 per cent in the United States in 1970 was around one-third of total income; the share of the bottom 60 per cent in the international distribution was less than 10 per cent. Moreover, comparing 1970 and 1949, there appears to have been a worsening over time in the position of the poorest countries, although some improvement has occurred in that of countries in the upper middle range relative to those at the top. The Lorenz curve has shifted outwards at the bottom and inwards at the top.

The method of comparing living standards in different countries on the basis of *per capita* incomes, as in Table 12·1, is open to a number of serious objections. Indeed, some people have gone so far as to argue that such international comparisons are meaningless.

The first obvious objection is that the quality of the underlying data is too poor to allow any comparison to be made. The figure for China, for example, is described by the World Bank as 'tentative' and there can be little doubt that the national accounts estimates are subject to substantial error particularly in the case of the less developed countries. There may also be considerable inaccuracies in the population figures. Bauer (1971), for example, refers to the official estimate of the population of Nigeria in 1963, which was 56 million, compared with an independent estimate of 37 million (the reason for the difference may have been that representation in the federal parliament depended on population, so that each region appeared to have 'padded' its population figure). This is probably an extreme case, and it is important to examine the likely magnitude of the errors and whether they are likely to lead to a systematic bias in the measurement of the gap between rich and poor countries. Kuznets (1966) suggests that the errors are likely to be in the direction of understatement and to be greater in less developed countries, but that the bias involved is probably not large:

with errors in the estimates for developed countries reasonably assumed to be no greater than 7·5 per cent and in those for underdeveloped countries no greater than 20 per cent (which may be too large an allowance), the true ratio of the *per capita* products of the two groups of countries is likely to be between a tenth and a seventh lower than that actually estimated (1966, p. 371).

The second objection is that the limited scope of national income accounts leads to a relative understatement of incomes in less developed countries, particularly through the exclusion of production for own consumption. The main example is the output of subsistence agriculture, which tends to be undervalued in national income statistics; since this sector is more important in poor countries, the size of the gap tends to be exaggerated. The same is probably true of the value of intra-family services (e.g. those of housewives), although there are other factors, such as the imputed services of consumer durables or public capital, which would work in the opposite direction. Kuznets (1966) makes an approximate estimate of the extent of this exaggeration. On the assumption that the net missing output would be a quarter of the total product of the agricultural sector, and that this in turn represents 40 per cent more of output in less developed countries, he concludes that their relative *per capita* income should be raised by roughly one-tenth.

The third objection concerns the use of exchange rates to convert all figures to a common standard, and it is widely recognized that exchange rates may be a poor guide to purchasing power. Even if they reflect the relative prices of goods entering foreign trade, they do not adequately represent goods and services which are not exchanged internationally (e.g. haircuts). This is important because there tends to

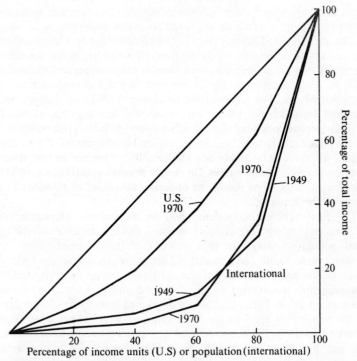

Fig. 12·1. International distribution of *per capita* income, 1949 and 1970
Source: See Tables 4·2 and 12·1, and Andic and Peacock (1961).

be a systematic relationship between the level of development and the extent to which the exchange rate differs from a rate of conversion reflecting purchasing power. The relative prices of goods not entering international trade tend to be lower in less developed countries, so that a given income will buy relatively more than the exchange rate would suggest.

A number of attempts have been made to calculate 'purchasing power parity' rates of conversion, using a common set of prices. From these it has been suggested (David, 1972) that the true gap between the United States and other countries is only four-ninths of that indicated by exchange rate conversions, where the 'gap' is defined as the difference in *per capita* incomes as a proportion of the income of the other country concerned. For example, the nominal gap between the United States and Uganda appears to be $37 - 1 = 36$ from the data in Table 12·1; the four-ninths rule would lead to an adjusted figure of 16, so that the adjusted ratio of *per capita* incomes would be $16 + 1 = 17$. This adjustment is subject to a number of reservations, since it relies on extrapolating estimates from advanced countries. Moreover, it is based on the use of United States prices, as the common method of valuation. This means that the four-ninths figure is likely to be on the low side: the use of the price in an advanced country for mangoes or a shoeshine leads to a wider disparity than if the price in a less developed country were employed. The comparison by Usher (1963) of Britain and Thailand illustrates this point, since he showed that the ratio of British to Thai incomes per head was 2·8 when valued at British prices, but 6·3 when valued at Thai prices. Usher argues for the use of the former figure, but there is no single best choice. All that we can do is to try to give upper and lower estimates. On certain assumptions (Balassa, 1973), this gives a range from the factor of four-ninths referred to above to a factor of three-quarters.

The final problem considered here is that of the allowance for differences in needs. The simple process of dividing national income by total population may not take account of its age composition, of differences in family and household structure, or of factors such as climate. The possible impact of the age structure may be illustrated by assuming that the average needs of a child under 15 are a quarter of those of an adult. If the typical less developed country has 40 per cent of its population aged under 15, compared with 25 per cent in an advanced country, the conversion on an equivalent adult basis reduces the gap by about one eighth. Since the allowance of a quarter is probably too low (see Table 3·2), this is likely to be an outside limit to the necessary adjustment. Climatic differences are taken into account by Usher (1963), who reduces the British income per head by about 15 per cent on account of the cost of keeping warm, although he makes no allowance for the cost of air conditioning in Thailand. This reflects the common observation that a lower need in one respect may be highly correlated with greater needs on other accounts; as Usher himself recognizes elsewhere, 'one environment is rarely better than another in every respect' (1966, p. 21).

This examination has suggested several ways in which the figures given in Table 12·1 may overstate the gap between rich and poor countries: the likely errors, the undervaluation of subsistence output, the use of foreign exchange rates and differences in age composition. We should not, however, conclude that the gap is non-existent or unimportant. If we take the larger adjustment factor (four-ninths) for differences in purchasing power, the ratio of *per capita* income in the United States to that of Uganda is reduced from 37:1 to 17:1. If we now allow for the effects of errors, for subsistence output and age composition, using the adjustments described above, we get

$$\text{Adjusted ratio} = 17 \times \underset{\text{errors}}{\frac{6}{7}} \times \underset{\text{subsis-}}{\underset{\text{tence}}{\frac{9}{10}}} \times \underset{\text{age}}{\frac{7}{8}} = 11\tfrac{1}{2}$$

If we were to apply the smaller adjustment factor (three-quarters) for differences in purchasing power, the ratio for the United States and Uganda would be reduced from 37 to 28, and then by further adjustments to approximately 19.[1] Applying the same kind of calculation to other less developed countries suggests that, in broad terms, the ratio of income per head in the United States to that of poor countries is reduced by a factor of between two and three.

Even with the larger of these adjustments, the gap between rich and poor countries remains very great. The problem cannot be made to disappear by statistical sleight of hand: 'the main effect of better statistics is not to make us change our views about the extent of poverty in the underdeveloped countries, but rather to make us attach different numbers to the scale of poverty and wealth' (Usher, 1966, p. 40).

One interesting attempt to derive such a different scale for the international distribution is that of Beckerman and Bacon (1970). They employed the purchasing power adjusted estimates of *per capita* real consumption where they exist, and extrapolated them to other countries using various non-monetary indicators which are widely available.[2] According to their results, real consumption per head may be predicted quite accurately if we know only the newsprint consumption and the number of installed telephones in a country. If these results are assumed to apply to all countries, and not just to those for which purchasing power adjusted estimates are available, which is clearly a strong assumption, then they can be used to examine the world distribution of real consumption. (It should be noted that these figures relate to *consumption* and not income, as discussed earlier.)

[1] The unadjusted gap is $37 - 1 = 36$, which becomes 27 on the three-quarters rule, giving a ratio of $27 + 1 = 28$, which is then multiplied by $\tfrac{6}{7} \times \tfrac{9}{10} \times \tfrac{7}{8}$. The general formula for the adjusted ratio y^* of the United States *per capita* income to that in a less developed country is

$$y^* = \frac{27}{40} \times ((1 + \theta \times (y-1)))$$

where y is the nominal ratio, as shown in Table 12·1, and θ takes the value $\tfrac{4}{9}$ or $\tfrac{3}{4}$ depending on the purchasing power conversion applied.

[2] In contrast to the four-ninths and other purchasing power adjustment rules, their method makes no use of national accounts statistics for extrapolation and thus avoids problems arising from their greater unreaiability in less developed countries. No adjustment is made for age composition.

The resulting estimates show, as expected, a larger share going to the poorer countries than in the income figures illustrated in Fig. 12·1, but the share of the bottom 40 per cent in 1962—3 was still only 7 per cent of total world consumption. Beckerman and Bacon conclude that the international distribution is far more unequal than that within any one country, such as the United States or Britain, and that there has been no significant change over time. This conclusion about the trend over time differs from that indicated by Fig. 12·1. This may in part reflect the different period (Beckerman and Bacon were comparing 1962—3 with 1954—5), but it may also be a result of the different method of estimation.

TABLE 12·2

Growth targets and achievement 1960—70

Countries (ranked in descending order of *per capita* income)	Growth rate of *per capita* income (% per annum) Required to reach by the year 2000			
	Per capita income of US	Half *per capita* income of US	Third of *per capita* income of US	Actual growth rate 1960—70
Venezuela	7·3	5·0	3·6	2·3
Singapore	7·5	5·1	3·8	5·2
Mexico	8·5	6·2	4·8	3·7
Brazil	10·1	7·8	6·4	2·4
Zambia	10·3	7·9	6·6	7·1
Malaysia	10·4	8·1	6·8	3·1
Phillipines	12·4	10·1	8·8	2·9
Egypt	12·4	10·1	8·8	1·7
Thailand	12·6	10·3	8·9	4·9
Kenya	13·5	11·2	9·8	3·6
Nigeria	14·3	12·0	10·6	0·1
Sri Lanka	14·6	12·3	10·9	1·5
India	14·6	12·3	10·9	1·2
Tanzania	14·9	12·6	11·2	3·6

Source: as Table 12·1.

In whatever way the evidence is viewed, the disparity between countries remains substantial. In order to close the gap, the standard of living of the developing countries has to rise at a much faster rate than that in the already developed countries. The magnitude of the task can be seen from Table 12·2, which shows the rates of growth of *per capita* income (i.e. growth in excess of the population increase) which would have to be attained to reach a given proportion of the *per capita* income of the United States by the year 2000, on the assumption that the United States' *per capita* income grows at a rate of 2 per cent per annum. The figures relate to *per capita* incomes converted at exchange rates, and hence are subject to the objections discussed above. For this reason a range of targets is presented; that of one-third may be seen as corresponding to the higher of the adjustment factors described above, and that of a half to the lower factor.

Setting a target of one-third would require a *per capita* growth rate in excess of 4 per cent per annum for all countries with average incomes below that of Singapore. Yet the Pearson Commission on International Development put forward a growth target of 6 per cent per annum, which with 2 per cent population growth would mean a 4 per cent growth of *per capita* income. At such a rate, all countries shown in the table, apart from Venezuela and Singapore, would still have *per capita* incomes less than one-third of the target. These calculations clearly depend crucially on the assumption about the United States growth rate; however, even if there were zero growth in the United States, a growth rate in excess of 4 per cent would still be required by all countries with average incomes below $500 in 1970.

Some countries have achieved growth rates considerably higher than 4 per cent, as is illustrated by Zambia, Singapore and Thailand in the table, to say nothing of the oil-producing states.[1] It is reasonable to hope that these countries will eventually catch up with the advanced nations. Eight of the fourteen countries shown, however, had average annual growth rates of less than the 3·2 per cent achieved by the United States over the decade. For them the First Development Decade allowed no catching up. Even if the United States did not grow at all, it would take over 200 years to close the gap between the United States and India on the basis of the experience of the 1960s. In many cases, of course, the growth rate of total income is substantially higher: in India the average annual rate was 3·5 per cent, in Egypt 4·2 per cent, and in Brazil 5·3 per cent. The increase in *per capita* incomes is substantially reduced by the persistence of high birth rates.

12·2 The world distribution and inequality within countries

The previous section was concerned with differences between countries in average *per capita* income, but this masks the inequality which exists *within* countries. When this is taken into account, the world distribution of income is seen to be even more concentrated. By treating each country as if incomes were equally distributed, we have undoubtedly understated by a substantial amount the degree of income differences

[1] It should be noted that the actual growth rates shown in Table 12·2 are based on a nominal exchange rate conversion, and—just as the gap is exaggerated by such a method—the speed of convergence towards the income level of the United States will be overstated.

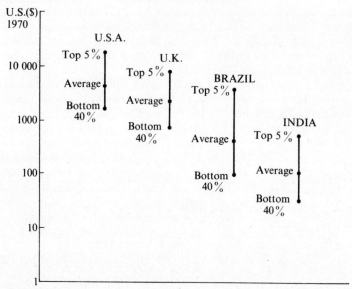

Fig. 12·2. The effect of income differences within countries on world distribution.

Source: Tables 12·1 and 12·3.

among the world's inhabitants. The oil sheikhdoms, deliberately left out of the earlier discussion, provide a vivid illustration. Their *per capita* income may well be the highest in the world, but they contain many people with extremely low incomes.

The impact of inequality within countries is illustrated by Fig. 12·2. This takes the average *per capita* incomes in nominal terms in 1970 for four countries, together with data for the distribution of income within those countries (discussed further below), and shows the position of the top 5 per cent and the bottom 40 per cent. It brings out the overlap between the poor in one country and the rich in another. The bottom 40 per cent in the United States come quite a long way down the income scale: they have an average income considerably less than that of the top 5 per cent in Brazil. The bottom 40 per cent in the United Kingdom have, on average, an income only one and a half times that of the top 5 per cent in India. On the other hand, the gap between the top and the bottom is clearly greater. If we take the top 5 per cent in the United States and the bottom 40 per cent in India, we find the gap widening to a ratio of 400:1. (Applying the adjustment factors derived in the previous section would give a ratio of between 125:1 and 200:1 in round terms.)

The income differences within developing countries have most important implications. They mean that a number of countries with average *per capita* incomes well above that of India—$110 in 1970—may still have a substantial fraction of their population below that level. If the bottom 40 per cent of the population in developing countries received on average a third of the national average (i.e. if their share in the total is around $13\frac{1}{3}$ per cent), then countries with *per capita* incomes up to $330 or higher would contain a large fraction of people below the *per capita* income of India. The countries with the lowest *per capita* incomes singled out for special consideration in various United Nations resolutions are undoubtedly those with the most urgent problems, but they are not the only ones of concern.

A feature of Fig. 12·2 is that the extent of income inequality is shown as being greater within the less developed countries, the line for Brazil, for example, being longer than that for the United Kingdom.[1] The question of international differences in income distributions has been examined in depth by Kuznets. According to his pioneering study, the share of the top groups in before tax income is distinctly higher in developing than in developed countries, the share of the top 5 per cent ranging from 30 per cent to 40 per cent in the former, and from 20 per cent to 25 per cent in the latter. At the same time, he found that the share of the larger, bottom group tended to be broadly similar in developing and developed countries. It was therefore the middle ranges whose share was lower in the developing countries.

More detailed information about the distribution of income is provided by Table 12·3, which covers those countries for which comparable data are available, ranked in approximately descending order of *per capita* incomes. Kuznets described his early work in this area as '5 per cent empirical information and 95 per cent speculation', and the figures given here must equally be regarded with considerable caution. As we have seen in Chapter 2, the comparison of income distributions across countries involves many problems and these are even more serious when comparing countries with such differences in social and economic structure. Moreover, the countries are not a random selection, although there is no reason to suppose that there is any systematic bias.

Bearing these qualifications in mind, we can see that the table provides some broad confirmation of Kuznets' analysis. Taking an arbitrary dividing line at Japan shows that in all the developed countries the share of the top 5 per cent was a quarter or less: whereas it was above a quarter in over half the developing countries shown. Moreover,

[1] Since the scale is logarithmic, the distance measures the ratio of the average income of the top 5 per cent to the average income of the bottom 40 per cent.

TABLE 12·3

Distribution of income within countries

Country	Date	Percentage share of Bottom 40 per cent	Top 20 per cent	Top 5 per cent
United States	1966	15	44	19
Canada	1965	20	40	14
France	1962	10	54	25
Australia	1966	20	39	14
United Kingdom	1964	15	44	19
Japan	1962	15	46	20
Puerto Rico	1963	14	51	22
Argentina	1961	17	52	29
Uruguay	1967	14	47	21
Chile	1968	15	52	23
Mexico	1963	10	59	29
Lebanon	1955–60	13	61	34
Brazil	1970	10	62	33
Zambia	1959	15	57	38
Phillipines	1965	12	55	30
Thailand	1962	13	58	34
Sudan	1969	15	48	17
Sri Lanka	1969–70	17	46	19
India	1964–5	17	49	25
Tanzania	1967	14	61	36
Pakistan and Bangladesh	1963–4	18	45	20

Source: Paukert (1973) and other sources referred to there. In certain cases the figures have been brought up to date or adjusted, and they have been rounded to the nearest per cent.

Note: the estimates are of varying degrees of reliability, but are standardized to relate to the distribution among households and cover the whole country.

the share of the bottom 40 per cent does not seem to be related to the level of development, lying between 12 and 18 per cent in all but five of the countries. At the same time, there is considerable diversity, particularly within the group of developing countries. The distribution in Sri Lanka, Sudan, and Uruguay appears to be little different from that in most of the developed countries, whereas that in certain other countries (e.g. Mexico, Brazil, Zambia, and Thailand) appears to be considerably more concentrated. It is important to remember, therefore, that while broad generalizations may have some truth, there is a great deal of variation between countries in the distribution of income; moreover, this variation may be exaggerated or understated by differences between the methods by which the statistics are compiled.

The elimination of world income differences depends, therefore, both on the growth of *per capita* income discussed in the previous section and on the cnanges in the distribution of income within countries. The cross-country comparison described above suggests at first sight that there are grounds to expect some redistribution away from the top groups as incomes rise. However, *cross-country* comparisons are not necessarily a reliable guide to the way in which the distribution is likely to change *over time*. Kuznets himself, on the basis of an examination of the historical experience of a number of countries, has argued that the distribution tends during the course of industrialization first to become more unequal and then to move in the direction of greater equality. He found that the degree of concentration in Britain had widened up to the middle of the nineteenth century and then narrowed; in the United States, the reversal took place later (around the time of the First World War).

The explanation by Kuznets of this pattern was based in large part on the sectoral structure of the economy and on the changing weights of different sectors. Any such attempt to identify the causes of changes in the distribution has clearly to be based on a simplified view of the development process, which does not apply with equal force to all countries. Nonetheless it may be useful to sketch some of the features which appear to be important. Kuznets stressed that the final distribution of income was the weighted average of two basically different distributions, for the agricultural and non-agricultural sectors of the economy. This classification may not be appropriate for some countries (for example, those with substantial plantation agriculture) but we can envisage a more general interpretation of a 'dual' economy with a traditional/advanced or rural/urban division. Typically, there is a substantial difference in average income between the two sectors, and the distribution within the modern sector exhibits greater dispersion than that within the traditional sector. If economic growth leads to an increased importance of the modern sector it is likely therefore to cause a rise in inequality. On the other hand, this may be offset by a reduction in the differential between the sectors, or by a decline in the degree of inequality within the modern sector. It was to this latter factor that Kuznets attributed the reversal of the trend towards concentration of incomes: 'the major offset to the widening of income inequality associated with the shift from agriculture and the country-side to industry and the city must have been a rise in the share of the lower groups within the non-agricultural sector of the population' (1955, p. 17).

As Kuznets points out, 'there is danger in simple analogies', and the experience of the developing countries need not follow that of the advanced countries. However, many authors have suggested that there will be a similar widening and then narrowing of income differences. To take one example, Baster (1970) suggested that there are three stages to the process. Below an average *per capita* income of around $300 'inequalities of income would be generated . . . as a result of . . . the sharp differences between the subsistence and modern sectors and the inequality within sectors'; there would then be a transitional stage between $300 and $500; and finally above this threshold the forces making for equality would be strengthened, incomes in agriculture rising, differences within sectors declining, and governments able to play a larger role in the process of income redistribution.

The evidence required to demonstrate the applicability of this hypothesis to the less developed countries is not available for a sufficient length of time and range of countries to allow any firm conclusions to be drawn. What fragments there are, however, are not encouraging. The study by Weisskoff (1970), for example, of three Latin American countries with average incomes well above $500 *per capita*, showed that while the share of the top 5 per cent fell between the 1950s and the early 1960s, the share of the bottom 40 per cent was also reduced. In the case of Puerto Rico, he concluded that the sectoral changes identified earlier were all working in the direction of increased concentration: 'the observation that country-wide equality declined . . . is consistent with the three major factors revealed by the sectoral study: first, divergences between average incomes in both sectors: second, increasing weight to the less equal sector; third, increasing inequality in both sectors' (1970, p. 326). The use of figures for single years and for a relatively short period is clearly subject to dangers. The period covered by the Argentine data, for example, was one of political revolution, abrupt changes in economic policy, and a major devaluation in 1959. It is nonetheless striking that three countries pursuing rather different development policies should exhibit the same pattern of changes in the distribution of income. It means, for these countries at least, either that they are still in the first stage of the process or that the hypothesis does not hold.

To sum up the evidence about inequality within countries, there are clearly substantial differences in income within less developed countries, and the world distribution of income is consequently more unequal than the international distribution discussed in the previous section. The direction in which the distribution within countries is changing is hard to establish, but there are structural reasons to expect an increase in concentration in the early stages of development. Whether this trend will be reversed as incomes rise is yet to be determined. Finally, it should not be forgotten that economic inequality is far wider than the distribution of income on which we have focused here. In most non-socialist low income countries, the distribution of wealth is much more concentrated than the distribution of income, and this is especially marked in the case of land-holdings.

12·3 Aid and world redistribution

Whatever the problems of measurement, there can be little doubt that the differences in incomes on a world scale are considerable. The gap between the average incomes of rich and poor countries is still substantial, even when allowance is made for the shortcomings of the figures usually quoted, and this is greatly accentuated by differences of income within countries. The evidence about changes over time is not encouraging. While some countries may well catch up with the standard of living of the industrialized nations, others stand little chance at the rates of growth achieved during the 1960s. While some countries may be in the second Kuznets phase, with a narrowing of income differentials, others appear to have experienced increasing concentration. These considerations lead us to examine the scope for world redistribution through foreign aid.

Foreign aid is one of the principal measures for world redistribution, but at present its impact is very limited. This is illustrated by the Pearson Commission on International Development, which in 1969 recommended as a target for overseas aid that rich countries should provide 1 per cent of their gross national product per annum by 1975, of which 0·7 per cent should be official aid. The potential significance of aid at such a level may be seen most simply from the estimate by the United Nations that 'a flow of capital representing 1 per cent of the incomes of the developed countries adds about 10 per cent to the national incomes of the underdeveloped countries and about 100 per cent to their present net capital formation' (1962). In other words, in terms of narrowing the differences in current incomes, such a transfer would have a scarcely significant effect. A 10 per cent rise in the income of India would still leave its *per capita* income at a mere 5–7½ per cent (on an adjusted basis) of that of the United States.

The increase in aid could make a significant addition to the resources available for capital formation, and hence could contribute to the accelerated growth of the developing countries (its effectiveness depends, of course, on any repercussions on domestic savings and on the extent to which there are other constraints on the rate of growth, such as limits to 'absorptive capacity' for investment). However, the Pearson target is in fact very modest. It aimed for a 6 per cent overall annual growth rate, but we have seen in the first section of this chapter that the achievement of this target would still mean that the gap between rich and poor nations closed at a very slow rate, if at all. For substantial progress to be made in narrowing international differences in *per capita* incomes by the end of the century, a much more rapid rate of progress has to be attained.

The Pearson Commission target would, therefore, neither make a substantial contribution to the narrowing of current living standards nor offer hope of rapid progress in this direction in the future. This target is, however, considerably higher than the current aid performance of most advanced countries and has not been met. In the United Kingdom official aid has been at a level of some 0·4 per cent of GNP, or slightly over half the target; in West Germany and the United States the figure has been 0·3 per cent; and in Japan 0·2 per cent.[1]

The small scale of current aid programmes is brought out even more starkly by comparison with proposals for redistribution at a national level. As we saw in the last chapter, there is active consideration in a number of advanced countries of ways of guaranteeing a minimum income through some form of negative income tax. This idea could be transferred to a world level as a means of determining international policy toward aid, as has been suggested by Weaver and Jones (1968). Suppose that we take a guaranteed minimum of $250 in 1970, or approximately one-third of the world average income, and a negative tax rate of 50 per cent. This would have meant, for example, that Ghana with a *per capita* income of $310, would have received aid *per capita* of $95 (or $250 minus 50 per cent of $310), and that Tanzania with a *per capita* income of $100 would have received aid of $200 a head. (In calculating the payments, adjustments to the national income figures would clearly be made.) Such an 'international negative income tax' scheme would mean a contribution from the countries above the break-even level of $500 of approximately 18 per cent of their total gross national product above that level—or many times the present level of aid. The burden would clearly be spread among donor countries in a progressive manner, and those not far above the break-even level (for example Mexico) could well be exempted. It would be possible to scale down the proposal. With the same break-even level, a negative tax rate of 20 per cent, for example, would cost donor countries 7 per cent of of gross national product in excess of $500, and would provide Tanzania with aid of $80 per head. Even this is many times higher than the Pearson target.

---

[1] Total aid is not the only factor of importance. The effective transfer depends on what proportion of the aid is provided in grants rather than commercial loans. (Concessionary loans—e.g. at low rates of interest—are regarded as containing a grant element.) While the repayment terms for loans have been improved in recent years, there has been a switch away from outright grants, so that the overall grant element in United Kingdom aid has been reduced. The value to the donor is also reduced when the aid is tied to the purchase of goods produced by the donor, as it is in many cases.

The effectiveness of aid as a means of world redistribution depends crucially on how it is allocated, both between and within countries. To have the greatest effect, aid should be channelled to those countries with the lowest *per capita* incomes, and should be used to finance projects which benefit the poorest within those countries. At present there seems little reason to believe that this is happening. The distribution of aid for a selection of countries is shown in Table 12·4. There appears to be no tendency for aid received per head to be inversely related to the level of *per capita* income, and indeed the study of Davenport (1970) suggested a *positive* relationship. There is no reason to suppose that a poorer country is like to receive more in *per capita* aid—if anything the reverse. There are, of course, other factors at work. The countries receiving large amounts of aid are those which are important to the donors for political or military reasons (Laos, Taiwan, and Jordan), which have close links with an ex-colonial power (particularly the French African states), and which are small in size (Malta, Swaziland). The same pattern is found at the level of the individual aid donor's policies. British aid allocation shows no correlation between aid per head and income per head, and even allowing for

TABLE 12·4

The distribution of aid

Country	Per capita income 1970, as in Table 12·1 ($)	Aid *per capita* 1965−8 annual average ($)
Malawi	80	7
Indonesia	80	2
Tanzania	100	3
India	110	2
Guinea	120	4
Laos	120	24
Nigeria	120	2
Mauritius	140	7
South Vietnam	200	25
Phillipines	210	3
South Korea	250	8
Ghana	310	8
Malaysia	380	5
Jamaica	670	9

Sources: Table 12·1 and OECD, *Resources for the developing world: the flow of financial resources to less-developed countries 1962−8*, Table 31.

the British preference towards Commonwealth or ex-Commonwealth countries, the poorest countries, such as India, receive on a *per capita* basis less than relatively well off countries, such as Jamaica and Malaysia (Elliott, 1974).

The allocation of aid *within* developing countries is a matter of grave importance. The impact of aid on income inequalities within countries is not well documented, but some authors have doubted whether its incidence is very progressive. Bauer has suggested that 'foreign aid benefits better-off people within the recipient countries, notably members of the urban population and especially politicians, civil servants, academics and certain sections of the business community' (1971, p. 115). Elliott (1974) has pointed out that one reason for this may be the tying of aid to purchases from the donor country, which biases the selection of projects towards those in the modern sector and towards large infra-structural projects, such as hydro-electricity and roads. The foreign exchange content of projects designed to benefit the poorest groups is often low. A good example is medical care, where a large part of British aid has gone to large urban hospitals and very much smaller sums have gone into preventive medicine or the provision of rural health centres. This kind of bias in the allocation of aid has been recognized in recent years by the World Bank and in 1973 Mr McNamara announced a re-orientation of priorities, giving more attention to problems of income distribution and emphasizing aid to the rural sector.

The fact that aid may have failed to provide most help to the poorest countries or to the poorest groups within a country is one of the reasons why it has been criticized by people on both the left and the right of the political spectrum. Bauer (1971), for example, has attacked the concept of aid as redistributive taxation on the grounds that, unlike domestic taxation, it is not redistribution between persons but redistribution between governments. (Hence the gibe that 'foreign aid is a process by which poor people in rich countries help rich people in poor countries'.) Whether this is a *necessary* feature of foreign aid is not clear. Its not being so depends on the scope for the donor countries to finance the transfer through progressive taxation, and on the degree of control exercised by donors over the domestic policies of the recipients. Bauer himself favours such increased control by the donor, both for this reason and to ensure that aid contributes most effectively to development.

The attack on foreign aid from the left has emphasized that aid policy is an important component in the foreign policy of the major industrial countries. President Kennedy may have said that the United States provided aid 'not because the Communists are doing it, not because we seek their votes, but because it is right', but in another speech he made no attempt to disguise the fact that 'foreign aid is a method by which the United States maintains a position of influence and control around the world'. This is reflected in the allocation of aid described earlier, and is embodied in such legislation as the Hickenlooper Amendment, which prohibits aid to countries which nationalize United States owned assets and fail to make appropriate compensation. From this it is argued that aid provided by countries with overt or covert political motives is unlikely to be to the long-run benefit of the less-developed countries. The analysis by Hayter (1971) of the impact of the World Bank in Latin America led her to suggest that the concern of international agencies for preserving economic and political stability has frequently conflicted with action to improve the conditions of life of the majority of Latin Americans.

Seers has drawn a parallel with the evolution of attitudes towards poverty in advanced countries:

We live in an age of archaic attitudes to international poverty. Once the main way of relieving poverty in Britain was by charity—whether from individuals or through charitable associations or the parishes. In retrospect, we can now see that, though charity undoubtedly alleviated some of the worst social miseries . . . it was in itself entirely inadequate to change the social structure . . . indeed . . . charity may well have helped to consolidate the *status quo* (1971, p. 346).

In this context we can interpret the proposal for an international negative income as corresponding to the growth at the domestic level of social insurance and redistribution through the tax system. It would represent a major change, not only in the magnitude of aid, but also in the form in which the transfers of resources was made. There would be no restrictions on membership of the scheme and the allocation would be determined solely by *per capita* income, adjusted to a comparable basis. The payments would not depend on political attitudes or foreign policies. The scheme would not, however, meet the objection that the recipient countries could use the aid to benefit their richest citizens— that the poor in the United States were being taxed to help wealthy mine-workers in Zambia or prosperous businessmen in Liberia. For the proposal to have any prospect of acceptance, it would have to incorporate certain restrictions on domestic policies. In this it would be closer to social insurance (for example, in the same way as receipt of unemployment benefit is conditional on seeking work) than to a negative income tax. Whether agreement could be reached on such a set of conditions is an open question. While both left and right agree that the present situation has serious shortcomings, their recommendations would in many cases involve moving in opposite directions.

Finally, the parallel drawn by Seers between the world redistribution and policies at a domestic level reminds us that such transfers can form only one component of a policy to lessen world income differences. Just as unions and state intervention have affected pre-redistribution incomes in domestic economies, so too, in an international context, changes in the world economic system—for example, in the trade relations between rich and poor countries, or in the regulation of multinational companies—may play an equally important role.

13
THE APPROACH TO THE ISSUES

The aim of this chapter is not to draw conclusions about the extent of inequality, or about the need for changes in policy. Its purpose is rather to emphasize the main features of the approach, and to draw together the threads of a book whose subject matter has ranged from fringe benefits for executives to subsistence output, from inheritance taxation to public assistance, from intelligence tests to trade union bargaining power.

The approach adopted to this wide range of topics has had certain common features. The first is the emphasis on quantitative aspects. Discussion of statistics may be dull, but 'looking at the figures' seems very much preferable to the frequently employed alternative of consulting one's prejudices. This need for quantitative analysis is brought out clearly where, as often happens, the readily available evidence is seriously deficient. In many cases, writers have tended to point to the difficulties and then simply conclude that nothing can be said. To take two examples, Titmuss (1962) detailed with great care the shortcomings of the income distribution statistics in Britain, but did not indicate their likely quantitative importance, and Bauer (1971) argued that the problems in an international comparison of incomes were such that it was doubtful whether it had any meaning.

In contrast to this nihilistic outlook, the approach followed here has been to examine the extent to which the figures are deficient and to try and assess how far this affects the conclusions drawn. One has to ask whether the observed differences in incomes could be eliminated by making allowance for factors missing from the conventional picture, or whether the differences would be increased. As described by Kuznets, the approach adopted here 'is needed not only to warn against uncritical reliance on the estimates as they are usually shown but, perhaps even more, to counter their complete dismissal because of the serious errors and biases in them' (1966, p. 386).

Emphasis on quantification should not be interpreted as a blind faith in items which can be measured; rather it reflects a concern with aspects of the distribution which are important. It is easy to point to features which are striking, even exotic, particularly at the upper tail of the distribution, but which are really relatively unimportant. Reference was made to the allowance for members of the House of Lords, and the high earnings of singers, film stars, and sportsmen probably come in the same category. In this book, the main focus has been on aspects of the distribution which affect a large number of people or substantial amounts of income and wealth. Chapter 8, for example, was concerned with a small fraction of the population (the top $0{\cdot}1$ per cent), but on the grounds that they held a considerably larger proportion of total wealth.

The relative importance of different factors affects judgements about the equity or otherwise of the distribution. There is a tendency for it to be argued that the observed differences in income do not indicate inequity, since they reflect differences in individual decisions, in age, or in tastes. For this to be convincing, it would have to be established that the observed differences in income can in fact be explained in this way—just pointing to the possibility is not enough. In this book we have taken certain examples, examining the contribution of decisions about human capital (Chapter 5), and the role of life-cycle savings (Chapter 7). It appears from the evidence that earnings differentials do not simply reflect decisions about education; nor do age differences explain more than part of the concentration of wealth.

The interpretation of differences in income and wealth in effect requires an understanding of the determinants of the distribution, and a major part of the book has been concerned with seeking such an explanation. What are the forces governing movements in the share of profits? How far are earnings explained by the institutions of the labour market, rather than by personal characteristics of workers? These problems not only are intellectually testing, but also must be resolved before we can make firm predictions about future developments or the impact of government policy. We have drawn attention to the danger of extrapolating from past trends without considering the underlying forces, and have stressed the dependence of policy recommendations (for example, minimum wage legislation) on particular views as to how the distribution is determined.

In seeking to understand the causes, however, we have time and time again come to phenomena for which no adequate explanation exists. Governments are facing distributional problems whose causes are not well understood and for which there are often no agreed policies. One of the aims of the book has been to demonstrate that far too little is known about this central subject. This is an indictment of economics, but it is also a challenge. There are fascinating and important questions to be answered.

NOTES ON SOURCES AND FURTHER READING

The aim of these notes is to provide fuller details of the main sources, and to suggest further reading. They are arranged by chapters, so as to facilitate reference from the text. No attempt has been made to be exhaustive, but those sources which contain good bibliographies have been indicated. The items marked with an asterisk are more technical.

Chapter 1 Introduction

There is very little in this book which is original, and it has drawn heavily on the work of others. This has, however, involved assembling material from different sources, since there have been very few books in recent years covering the same wide range of topics. The classic studies of Dalton (1920) and Cannan (1914) have no modern counterparts. The nearest perhaps is Pen's book on income distribution, which covers similar ground to our Chapters 1–6 and 9. His exposition is remarkable (and has been borrowed in Chapter 2), although the housewives to whom the book is partly addressed may be put off by there being considerably more mathematics than here (although fewer statistics). The recent books on income distribution by Bronfenbrenner (1971) and Johnson (1973) are, as noted in the text, concerned largely with factor shares.

There are several books of readings relevant to the field. Budd (1967) has selections on the goal of equality, on the distribution of income and wealth in the United States, on the determinants of inequality, and on poverty, as well as a useful bibliography. Scoville (1971) covers similar ground, but is more directed at policy, with selections on the tax system, labour market policy, and income maintenance. Atkinson (1973) was designed to accompany the course of lectures in which this book originated. (Other books of readings on specific topics, for example on poverty, are referred to under the relevant chapters.)

For an excellent introduction to some of the issues involved in the definition of inequality, and further reference to the literature, see Sen (1973). See also Bauer and Prest (1973), and the exchange between Thurow (1973) and Posner (1973).

A small selection from the many sources dealing with the relationship between economic inequality and wider social inequality are Tawney (1964), Miller and Roby (1970), Runciman (1966), Goldthorpe (1974), and Reissman (1973). See also the readings edited by Béteille (1969), Rainwater (1974), and Urry and Wakeford (1973).

Chapter 2

A general review of some of the main features of the distribution of income and wealth can be found in some, but not all, introductory textbooks: for example, in the case of Britain, Brown (1970), Chapter 4, Hicks (1971), Chapter 18, and Prest (1970), Chapter 5. For similar material on the United States, see, among others, Miller (1964), Samuelson (1973), Chapters 5, 9 and 39, Fusfeld (1972), Chapters 36 and 37, Thurow and Lucas (1972), Edwards, Reich, and Weisskopf (1972), Chapter 5, and *Toward a Social Report* (US Department of Health, Education, and Welfare, 1969).

References to further reading on the topics discussed are to be found below under the relevant chapters.

Chapter 3

The definition of resources, with particular reference to taxation, is discussed by Simons (1938), Kaldor (1955), Vickrey (1947), and the Royal Commission on the Taxation of Profits and Income (1955). Extracts from this literature are conveniently reprinted in Houghton (1970).

The effect of income variability and the choice of different assessment periods was brought out in Friedman's study of the consumption function (1957). The application to income distribution data, and the relationship to the individual life-cycle, have been discussed by Lydall (1955) and Morgan (1962) and (1965), the latter being reprinted in part in Atkinson (1973). The concept of lifetime income is discussed in Layard (1974). A clear description of the process of discounting used in calculating lifetime incomes is given by Rowan (1968), pp. 186–7 (his example relates to an investment project, but the same principles apply).

The choice of unit for analysis is treated by Morgan *et al.* (1962), Chapter 20 and by Morgan (1965). See also Atkinson (1974). The work of Rowntree determining equivalence scales is discussed further in Chapter 10. The alternative approach to equivalence scales is represented by the work of Nicholson (1949) and Henderson (1949). For recent reviews of the literature, see Abel-Smith and Bagley (1970) and *Brown and Deaton (1972), pp. 1178–86.

For more details on the methodology of measuring inequality, see the pioneering article by Dalton (1920a), *Kolm (1969), *Champernowne (1973), and *Atkinson (1970). For the mathematical representation of the Gini coefficient and discussion of standard errors, see *Kendall and Stuart (1969), Chapters 2 and 10, and for a straightforward method of calculation, see the appendix to Morgan (1962).

Chapter 4

The first reference in the British context must be to Titmuss (1962), whose critique of the official statistics has had considerable influence, although it was far from universally acclaimed (see, for example, the review by Prest (1963)). In the United States, important references are Kuznets (1953), Morgan (1962), Kravis (1962), and Miller (1966). (An extract from the last is reprinted in Atkinson (1973).)

In Britain, the main studies of income distribution since the Second World War have been (in chronological order) Paish (1957), Allen (1957), Lydall (1959), Brittain (1960), R. J. Nicholson (1967) (reprinted in Atkinson (1973)), Prest and Stark (1967), Stewart (1972), and Stark (1972). For an excellent survey of the available data in Britain, see Stark (forthcoming). For references to more technical points, see *Harrison (1975) on the use of the Pareto index and *Muellbauer (1974) on the change in relative prices.

In the United States, the principal references include Goldsmith et al. (1954), Solow (1960) (reprinted in part in Budd (1967)), Schultz (1964), Miller (1966), Haley (1968) (reprinted in Scoville (1971)), Budd (1970), Brimmer (1971), and Taussig (1973). This is only a partial list and further references are contained in Budd (1967).

The literature on the effect of the government budget on the distribution of income is represented by J. L. Nicholson (1965) in Britain and Gillespie (1965) in the United States. For recent results, see Nicholson (1974) and Okner and Pechman (1974) for the respective countries. For criticism of the methods employed, see, among others, *Aaron and McGuire (1970), Thurow (1971), Chapter 4, and Michelson (1970).

Chapter 5

This and the next chapter draw heavily on the work of labour economics. Reference should be made at the outset to Lydall (1968), which is particularly relevant to Chapter 5. Rees (1973), Hunter and Robertson (1969), Fleisher (1970), and Phelps Brown (1962) are more general in their coverage. For a rather briefer introduction, the reader is referred to McCormick (1969).

The evidence about the distribution of earnings is summarized very clearly in Lydall (1968), who describes more fully the meaning of lognormal and Pareto distributions. Valuable sources of information about earnings differentials over time in Britain are Routh (1965) and Thatcher (1968).

The human capital theory is clearly set out in the original article by Mincer (1958) (reprinted in Atkinson (1973)), and in Becker (1964). Mincer has surveyed more recent developments in (1970) and has made a substantial extension of the empirical results in (1974). Other expositions are contained in Blaug (1970) and Fisher (1971). The early study by Friedman and Kuznets (1945) is still of interest, and Hanoch (1967) is one of a number of recent attempts to examine the relationship between human capital and earnings. The relationship between ability, opportunity, and human capital is set out in Becker (1967).

The determinants of earnings, and the relative contribution of schooling, ability, and social class background, has been an active area for research. The work of Bowles and associates is reported in (1972), (1973), Bowles and Gintis (1973), and Bowles and Nelson (1974). Other important studies include Taubman (1974), Hause (1972), and Griliches and Mason (1972). The book by Jencks (1972) is wide-ranging but needs careful reading.

Chapter 6

In addition to general textbooks on the economics of labour, referred to above, there is a range of specialist studies on the institutions of the labour market. Lewis (1963) is the classic reference on the impact of unionization in the United States; in Britain, the reader is referred to the work of Turner, for example (1957), and, for a sceptical view of economists, Wootton (1962). A theoretical analysis of the impact of unionization is contained in *Johnson (1973), Chapter 10.

The concept of the internal labour market is described in Doeringer and Piore (1971), which refers to earlier writers, such as Kerr (1950). The following recent studies refer to similar features, although they differ in a number of respects: Thurow and Lucas (1972), Feldstein (1973), Hall (1971), and Bluestone (1970). For the application of the concept to Britain, see Bosanquet and Doeringer (1973). For summaries of the evidence on sex differentials in earnings in the United States, see for example Oaxaca (1973) and Council of Economic Advisers (1973), the latter having been reviewed by Bergmann and Adelman (1973).

The question of low pay in the United States is discussed further by Perrella (1967), Bluestone (1968), and Wachtel and Betsy (1972). The dual labour market hypothesis is described in Doeringer and Piore (1971) and Gordon (1972). On low pay in Britain, see Field (1973).

Chapter 7

The estate duty method of estimating the distribution of wealth is well described by Langley (1950) and Lampman (1962), and some of the problems with the choice of multipliers are examined by Revell (1967). The three different approaches are described in Atkinson (1972).

The main academic studies of the distribution of wealth have been Clay (1925), Daniels and Campion (1936), Campion (1939), Langley (1951), and Lydall and Tipping (1961). The last of these is reprinted in Atkinson (1973). More recent estimates are given in Polanyi and Wood (1974), which is an attack on Atkinson (1972), and in Atkinson and Harrison (1974).

In the United States, the main reference is to Lampman (1959) and (1962). Extracts from these are included in Budd (1967), Scoville (1971), and Atkinson (1973). See also the recent work of Smith (1974), Smith and Franklin (1974), and the sample survey evidence in Federal Reserve Board (1966).

The life-cycle aspects of asset-holding are discussed in Lydall (1955), *Atkinson (1971), and Atkinson (1972).

Chapter 8

An excellent discussion of the forces underlying the distribution of wealth and the effect of taxation is Meade (1964). Extracts from this are reprinted in Budd (1967) and Atkinson (1973), and the latter also contains a mathematical treatment by *Stiglitz (1969). Meade has recently returned to this subject in Meade (1973).

The importance of inheritance has been examined by Wedgwood (1929), Harbury (1962), which is reprinted in Atkinson (1973), Harbury and McMahon (1973), and Rubinstein (1974). For evidence on the American rich, see for example Lundberg (1968) and Tuckman (1973).

A great deal has been written on the taxation of wealth. In Britain, a selection of references are Peacock (1963), Tait (1967), and Sandford (1971). More recently there is the British Government Green Paper on the wealth tax (Cmnd. 5704) and contributions to the debate such as Flemming and Little (1974), which is provocative and complete with pictures of stately homes. In the United States taxes on wealth and wealth transfer have been less debated, but see Shoup (1966) and Thurow (1971), Chapter 7.

Chapter 9

There are a relatively large number of books dealing with the subject of factor shares. Reference has been made to Johnson (1973) and Bronfenbrenner (1971), which cover the field extensively. Phelps Brown (1968) provides a clear summary of the main features of different theories and comments on their relevance. Two earlier surveys of the field are Davidson (1960) and Scitovsky (1968).

A useful collection of articles on recent trends in factor shares is Marchal and Ducros (1968), which includes studies by Feinstein of the

United Kingdom, Haley of the United States, Ohkawa of Japan, and Jeck of West Germany. Phelps Brown and Browne (1968) contains data on France, Germany, Sweden, the United Kingdom, and the United States. Recent evidence on seventeen advanced countries is given by Heidensohn (1969). The study by Kravis (1959) brings out many of the methodological problems.

A clear statement of, and apology for, orthodox theory is given in Ferguson (1969), and it is also described in detail in the textbooks referred to earlier. There is a large volume of criticism and for a selection the reader is referred to the readings edited by Hunt and Schwartz (1972): for example, the contributions by Robinson and Nuti. For a critique from a rather different perspective, see the preface to *Hahn (1972).

Kalecki first presented his degree of monopoly theory in 1938–9 (Kalecki, 1939), and this is the version discussed in the text. In later writing, the emphasis shifted and he interpreted the index of monopoly power, m, in a more general way. The Kaldorian theory has also been presented in a variety of forms. The text follows the original (Kaldor, 1955a); for a more recent statement of his views, see (1966). The radical approach is described in Sherman (1972), Gurley (1971), and Hunt and Sherman (1972). For an outsider's view, see Lindbeck (1971) and Solow's reply to Gurley (1971). An excellent introduction to Marxian economic theory is Desai (1974), as is Morishima (1973). For a test of the relationship between the exploitation of labour and variables such as union strength, see Persky and Tsang (1974).

Chapter 10

There are a number of books dealing with poverty in general. In Britain, recent books include Jackson (1972) and Kincaid (1973); in the United States, to choose from a wider selection, there are Batchelder (1972), Gordon (1972), and Schiller (1973), as well as a number of useful volumes of readings, such as Weisbrod (1965), Scoville (1971), and Ferman, Kornbluh, and Haber (1968). A useful source of references is the journal *Poverty and Human Resources* (Abstracts).

The definition of poverty adopted by Rowntree (1901) and (1941), and Rowntree and Lavers (1951) is criticized by Townsend (1954) and (1962), and a more general discussion is provided by the Social Science Research Council (1968). The definition of poverty applied in the United States is developed in Orshansky (1965), and has been criticized by Friedman (1965), Haber (1966), and Rein (1970), the last having been reprinted in Ferman *et al.* (1968). An alternative relative concept of poverty has been put forward by Fuchs (1969). For a review of the concepts of minimum living standards applied in different countries, see

Franklin (1967). Some of the theoretical issues in the measurement of poverty are analysed in *Sen (1974). For discussion of some of the broader issues, see Reissman (1973), and the readings edited by Roach and Roach (1972).

The recent concern about poverty in Britain stems largely from the work of Wedderburn (1962) and Abel-Smith and Townsend (1965). A summary of the evidence available at the end of the 1960s is given in Lafitte (1970) and Atkinson (1969), (1974). The trends in poverty in the late 1960s were the subject of debate between the Child Poverty Action Group and the Labour government—see Child Poverty Action Group (1970) and Stewart (1972). Discussion of the changes in more recent years is contained in Young (1974) and Field (1973). The incomes of old people are examined in Townsend and Wedderburn (1965) and the Ministry of Pensions and National Insurance (1966). Family poverty is the subject of Bull (1971), Department of Health and Social Security (1971), Land (1970), Ministry of Social Security (1967), and Wynn (1970). Single parent families are discussed in Marsden (1969), and the unemployed by Sinfield (1970) and Hill et al. (1973). See also Department of Health and Social Security (1972). The problems of poverty in a particular area are brought out very clearly in the study of St Ann's, Nottingham, by Coates and Silburn (1970).

The revival of interest in the United States in the 1960s owed much to Harrington (1962). The official analysis of poverty began with the Council of Economic Advisers (1964), extracts from which are reprinted in Scoville (1971) and Atkinson (1973), and the position in 1969 was summarized by the President's Commission on Income Maintenance Programs (1969). Government estimates of its extent and composition are published regularly by the US Bureau of the Census, in their series of Current Population Reports, under the title *Characteristics of the low income population*.

Poverty in Canada has been the subject of a Special Senate Committee on Poverty, as well as independent studies, such as Adams, Cameron, Hill and Penz (1971), who were critical of the official report, and Rose (1969). In Australia, the results of a survey in Melbourne are described in Henderson, Harcourt, and Harper (1970), which represented the first attempt to measure the extent of income inadequacy.

A general discussion of racial discrimination and poverty is provided by Thurow (1969) and readings contained in Kain (1969) and Vatter and Palm (1972). For statistical and street-corner views respectively, see US Department of Labor (1971) and Liebow (1967). Theories of racial discrimination have been presented by *Becker (1957), which has been extended by Krueger (1963) and criticized by *Arrow (1972). See also Ashenfelter and Rees (1973), and Stiglitz (1973). Evidence about the changes in discrimination over time is examined by Batchelder (1964), Rasmussen (1970), Ashenfelter (1970), and Farley and Hermalin (1972). The *Review of Black Political Economy* has contained a number of theoretical and empirical articles on discrimination.

Chapter 11

For general discussion of policy towards income maintenance, with particular reference to the United States, see Green (1967), Levitan (1973), and the readings edited by Marmor (1971). Barth *et al.* (1974) provide an excellent recent review of the issues. In Britain, see Culyer (1973), Kincaid (1973), and Atkinson (1969).

Present income maintenance policies in Britain are described in (among others) Maynard (1973) and George (1968), the latter containing useful detail about the organization of social security. In the United States, valuable sources are Kershaw (1970) and Levitan (1973).

The problems with means-tested programmes in the United States are well described in Stein (1971), Steiner (1971), and Aaron (1973). In Britain, see Meacher (1973) and Bull (1971).

There is an extensive literature on the negative income tax and related proposals. For a selection in the United States, see Green (1967), Tobin (1968), and Tobin, Pechman, and Mieszkowski (1967). In Britain, see Meade (1972) and the Institute of Economic Affairs (1970). The British government's plans for a tax credit scheme were set out in a Green Paper *Proposals for a tax-credit system*, Cmnd. 5116. For a critical view of the scheme see Atkinson (1973a); for a more sympathetic view, see Barr and Roper (1974).

For references to the negative income tax experiments in the United States and analysis of the effect on work incentives, see Watts (1969) and the forthcoming volume to be published by the Brookings Institution. For a survey of other evidence on work incentives, see Cain and Watts (1973).

Chapter 12

The literature on world income differences and development is enormous. From a very wide selection of introductory books, Bhagwati (1966), Kindleberger (1965), Seers and Joy (1971), and the readings edited by Meier (1969) may provide an introduction to the subject.

The gap between nations is well discussed in Kuznets (1966), in Hagen and Hawrylyshyn (1969), in Usher (1966), and by several authors in Ranis (1972). Criticism of such international comparisons is made by Bauer (1971). The adjustments to the nominal income gap for understatement are based on Kuznets (1966), and the treatment of purchasing power parities on that by *David (1972) and *Balassa (1973), who give further references. The underlying theory is set out clearly in Samuelson (1974). Beckerman and Bacon (1970) adopt a rather different approach.

The classic reference on the relationship between economic growth and income inequality is Kuznets (1955). More recent data are given in Paukert (1973).

For a range of views on aid, see Bauer (1971), Hayter (1971), and Pearson (1970).

REFERENCES

Aaron, H. J. (1973). *Why is welfare so hard to reform?*, Brookings Institution, Washington, DC.

Aaron, H. and McGuire, M. (1970). 'Public goods and income distribution', *Econometrica*, Vol. 38.

Abel-Smith, B. and Bagley, C. (1970). 'The Problem of Establishing Equivalent Standards of Living for Families of Different Composition' in Townsend (1970).

Abel-Smith, B. and Townsend, P. (1965). *The poor and the poorest*, Occasional Papers on Social Administration, No. 17, Bell and Sons, London.

Ackerman, F., Birnbaum, H., Wetzler, J. and Zimbalist, A. (1971). 'Income distribution in the United States', *Review of Radical Political Economics*, Vol. 3.

Adams, F. G. (1958). 'The size of individual incomes: socio-economic variables and chance variation', *Review of Economics and Statistics*, Vol. 40.

Adams, I., Cameron, W., Hill, B. and Penz, P. (1971). *The real poverty report*, M. G. Hurtig, Edmonton, Alberta.

Alcaly, R. E. and Klevorick, A. K. (1971). 'Food prices in relation to income levels in New York City', *Journal of Business*, Vol. 44.

Allen, R. G. D. (1957). 'Changes in the distribution of higher incomes', *Economica*, Vol. 24.

Andic, S. and Peacock, A. T. (1961). 'The International Distribution of Income', *Journal of the Royal Statistical Society*, vol. 124, series A.

Arrow, K. J. (1972). 'Models of job discrimination'. *In Racial discrimination in economic life* (ed. A. H. Pascal), D. C. Heath, Lexington, Massachusetts.

Ashenfelter, O. (1970). 'Changes in labor market discrimination over time', *Journal of Human Resources*, Vol. 5.

Ashenfelter, O. and Rees, A. (1973). *Discrimination in labor markets*, Princeton University Press, Princeton, New Jersey.

Atkinson, A. B. (1969). *Poverty in Britain and the reform of social security*, Cambridge University Press, London.

Atkinson, A. B. (1970). 'On the measurement of inequality', *Journal of Economic Theory*, Vol. 2.

Atkinson, A. B. (1971). 'The distribution of wealth and the individual life-cycle', *Oxford Economic Papers*, Vol. 23.

Atkinson, A. B. (1972). *Unequal shares—the distribution of wealth in Britain*, Allen Lane, London.

Atkinson, A. B. (ed.) (1973). *Wealth, income and inequality*, Penguin, London.

Atkinson, A. B. (1973*a*). *The tax credit scheme and the redistribution of income*, Institute for Fiscal Studies, London.

Atkinson, A. B. (1974). 'Poverty and income inequality in Britain', in *Poverty, inequality and class structure* (ed. D. Wedderburn), Cambridge University Press, London.

Atkinson, A. B. (1974*a*). 'The distribution of wealth in Britain in the 1960s—the estate duty method re-examined', in *Personal distributions of income and wealth* (ed. J. Smith), National Bureau of Economic Research, New York.

Atkinson, A. B. and Harrison, A. J. (1974). 'Wealth distribution and investment income in Britain', *Review of Income and Wealth*, Vol. 20.

Atkinson, A. B. and Harrison, A. J. (forthcoming). *The distribution of personal wealth in Britain*, Cambridge University Press, London.

Bach, G. and Stephenson, J. (1974). 'Inflation and the redistribution of wealth', *Review of Economics and Statistics*, Vol. 56.

Balassa, B. (1973). 'Just how misleading are official exchange rate conversions? A comment', *Economic Journal*, Vol. 83.

Barlow, R., Brazer, H. E. and Morgan, J. N. (1966). *Economic behavior of the affluent*, Brookings Institution, Washington, DC.

Barr, N. and Roper, J. (1974). 'Tax credits', *Three Banks Review*, No. 101.

Barth, M. C., Carcagno, G. J., Palmer, J. L. and Garfinkel, I. (1974). *Toward an effective income support system*, Institute for Research on Poverty, Madison, Wisconsin.

Baster, N. (1970). *Distribution of income and economic growth: concepts and issues*, United Nations Research Institute for Social Development, Geneva.

Batchelder, A. B. (1964). 'The decline in the relative income of Negro men', *Quarterly Journal of Economics*, Vol. 78.

(1972). *The economics of poverty* (2nd ed.), John Wiley, New York.

Bauer, P. T. (1971). *Dissent on development*, Weidenfeld and Nicolson, London.

Bauer, P. T. and Prest, A. R. (1973). 'Income differences and inequalities', *Moorgate and Wall Stree Journal*.

Becker, G. (1957). *The economics of discrimination* (2nd ed., 1971). University of Chicago Press, Chicago.

Human capital. National Bureau of Economic Research, New York.

(1967). *Human capital and the personal distribution of income*, University of Michigan, Ann Arbor, Michigan.

Beckerman, W. and Bacon, R. (1970). 'The international distribution of incomes', in *Unfashionable economics* (ed. P. Streeten), Weidenfeld and Nicolson, London.

Bergmann, B. and Adelman, I. (1973). 'The economic role of women', *American Economic Review*, Vol. 63.

Béteille, A. (ed.) (1969). *Social inequality*, Penguin, London.

Beveridge, Lord (1942). *Social insurance and allied services*, HMSO, London.

Bhagwati, J. (1966). *The economics of underdeveloped countries*, Weidenfeld and Nicolson, London.

Bhatia, K. B. (1974). 'Capital gains and the distribution of income', *Review of Income and Wealth*, Vol. 20.

Blaug, M. (1970). *An introduction to the economics of education*, Allen Lane, London.

Bliss, C. J. (1975). *Capital theory and the distribution of income*, North-Holland, Amsterdam.

Bluestone, B. (1968). 'Low wage industries and the working poor', *Poverty and Human Resources Abstracts*, Vol. 3.

Bluestone, B. (1970). 'The tripartite economy: labor markets and the working poor', *Poverty and Human Resources Abstracts*, Vol. 5.

Bosanquet, N. and Doeringer, P. B. (1973). 'Is there a dual labour market in Britain?', *Economic Journal*, Vol. 83.

Boskin, M. J. (1972). 'Unions and relative real wages', *American Economic Review*, Vol. 62.

Boulding, K. E. and Pfaff, M. (eds.) (1972). *Redistribution to the rich and the poor*, Wadsworth, Belmont, California.

Bowles, S. (1972). 'Schooling and inequality from generation to generation', *Journal of Political Economy*, Vol. 80.

Bowles, S. (1973). 'Understanding unequal economic inequality', *American Economic Review, Papers and Proceedings*, Vol. 63.

Bowles, S. and Gintis, H. (1973). 'IQ in the US class structure', *Social Policy*, Vol. 3.

Bowles, S. and Nelson, V. (1974). 'The "inheritance of IQ" and the intergenerational reproduction of economic inequality', *Review of Economics and Statistics*, Vol. 56.

Brimmer, A. (1971). 'Inflation and income distribution in the United States', *Review of Economics and Statistics*, Vol. 53.

Brittain, J. A. (1960). 'Some neglected features of Britain's income levelling', *American Economic Review, Papers and Proceedings*, Vol. 50.

Brittain, J. A. (1973). 'Research on the transmission of material wealth', *American Economic Review, Papers and Proceedings*, Vol. 63.

Bronfenbrenner, M. (1971). *Income distribution theory*, Macmillan, London.

Brown, A. and Deaton, A. (1972). 'Models of consumer behaviour: a survey', *Economic Journal*, Vol. 82.

Brown, M. B. (1970). *What economics is about*, Weidenfeld and Nicolson, London.

Budd, E. C. (ed.) (1967). *Inequality and poverty*, Norton, New York.

Budd, E. C. (1970). 'Postwar changes in the size distribution of income in the US', *American Economic Review, Papers and Proceedings*, Vol. 60.

Budd, E. C. and Seiders, D. F. (1971). 'The impact of inflation on the distribution of income and wealth', *American Economic Review, Papers and Proceedings*, Vol. 61.

Bull, D. (ed.) (1971). *Family poverty*, Duckworth, London.

Cain, G. and Watts, H. W. (eds.) (1973). *Econometric studies of labor supply*, Academic Press, New York.

Campion, H. (1939). *Public and private property in Great Britain*, Oxford University Press, London.

Cannan, E. (1914). *Wealth* (3rd ed., 1928), Staples Press, London.

Caplovitz, D. (1963). *The poor pay more: consumer practices of low-income families*, Free Press, New York.

Cartter, A. M. (1955). *The redistribution of income in postwar Britain*, Yale University Press, New Haven, Connecticut.

Champernowne, D. G. (1953). 'The production function and the theory of capital: a comment', *Review of Economic Studies*, Vol. 21.

Champernowne, D. G. (1973). *The distribution of income*, Cambridge University Press, London.

Child Poverty Action Group (1970). *Poverty and the labour government*, CPAG, London.

Chiswick, B. (1969). 'Minimum schooling legislation and the cross-sectional distribution of income', *Economic Journal*, Vol. 79.

Clay, H. (1925). 'The distribution of capital in England and Wales', *Transactions of the Manchester Statistical Society*, Vol. 92.

Coates, K. and Silburn, R. (1970). *Poverty: the forgotten Englishmen*, Penguin, London.

Cole (Wedderburn), D. and Utting, J. E. G. (1957). 'The distribution of household and individual income', *Income and Wealth*, Vol. 6.

Cole (Wedderburn), D. and Utting, J. E. G. (1962). *The economic circumstances of old people*, Codicote Press, London.

Copeman, G. and Rumble, T. (1972). *Capital as an incentive*, Leviathan House, London.

Council of Economic Advisers (1964). *Economic report of the President 1964*, US Government Printing Office, Washington, DC.

Council of Economic Advisers (1973). *Economic report of the President 1973*, US Government Printing Office, Washington, DC.

Crosland, C. A. R. (1964). *Future of socialism*, Cape, London.

Culyer, A. J. (1973). *The economics of social policy*, Martin Robertson, London.

Dalton, H. (1920). *The inequality of incomes*, Routledge, London.

Dalton, H. (1920a). 'The measurement of the inequality of incomes', *Economic Journal*, Vol. 30.

Daniel, W. W. (1968). 'Personal taxation and occupational incentives', *Banker*, Vol. 118.

Daniels, G. W. and Campion, H. (1936). *Distribution of national capital*, Manchester University Press, Manchester.

Davenport, M. (1970). 'The allocation of foreign aid: a cross-section study', *Yorkshire Bulletin of Economic Research*, Vol. 22.

David, P. A. (1972). 'Just how misleading are official exchange rate conversions?', *Economic Journal*, Vol. 82.

Davidson, P. (1960). *Theories of aggregate income distribution*, Rutgers University Press, New Brunswick.

Department of Employment (1973). *Family expenditure survey*, HMSO, London.

Department of Health and Social Security (1969). *National superannuation and social insurance*, HMSO, London.

Department of Health and Social Security (1971). *Two-parent families*, HMSO, London.

Department of Health and Social Security (1972). *Families receiving supplementary benefit*, HMSO, London.

Desai, M. (1974). *Marxian economic theory*, Gray-Mills, London.

Doeringer, P. B. and Piore, M. J. (1971). *Internal labor markets and manpower analysis*, D. C. Heath, Lexington, Massachusetts.

Douglas, P. H. (1934). *Theory of wages*, Macmillan, London.

Duncan, O. D. (1968). 'Inheritance of poverty or inheritance of race?', in *On understanding poverty* (ed. D. P. Moynihan), Basic Books, New York.

Economic Commission for Europe (1967). *Incomes in postwar Europe*, United Nations, Geneva.

Economic Trends (1971). 'The incidence of taxes and social security benefits', *Economic Trends*, No. 208.

Edwards, R., Reich, M. and Weisskopf, T. (eds.) (1972). *The capitalist system*, Prentice Hall, Englewood Cliffs, New Jersey.

Elliott, C. (1974). 'The international context of British poverty', in Young, (1974).

Engels, F. (1892). *The conditions of the working class in England*, Allen and Unwin, London.

Farley, R. and Hermalin, A. (1972). 'The 1960s: decade of progress for blacks?', *Demography*, Vol. 9 (reprinted in Rainwater, 1974).

Federal Reserve Board (D. S. Projector and G. S. Weiss) (1966). *Survey of financial characteristics of consumers*, Board of Governors of the Federal Reserve System, Washington, DC.

Feinstein, C. H. (1968). 'Changes in the distribution of national income in the United Kingdom since 1860', in Marchal and Ducros, (1968).

Feldstein, M. S. (1973). *Lowering the permanent rate of unemployment*, Joint Economic Committee, US Government Printing Office, Washington, DC.

Ferguson, C. E. (1969). *The neoclassical theory of production and distribution*, Cambridge University Press, London.

Ferguson, C. E. and Nell, E. J. (1972). 'Two books on the theory of income distribution: a review article', *Journal of Economic Literature*, Vol. 10.

Ferman, L. A., Kornbluh, J. L. and Haber, A. (eds.) (1968). *Poverty in America*(2nd ed.), University of Michigan Press, Ann Arbor.

Field, F. (ed.) (1973). *Low pay*, Arrow Books, London.

Finer, M. (1974). *Report of the committee on one-parent families*, HMSO, London.

Fisher, M. R. (1971). *The economic analysis of labour*, Weidenfeld and Nicolson, London.

Fleisher, B. (1970). *Labor economics: theory and evidence*, Prentice-Hall, Englewood Cliffs, New Jersey.

Flemming, J. S. and Little, I. M. D. (1974). *Why we need a wealth tax*, Methuen, London.

Franklin, N. N. (1967). 'The concept and measurement of minimum living standards', *International Labour Review*, Vol. 96.

Freeman, R. B. (1973). 'Decline of labor market discrimination and economic analysis', *American Economic Review, Papers and Proceedings*, Vol. 63.

Fried, E. R., Rivlin, A. M., Schultze, C. L. and Teeters, N. H. (1973). *Setting national priorities, the 1974 budget*, Brookings Institution, Washington, DC.

Friedman, M. (1954). 'Some comments on the significance of labor unions for economic policy', in *The impact of the union* (ed. D. McCord Wright), Kelley and Millman, New York.

Friedman, M. (1957). *A theory of the consumption function*, Princeton University Press, Princeton, New Jersey.

Friedman, M. (1962). *Capitalism and freedom*, University of Chicago Press, Chicago.

Friedman, M. and Kuznets, S. (1945). *Income from independent professional practice*, National Bureau of Economic Research, New York.

Friedman, R. D. (1965). *Poverty: definition and perspective*, American Enterprise Institute for Public Policy Research, Washington, DC.

Fuchs, V. (1969). 'Comment on measuring the size of the low-income population', in *Six papers on the size distribution of wealth and income* (ed. L. Soltow), National Bureau of Economic Research, New York.

Fusfeld, D. (1972). *Economics*, D. C. Heath, Lexington, Massachusetts.

George, V. N. (1968). *Social security: Beveridge and after*, Routledge and Kegan Paul, London.

Gillespie, W. I. (1965). 'The effect of public expenditures on the distribution of income', in *Essays on fiscal federalism* (ed. R. A. Musgrave), Brookings Institution, Washington, DC.

Glyn, A. and Sutcliffe, B. (1972). *British capitalism, workers and the profits squeeze*, Penguin, London.

Goldsmith, S. F. *et al.* (1954). 'Size distribution of income since the mid-thirties', *Review of Economics and Statistics*, Vol. 36.

Goldthorpe, J. (1974). 'Social inequality and social integration in modern Britain', in *Poverty, inequality and class structure* (ed. D. Wedderburn), Cambridge University Press, London.

Gordon, D. M. (1972). *Theories of poverty and underemployment*, D. C. Heath, Lexington, Massachusetts.

Gordon, M. S. (ed.) (1965). *Poverty in America*, Chandler, San Francisco.

Gough, I. and Stark, T. (1968). 'Low incomes in the United Kingdom', *Manchester School*, Vol. 36.

Green, C. (1967). *Negative taxes and the poverty problem*, Brookings Institution, Washington, DC.

Griliches, Z. and Mason, W. M. (1972). 'Education, income, and ability', *Journal of Political Economy*, Vol. 80.

Gurley, J. (1971). 'The state of political economics', *American Economic Review, Papers and Proceedings*, Vol. 61, and comment by R. M. Solow.

Haber, A. (1966). 'Poverty budgets: how much is enough?', *Poverty and Human Resources Abstracts*, Vol. 1.

Hagen, E. E. and Hawrylyshyn, O. (1969). 'Analysis of world income and growth 1955–1965', *Economic Development and Cultural Change*, Vol. 18.

Hahn, F. H. (1972). *The share of wages in the national income*, Weidenfeld and Nicolson, London.

Hahn, F. H. and Matthews, R. C. O. (1965). 'The theory of economic growth: a survey', in *Surveys of economic theory* (vol. 2), Macmillan, London.

Haley, B. F. (1968). 'Changes in the distribution of income in the United States', in Marchal and Ducros (1968).

Hall, R. E. (1971). 'Prospects for shifting the Phillips curve through manpower policy', *Brookings Papers on Economic Activity*, Vol. 2.

Hanoch, G. (1967). 'An economic analysis of earnings and schooling', *Journal of Human Resources*, Vol. 2.

Hansen, W. L. (1967). 'The economics of scientific and engineering manpower', *Journal of Human Resources*, Vol. 2.

Harbury, C. D. (1962). 'Inheritance and the distribution of personal wealth in Britain', *Economic Journal*, Vol. 72.

Harbury, C. D. and McMahon, P. C. (1973). 'Inheritance and the characteristics of top wealth leavers in Britain', *Economic Journal*, Vol. 83.

Harrington, M. (1962). *The other America*, Macmillan and Penguin, London.

Harrison, A. J. (1975). 'Inequality of income and the Champernowne distribution', *University of Essex, Department of Economics Discussion Paper*, No. 54.

Hause, J. C. (1972). 'Earnings profile: ability and schooling', *Journal of Political Economy*, Vol. 80.

Hayter, T. (1971). *Aid as imperialism*, Penguin, London.

Heidensohn, K. (1969). 'Labour's share in national income—a constant?', *Manchester School*, Vol. 37.

Henderson, A. M. (1949). 'The cost of children', Parts I–III, *Population Studies*, Vols. 3–4.

Henderson, R. F., Harcourt, A. and Harper, R. V. A. (1970). *People in poverty: a Melbourne survey*, Cheshire, Melbourne.

Henle, P. (1972). 'Recent trends in retirement benefits related to earnings', *Monthly Labour Review*, Vol. 95.

Herriot, R. A. and Miller, H. P. (1972). 'Tax changes among income groups', *Business Horizons*, February 1972.

Hicks, J. R. (1971). *The social framework* (4th ed.), Oxford University Press, London.

Hill, M. J., Harrison, R. M., Sargeant, A. V. and Talbot, V. (1973). *Men out of work*, Cambridge University Press, London.

Hollister, R. G. and Palmer, J. L. (1972). 'The impact of inflation on the poor', in Boulding and Pfaff (1972).

Houghton, R. W. (ed.) (1970). *Public finance*, Penguin, London.

Hughes, J. and Moore, R. (1972). *A special case?*, Penguin, London.

Hunt, E. K. and Schwartz, J. G. (eds.) (1972). *A critique of economic theory*, Penguin, London.

Hunt, E. K. and Sherman, H. J. (1972). *Economics: an introduction to traditional and radical views*, Harper and Row, New York.

Hunter, L. C. and Robertson, D. J. (1969). *Economics of wages and labour*, Macmillan, London.

Inland Revenue (1972). *Inland Revenue statistics*, HMSO, London.

Institute of Economic Affairs (1970). *Policy for poverty*, IEA, London.

Jackson, D. (1972). *Poverty*, Macmillan, London.

Jackson, D., Turner, H. A. and Wilkinson, F. (1972). *Do trade unions cause inflation?*, Cambridge University Press, London.

Jencks, C. (1972). *Inequality*, Basic Books, New York.

Jensen, A. (1969). 'How much can we boost IQ and scholastic achievement?', *Harvard Educational Review*, Vol. 39.

Johnson, H. G. (1973). *The theory of income distribution*, Gray-Mills, London.

Kain, J. F. (ed.) (1969). *Race and poverty*, Prentice-Hall, Englewood Cliffs, New Jersey.

Kain, J. F. and Quigley, J. M. (1972). 'Housing market discrimination, home ownership and savings behavior', *American Economic Review*, Vol. 62.

Kaldor, N. (1955). *An expenditure tax*, Allen and Unwin, London.

Kaldor, N. (1955a). 'Alternative theories of distribution', *Review of Economic studies*, Vol. 23.

Kaldor, N. (1966). 'Marginal productivity and the macro-economic theories of distribution', *Review of Economic Studies*, Vol. 33.

Kalecki, M. (1939). *Essays in the theory of economic fluctuations*, Allen and Unwin, London.

Kendall, M. G. and Stuart, A. (1969). *The advanced theory of statistics*, Vol. 1, Griffin, London.

Kerr, C. (1950). 'Labor markets: their character and consequences', *American Economic Review, Papers and Proceedings*, Vol. 40.

Kershaw, J. A. (1965) 'The attack on Poverty', in *Poverty in America* (ed. M. S. Gordon). Chandler, San Francisco.

Kershaw, J. A. (1970). *Government against poverty*, Brookings Institution, Washington, DC.

Kesselman, J. (1973). 'A comprehensive approach to income maintenance: Swift', *Journal of Public Economics*, Vol. 2.

Keynes, J. M. (1939). 'The income and fiscal potential of Great Britain', *Economic Journal*, Vol. 49.

Kincaid, J. C. (1973). *Poverty and equality in Britain*, Penguin, London.

Kindleberger, C. (1965). *Economic development*, McGraw-Hill, New York.

Kolko, G. (1962). *Wealth and power in America*, Praeger, New York.

Kolm, S. Ch. (1969). 'The optimal production of social justice', in *Public economics* (ed. J. Margolis and H. Guitton), Macmillan, London.

Kolm, S. Ch. (1972). *Justice et équité*, CNRS, Paris.

Kosters, M. and Welch, F. (1972). 'The effects of minimum wages on the distribution of changes in aggregate employment', *American Economic Review*, Vol. 62.

Kravis, I. B. (1959). 'Relative income shares in fact and theory', *American Economic Review*, Vol. 49.

Kravis, I. B. (1962). *The structure of income*, University of Pennsylvania Press, Philadelphia.

Krueger, A. O. (1963). 'The economics of discrimination', *Journal of Political Economy*, Vol. 71.

Kuh, E. (1965). 'Cyclical and secular labor productivity in US manufacturing', *Review of Economics and Statistics*, Vol. 47.

Kuznets, S. (1953). *Share of upper income groups in income and savings*, National Bureau of Economic Research, New York.

Kuznets, S. (1955). 'Economic growth and income inequality', *American Economic Review*, Vol. 45.

Kuznets, S. (1963). 'Quantitative aspects of the economic growth of nations: part VIII, distribution of income by size', *Economic Development and Cultural Change*, Vol. 11.

Kuznets, S. (1966). *Modern economic growth*, Yale University Press, New Haven, Connecticut.

Lafitte, F. (1970). 'Income deprivation', in *Socially deprived families in Britain* (ed. R. Holman), Bedford Square Press, London.

Lampman, R. J. (1959). 'Changes in the share of wealth held by top wealth-holders, 1922–1956', *Review of Economics and Statistics*, Vol. 41.

Lampman, R. J. (1962). *The share of top wealth-holders in national wealth, 1922–1956*. Princeton University Press, Princeton, New Jersey.

Lampman, R. J. (1971). *Ends and means of reducing income poverty*, Markham, Chicago.

Land, H. (1970). *Large families in London*, Bell, London.

Langley, K. M. (1950). 'The distribution of capital in private hands in 1936–1938 and 1946–1947, Part I', *Bulletin of the Oxford Institute of Economics and Statistics*, Vol. 12.

Langley, K. M. (1951). 'The distribution of capital in private hands in

1936–1938 and 1946–1947, Part II', *Bulletin of the Oxford Institute of Economics and Statistics*, Vol. 13.

Layard, P. R. G. (1974). 'The lifetime redistribution of income', paper presented at International Economic Association conference, forthcoming conference volume (ed. M. S. Feldstein), Macmillan, London.

Lester, R. A. (1964). *Economics of labour* (2nd ed.), Macmillan, London.

Levitan, S. (1973). *Programs in aid of the poor for the 1970s*, Johns Hopkins University Press, Baltimore, Maryland.

Lewis, H. G. (1963). *Unionism and relative wages in the United States*, University of Chicago Press, Chicago.

Liebow, E. (1967). *Tally's corner: a study of streetcorner men*, Little, Brown & Co., Boston, Massachusetts.

Lindbeck, A. (1971). *The political economy of the new left*, Harper and Row, New York.

Lipsey, R. G. (1964). *An introduction to positive economics*, Weidenfeld and Nicolson, London.

Lister, R. (1972). *The administration of the wage stop*, Child Poverty Action Group, London.

Lundberg, F. (1968). *The rich and the super rich*, Lyle Stuart, New York.

Lydall, H. F. (1955). 'The life-cycle in income, saving, and asset ownership', *Econometrica*, Vol. 23.

Lydall, H. F. (1959). 'The long-term trend in the size distribution of income', *Journal of the Royal Statistical Society*, Vol. 122, Series A.

Lydall, H. F. (1968). *The structure of earnings*, Oxford University Press, Oxford.

Lydall, H. F. and Lansing, J. B. (1959). 'A comparison of the distribution of personal income and wealth in the United States and Great Britain', *American Economic Review*, Vol. 49.

Lydall, H. F. and Tipping, D. G. (1961). 'The distribution of personal wealth in Britain', *Bulletin of the Oxford Institute of Economics and Statistics*, Vol. 23.

Lyons, P. M. (1974). 'The size distribution of personal wealth in the Republic of Ireland', *Review of Income and Wealth*, Vol. 20.

Macaulay, H. H. (1959). *Fringe benefits and their federal tax treatment*, Columbia University Press, New York.

Marchal, J. and Ducros, B. (eds.) (1968). *The distribution of national income*, Macmillan, London.

Marmor, T. (ed.) (1971). *Poverty policy*, Aldine, Chicago.

Marsden, D. (1969). *Mothers alone: poverty and the fatherless family*, Allen Lane, London.

Mayer, T. (1960). 'The distribution of ability and earnings', *Review of Economics and Statistics*, Vol. 42.

Maynard, A. K. (1973). 'A survey of social security in the UK', *Social and Economic Administration*, Vol. 7.

McCormick, B. J. (1969). *Wages*, Penguin, London.

Meacher, M. (1973). *Rate rebates: a study of the effectiveness of means tests*, Child Poverty Action Group, London.

Meade, J. E. (1964). *Efficiency, equality and the ownership of property*, Allen and Unwin, London.

Meade, J. E. (1972). 'Poverty in the welfare state', *Oxford Economic Papers*, Vol. 24.

Meade, J. E. (1973). 'The inheritance of inequalities', *Proceedings of British Academy*, Vol. 59.

Meier, G. M. (ed.) (1969). *Leading issues in development economics*, Oxford University Press, New York.

Metcalf, C. E. (1969). 'The size distribution of personal income during the business cycle', *American Economic Review*, Vol. 59.

Michelson, S. (1970). 'The economics of real income distribution', *Review of Radical Political Economics*, Vol. 2.

Miller, H. P. (1964). *Rich man, poor man*, Signet Press, New York.

Miller, H. P. (1966). *Income distribution in the United States*, US Government Printing Office, Washington, DC.

Miller, S. M. and Roby, P. (1970). *The future of inequality*, Basic Books, New York.

Mincer, J. (1958). 'Investment in human capital and personal income distribution', *Journal of Political Economy*, Vol. 66.

Mincer, J. (1970). 'The distribution of labor incomes–a survey', *Journal of Economic Literature*, Vol. 8.

Mincer, J. (1974). *Schooling, experience, and earnings*, Columbia University Press, New York.

Mincer, J. and Polachek, S. (1974). 'Family investments in human capital: earnings of women', *Journal of Political Economy*, Vol. 82.

Ministry of Labour (1964). *Sick pay schemes*, HMSO, London.

Ministry of Pensions and National Insurance (1966). *Financial and other circumstances of retirement pensioners*, HMSO, London.

Ministry of Social Security (1967). *Circumstances of families*, HMSO, London.

Morgan, J. N. (1962). 'The anatomy of income distribution', *Review of Economics and Statistics*, Vol. 44.

Morgan, J. N. (1965). 'Measuring the economic status of the aged', *International Economic Review*, Vol. 6.

Morgan, J. N. (1974). *Five thousand American families*, University of Michigan Press, Ann Arbor.

Morgan, J. N., David, M. H., Cohen, W. J. and Brazer, H. E. (1962). *Income and welfare in the United States*, McGraw-Hill, New York.

Morishima, M. (1973). *Marx's Economics*, Cambridge University Press, London.

Muellbauer, J. (1974). 'Prices and inequality: the United Kingdom experience', *Economic Journal*, Vol. 84.

Musgrave, R. A. and Musgrave, P. B. (1973). *Public finance in theory and practice*, McGraw-Hill, New York.

Myrdal, G. (1968). *Asian drama*, Twentieth Century Fund, New York.

National Board for Prices and Incomes (1971). *General problems of low pay*, HMSO, London.

Neild, R. R. (1963). *Pricing and employment in the trade cycle*, Cambridge University Press, London.

Nicholson, J. L. (1949). 'Variations in working-class family expenditure', *Journal of Royal Statistical Society*, Vol. 112, Series A.

Nicholson, J. L. (1965). *Redistribution of income in the United Kingdom in 1959, 1957 and 1953*, Bowes and Bowes, Cambridge.

Nicholson, J. L. (1970). 'Redistribution of income: notes on some problems and puzzles', *Review of Income and Wealth*, Vol. 16.

Nicholson, J. L. (1974). 'The distribution and redistribution of income in the United Kingdom', in *Poverty, inequality and class structure* (ed. D. Wedderburn), Cambridge University Press, London.

Nicholson, R. J. (1967). 'The distribution of personal income', *Lloyds Bank Review*, January, 1967.

Nordhaus, W. D. (1972). 'The effect of inflation on the distribution of economic welfare', *Cowles Foundation Discussion Paper*, No. 329.

Oaxaca, R. (1973). 'Male–female wage differentials in urban labor markets', *International Economic Review*, Vol. 14.

Okner, B. A. (1974). 'Individual taxes and the distribution of income', in *Personal distributions of income and wealth* (ed. J. Smith), National Bureau of Economic Research, New York.

Okner, B. A. and Pechman, J. A. (1974). *Who bears the tax burden?*, Brookings Institution, Washington, DC.

Okonkwo, U. (1973). 'Economics of ethnic discrimination', *Review of Black Political Economy*, Vol. 3.

Orshansky, M. (1965). 'Counting the poor: another look at the poverty profile', *Social Security Bulletin*, Vol. 28.

Oshima, H. T. (1970). 'Income inequality and economic growth: the postwar experience of Asian countries', *Malayan Economic Review*, Vol. 15.

Paish, F. W. (1957). 'The real incidence of personal taxation', *Lloyds Bank Review*, No. 43.

Pasinetti, L. (1961). 'Rate of profit and income distribution in relation to the rate of economic growth', *Review of Economic Studies*, Vol. 29.

Paukert, F. (1973). 'Income distribution: a survey of the evidence', *International Labour Review*, Vol. 108.

Peacock, A. T. (1963). 'The economics of a net worth tax for Britain', *British Tax Review*.

Pearson, L. B. (1970). *Partners in development*, Pall Mall Press, New York.

Pen, J. (1971). *Income distribution*, Allen Lane, London.

Penceval, J. H. (1974). 'Relative wages and trade unions in the United Kingdom', *Economica*, Vol. 41.

Perrella, V. C. (1967). 'Low earners and their incomes', *Monthly Labour Review*, Vol. 90. US Department of Labor. Bureau of Labour Statistics.

Persky, J. and Tsang, H. (1974). 'Pigouvian exploitation of labour', *Review of Economics and Statistics*, Vol. 56.

Phelps Brown, E. H. (1962). *The economics of labor*, Yale University Press, New Haven, Connecticut.

Phelps Brown, E. H. (1968). *Pay and profits*, Manchester University Press, Manchester.

Phelps Brown, E. H. and Browne, M. H. (1968). *A century of pay*, Macmillan, London.

Phelps Brown, E. H. and Hart, P. E. (1952). 'Share of wages in the national income', *Economic Journal*, Vol. 62.

Phelps Brown, E. H. and Hopkins, S. V. (1955). 'Seven centuries of building wages', *Economica*, Vol. 23.

Piachaud, D. (1974). *Do the poor pay more?*, Child Poverty Action Group, Poverty Research Series 3, London

Pigou, A. C. (1952). *The economics of welfare* (1952 ed.), Macmillan, London.

Polanyi, G. and Wood, J. B. (1974). *How much inequality?* Institute of Economic Affairs, London.

Posner, R. A. (1973). 'Economic justice and the economist', *Public Interest*, No. 33, and reply by L. Thurow.

President's Commission on Income maintenance Programs (1969). *Poverty amid plenty*, US Government Printing Office, Washington, DC.

Prest, A. R. (1963), 'Review of Titmuss (1962)', *British Tax Review*.

Prest, A. R. (ed.) (1970). *The UK economy: a manual of applied economics* (3rd ed.), Weidenfeld and Nicolson, London.

Prest, A. R. and Stark, T. (1967). 'Some aspects of income distribution in the UK since World War II', *Manchester School*, Vol. 35.

Projector, D. S. (1968). *Survey of changes in family finances*, Board of Governors of the Federal Reserve System, Washington, DC.

Psacharopoulos, G. (1973). *Returns to education*, Elsevier, Amsterdam.

Rainwater, L. (ed.) (1974). *Inequality and justice*, Aldine, Chicago.

Ranis, G. (ed.) (1972). *The gap between rich and poor nations*, Macmillan, London.

Rasmussen, D. W. (1970). 'A note on the relative income of nonwhite men 1948–1964', *Quarterly Journal of Economics*, Vol. 84.

Rawls, J. (1972). *A theory of justice*, Clarendon Press, Oxford.

Reder, M. W. (1959). 'Alternative theories of labor's share', in *The allocation of economic resources* (by M. Abramovitz *et al.*), Stanford University Press, Stanford, California.

Rees, A. (1973). *The economics of work and pay*, Harper and Row, New York.

Rein, M. (1970). 'Problems in the definition and measurement of poverty', in Townsend (1970).

Reissman, L. (1973). *Inequality in American society*, Scott, Foresman and Co., Glenview, Illinois.

Revell, J. R. S. (1965). 'Changes in the social distribution of property in Britain during the twentieth century', *Actes du troisième congrès international d'histoire economique*.

Revell, J. R. S. (1967). *The wealth of the nation*, Cambridge University Press, London.

Ricardo, D. (1821). *The principles of taxation and political economy*, Dent, London.

Roach, J. L. and J. K. (eds.) (1972). *Poverty*, Penguin, London.

Robinson, J. (1933). *Economics of imperfect competition*, Macmillan, London.

Robinson, J. (1953). 'The production function and the theory of capital', *Review of Economic Studies*, Vol. 21.

Robinson, J. (1966). *An essay on Marxian economics* (2nd ed.), Macmillan, London.

Rose, A. (1969). 'Poverty in Canada', *Social Service Review*, Vol. 43.

Rosen, S. (1970). 'Unionism and the occupational wage structure in the United States', *International Economic Review*, Vol. 11.

Routh, G. (1965). *Occupation and pay in Great Britain 1906–1960*, Cambridge University Press, London.

Rowan, D. C. (1968). *Output, inflation, and growth*, Macmillan, London.

Rowntree, B. S. (1901). *Poverty–a study of town life* (1922 ed.), Macmillan, London.

Rowntree, B. S. (1941). *Poverty and progress*, Longmans, London.

Rowntree, B. S. and Lavers, G. R. (1951). *Poverty and the welfare state*, Longmans, London.

Roy, A. D. (1950). 'The distribution of earnings and of individual output', *Economic Journal*, Vol. 60.

Royal Commission on the Taxation of Profits and Income (1955). *Final report*, HMSO, London.

Rubinstein, W. D. (1971). 'Occupations among British millionaires, 1857–1969', *Review of Income and Wealth*, Vol. 17.

Rubinstein, W. D. (1974). 'Men of property: some aspects of occupation, inheritance and power among top British wealth-holders', in *Elites and power in British society* (ed. P. Stanworth and A. Giddens), Cambridge University Press, London.

Runciman, W. G. (1966). *Relative deprivation and social justice*, Routledge and Kegan Paul, London.

Runciman, W. G. (1972). 'Who's rich?', *Listener*, 14 December.

Runciman, W. G. (1974). 'Occupational class and the assessment of economic inequality in Britain', in *Poverty, inequality and class structure* (ed. D. Wedderburn), Cambridge University Press, London.

Samuelson, P. A. (1967) and (1973). *Economics* (7th and 9th eds.), McGraw-Hill, New York.

Samuelson, P. A. (1974). 'Analytical notes on international real-income measures', *Economic Journal*, Vol. 84.

Sandford, C. T. (1971). *Taxing personal wealth*, Allen and Unwin, London.

Sandford, C. T., Willis, J. R. M. and Ironside, D. J. (1973). *An accessions tax*, Institute for Fiscal Studies, London.

Schiller, B. (1973). *The economics of poverty and discrimination*, Prentice-Hall, Englewood Cliffs, New Jersey.

Schultz, T. P. (1964). *The distribution of personal income*, US Government Printing Office, Washington, DC.

Schultz, T. P. (1969). 'Secular trends and cyclical behavior of income distribution in the United States: 1944–1965', in *Six papers on the size distribution of wealth and income* (ed. L. Soltow), Columbia University Press, New York.

Scitovsky, T. (1968). 'A survey of some theories of distribution', in *The behavior of income shares*, National Bureau of Economic Research, New York.

Scitovsky, T. (1973). 'Inequalities: open and hidden, measured and immeasurable', *Annals of the American Academy of Political and Social Science*, Vol. 409.

Scoville, J. G. (ed.) (1971). *Perspectives on poverty and income distribution*, D. C. Heath, Lexington, Massachusetts.

Seers, D. (1971). 'The total relationship', in Seers and Joy, (1971).

Seers, D. and Joy, L. (eds.) (1971). *Development in a divided world*, Penguin, London.

Select Committee on Tax-Credit (1973). *Report and proceedings of the Committee*, HMSO, London.

Sen, A. K. (1973). *On economic inequality*, Clarendon Press, Oxford.

Sen, A. K. (1974). 'Poverty: an ordinal approach to measurement', unpublished paper.

Sheahan, J. (1967). *The wage–price guideposts*, Brookings Institution, Washington, DC.

Sherman, H. J. (1972). *Radical political economy*, Basic Books, New York.

Shoup, C. S. (1966). *Federal estate and gift taxes,*, Brookings Institution, Washington, DC.

Simon, H. A. (1957). 'The compensation of executives', *Sociometry*, Vol. 20.

Simons, H. (1938). *Personal income taxation*, University of Chicago Press, Chicago.

Sinfield, A. (1970). 'Poor and out of work in Shields', in Townsend (1970).

Sloan, F. A. (1970). 'Lifetime earnings and physicians' choice of specialty', *Industrial and Labor Relations Review*, Vol. 24.

Smith, A. (1776). *An inquiry into the nature and causes of the wealth of nations* (1892 ed.), Routledge, London.

Smith, J. D. (1974). 'The concentration of personal wealth in America 1969', *Review of Income and Wealth*, Vol. 20.

Smith, J. D. and Franklin, S. D. (1974). 'The concentration of personal wealth, 1922–1969', *American Economic Review, Papers and Proceedings*, Vol. 64.

Social Science Research Council (1968). *Research on poverty*, Heinemann, London.

Solow, R. M. (1958). 'A skeptical note on the constancy of relative shares', *American Economic Review*, Vol. 48.

Solow, R. M. (1960). 'Income inequality since the war', in *Postwar economic trends in the United States* (ed. R. E. Freeman), Harper, New York.

Soltow, L. (1965). *Toward income equality in Norway*, University of Wisconsin Press, Madison.

Soltow, L. (1968). 'Long-run changes in British income inequality', *Economic History Review*, Vol. 21.

Stark, T. (1972). *The distribution of personal income in the United Kingdom 1949–1963*, Cambridge University Press, London.

Stark, T. (forthcoming). *A survey of personal income statistics*, Heinemann, London.

Stein, B. (1971). *On relief*, Basic Books, New York.

Steiner, G. (1971). *The state of welfare*, Brookings Institution, Washington, DC.

Stephen, D. (1973). 'Immigrant workers and low pay' in *Low Pay* (ed. F. Field), Arrow Books, London.

Stewart, M. (1972). 'The distribution of income', in *Labour's economic record* (ed. W. Beckerman), Duckworth, London.

Stigler, G. J. (1945). 'The Cost of Subsistence', *Journal of Farm Economics*, Vol. 27.

Stigler, G. J. (1946). 'The economics of minimum wage legislation', *American Economic Review*, Vol. 36.

Stiglitz, J. E. (1969). 'Distribution of income and wealth among individuals', *Econometrica*, Vol. 37.

Stiglitz, J. E. (1973). 'Approaches to the economics of discrimination', *American Economic Review, Papers and Proceedings*, Vol. 63.

Swamy, S. (1967). 'Structural changes and the distribution of income by size: the case of India', *Review of Income and Wealth*, Vol. 13.

Tait, A. A. (1967). *The taxation of personal wealth*, University of Illinois Press, Urbana.

Taubman, P. (1974). *Schooling, ability, nonpecuniary rewards, socioeconomic background, and the lifetime distribution of earnings*, National Bureau of Economic Research, New York.

Taussig, M. K. (1973). *Alternative measures of the distribution of economic welfare*, Industrial Relations Section, Princeton University, Princeton, New Jersey.

Tawney, R. H. (1964). *Equality* (new edition with Introduction by R. M. Titmuss), Allen and Unwin, London.

Thatcher, A. R. (1968). 'The distribution of earnings of employees in Great Britain', *Journal of the Royal Statistical Society*, Vol. 131, Series A.

Thurow, L. (1968). 'Disequilibrium and the marginal productivity of capital and labor', *Review of Economics and Statistics*, Vol. 50.

Thurow, L. (1969). *Poverty and discrimination*, Brookings Institution, Washington, DC.

Thurow, L. C. (1971). *The impact of taxes on the American economy*, Praeger, New York.

Thurow, L. C. (1973). 'Toward a definition of economic justice', *Public Interest*, No. 31.

Thurow, L. C. and Lucas, R. E. B. (1972). *The American distribution of income: a structural problem*, US Government Printing Office, Washington, DC.

Tipping, D. G. (1970). 'Price changes and income distribution', *Applied Statistics*, Vol. 19.

Titmuss, R. M. (1958). *Essays on 'the welfare state'*, Allen and Unwin, London.

Titmuss, R. M. (1962). *Income distribution and social change*, Allen and Unwin, London.

Tobin, J. (1968). 'Raising the incomes of the poor', in *Agenda for the Nation* (ed. K. Gordon), Brookings Institution, Washington, DC.

Tobin, J., Pechman, J. and Mieszkowski, P. (1967). 'Is a negative income tax practical?', *Yale Law Journal*, Vol. 77.

Townsend, P. (1954). 'Measuring poverty', *British Journal of Sociology*, Vol. 5, reprinted in Townsend (1973).

Townsend, P. (1962). 'The meaning of poverty', *British Journal of Sociology*, Vol. 13, reprinted in Townsend (1973).

Townsend, P. (ed.) (1970). *The concept of poverty*, Heinemann, London.

Townsend, P. (1973). *The social minority*, Allen Lane, London.

Townsend, P. and Wedderburn, D. (1965). *The aged in the welfare state*, Bell, London.

Tuckman, H. P. (1973). *The economics of the rich*, Random House, New York.

Turner, H. A. (1957). 'Inflation and wage differentials in Great Britain', in *Theory of wage determination* (ed. J. Dunlop), Macmillan, London.

United Nations (1962). *United Nations Development Decade— Proposals for Action*, United Nations, New York.

Urry, J. and Wakeford, J. (1973). *Power in Britain*, Heinemann, London.

US Bureau of the Census (1972). *Characteristics of the low-income population 1971*, US Government Printing Office, Washington, DC.

US Bureau of the Census (1973). *Characteristics of the low-income population 1972*, US Government Printing Office, Washington, DC.

US Bureau of the Census (1973a). *Household Money Income in 1972*, US Government Printing Office, Washington, DC.

US Department of Health, Education, and Welfare (1969). *Toward a social report*, US Government Printing Office, Washington, DC.

US Department of Labor (1970). *Manpower report of the President 1970*, US Government Printing Office, Washington, DC

US Department of Labor (1971). *Black Americans: a chartbook*, US Government Printing Office, Washington, DC.

Usher, D. (1963). 'The Thai national income at United Kingdom prices', *Bulletin of the Oxford University Institute of Economics and Statistics*, Vol. 25.

Usher, D. (1966). *Rich and poor countries*, Institute of Economic Affairs, London.

Vatter, H. G. and Palm, T. (eds.) (1972). *The economics of black America*, Harcourt, Brace, Jovanovich, New York.

Vickrey, W. (1947). *Agenda for progressive taxation*, Ronald Press, New York.

Wachtel, H. M. and Betsy, C. (1972). 'Employment at low wages', *Review of Economics and Statistics*, Vol. 54.

Watts, H. W. (1969). 'Graduated work incentives: an experiment in negative income taxation', *American Economic Review, Papers and Proceedings*, Vol. 59.

Weaver, J. H. and Jones, L. P. (1968). 'An international negative income tax', *Conference Papers of the Union for Radical Political Economics*, December 1968.

Webb, A. and Sieve, J. (1971). *Income redistribution and the welfare state*, Bell, London.

Wedderburn, D. (1962). 'Poverty in Britain today—the evidence', *Sociological Review*, Vol. 10.

Wedgwood, J. (1929). *The economics of inheritance*, Routledge, London.

Weeks, J. (1971). 'Political economy and the politics of economists', *Review of Radical Political Economics*, Vol. 3.

Weisbrod, B. (ed.) (1965). *The economics of poverty*, Prentice-Hall, Englewood Cliffs, New Jersey.

Weisbrod, B. A. and Hansen, W. L. (1968). 'An income—net worth approach to measuring economic welfare', *American Economic Review*, Vol. 58.

Weiss, L. (1966). 'Concentration and labor earnings', *American Economic Review*, Vol. 56.

Weisskoff, R. (1970). 'Income distribution and economic growth in Puerto Rico, Argentina, and Mexico', *Review of Income and Wealth*, Vol. 16.

Wiles, P. J. D. (1974). *Income distribution, East and West*, North-Holland, Amsterdam.

Wiles, P. J. D. and Markowski, S. (1971). 'Income distribution under Communism and Capitalism', *Soviet Studies*, Vol. 22.

Wilkinson, B. (1966). 'Present values of lifetime earnings in different occupations', *Journal of Political Economy*, Vol. 74. University of Chicago Press.

Wilson, J. (1966). *Equality*, Hutchinson, London.

Wootton, B. (1962). *The social foundations of wage policy* (2nd ed.), Allen and Unwin, London.

Wynn, M. (1970). *Family policy*, Michael Joseph, London.

Young, M. (ed.) (1974). *Poverty report 1974*, Temple Smith, London.

Zeckhauser, R. J. (1971). 'Optimal mechanisms for income transfer', *American Economic Review*, Vol. 61.

INDEX